Protecting Your Assets

Strategies for Successful Business Operation in a Litigious Society

Wayne S. Hyatt

W9-ANU-742

Urban Land Institute

About ULI– The Urban Land Institute

ULI–the Urban Land Institute is a nonprofit education and research institute that is supported and directed by its members. Its mission is to provide responsible leadership in the use of land in order to enhance the total environment.

ULI sponsors educational programs and forums to encourage an open international exchange of ideas and sharing of experience; initiates research that anticipates emerging land use trends and issues and proposes creative solutions based on this research; provides advisory serves; and publishes a wide variety of materials to disseminate information on land use and development.

Established in 1936, the Institute today has over 13,000 members and associates from more than 50 countries representing the entire spectrum of the land use and development disciplines. They include developers, builders, property owners, investors, architects, public officials, planners, real estate brokers, appraisers, attorneys, engineers, financiers, academics, students, and librarians. ULI members contribute to higher standards of land use by sharing their knowledge and experience. The Institute has long been recognized as one of America's most respected and widely quoted sources of objective information on urban planning, growth, and development.

Richard M. Rosan
Executive Vice President

Recommended bibliographic listing:

ULI–the Urban Land Institute. *Protecting Your Assets: Strategies for Successful Business Operation in a Litigious Society.* Washington, D.C.: ULI–the Urban Land Institute, 1997.

ULI Catalog Number: P11
International Standard Book
  Number: 0-87420-797-5
Library of Congress Catalog Card
  Number: 97-61909

Copyright 1997 by
ULI–the Urban Land Institute
1025 Thomas Jefferson Street, N.W.
Suite 500 West
Washington, D.C. 20007-5201

Printed in the United States of America. All rights reserved. No part of this book may be reproduced in any form or by any means, electronic or mechanical, including photocopying, recording, or by any information storage and retrieval system, without written permission of the publisher.

ULI Project Staff

Rachelle L. Levitt
*Senior Vice President
Policy and Practice*

David W. Parham
Project Director

Nancy H. Stewart
Director, Book Program

Carol E. Soble
Copy Editor

Joanne Nanez
Book Design/Layout

Meg Batdorff
Cover Design

Diann Stanley-Austin
*Associate Director for
Publishing Operations*

Review Committee

Linda J. Bozung
Partner
Brobeck, Phleger & Harrison
Los Angeles, California

Randall W. Lewis
Executive Vice President
Lewis Homes Management Corp.
Upland, California

Daniel C. Van Epp
Executive Vice President
The Howard Hughes Corporation
Summerlin Division
Las Vegas, Nevada

Preface

This book is about risk and litigation. But it is not a "lawyer's" book, at least not a lawyer's book alone. It is a book written for businesspeople, lawyers, other professionals, and anyone in business who wants to avoid litigation. Although written by lawyers, the book is designed both to introduce the most common areas of risk and explain how to minimize, if not avoid, them in a manner that serves the needs of and "speaks to" nonlawyers.

Protecting Your Assets grew out of a workshop presented by the Urban Land Institute for anyone in real estate or a related business interested in avoiding litigation and learning about proven, practical techniques to manage the risk of litigation. While the program was designed for nonlawyers, the presenters learned during the course of the workshop that its greatest utility was in reaching both the lawyer and the nonlawyer. Both need to hear about and be a part of the same avoidance process. Accordingly, this book seeks to be of value to lawyers and nonlawyers.

Writing a book is a unique challenge for a practicing attorney. It not only consumes considerable time and energy, but it also forces the author to avoid the traditional role of advocate, which is so much part of the typical attorney's professional life. In writing and editing this book, I have, for the most part, attempted to move beyond my traditional role. At times, however, it was appropriate, indeed desirable, to argue a position in order to advance an idea or position that I perceive as correct and desirable and in the industry's best interest. It is good, therefore, to disclose that bias so that the reader will know that this book is a lawyer's statement that litigation is not the answer and that there are ways to avoid it. Some might say that they avoided a lawsuit because good luck was with them. But others say that "luck is where preparation meets opportunity." It is the goal of this book to help the reader be prepared for situations that might lead to litigation.

The author expresses sincere appreciation to the two attorneys who contributed significant portions to this book. John D. Hagner, managing partner of the Washington, D.C., firm of David & Hagner, wrote the chapters on the nonresidential developer and related professionals. James B. Rhoads, partner in the Atlanta office of the Birmingham, Alabama, firm of Burr & Forman, LLP, wrote the chapter on alternative dispute resolution. Both able attorneys also participated in the ULI workshop that gave rise to *Protecting Your Assets*. For their assistance and contributions, the author remains deeply grateful.

Wayne S. Hyatt

Contents

Chapter 1. Introduction   1

**Chapter 2. Risk Management and Prevention:
Basic Strategies for Avoiding Litigation   3**
- The Causes of Litigation   4
- Some Counterapproaches   6

**Chapter 3. Litigation Risk and Avoidance Strategies
for the Residential Developer   15**
- What Business Are You Really In?   15
- Marketing and Representations   16
- Construction   22
- Operation of Community Associations   32
- Amenity Ownership, Operation, and Disposition   42
- State and Federal Land Sales Regulation   56

**Chapter 4. Litigation Risk and Avoidance Strategies
for the Nonresidential Developer   61**
- Definition of the Nonresidential Developer   61
- Risk Situations That Often Generate Disputes   64
- Investing with Others in Joint Ventures,
Partnerships, Corporations, and Limited-
Liability Companies   82
- Leasing   87
- Operating/Managing   89
- Dispute and Litigation Avoidance Strategies   90

**Chapter 5. Litigation Risk and Avoidance Strategies for
Lenders, Contractors, and Professionals
Serving the Nonresidential Developer   99**
- Dispute and Litigation Risks for Lenders   99
- Selection of Borrowers and Loan Commitments   100

- Loan Documents and Closing 102
- Loan Administration and Enforcement 104
- Dispute and Litigation Risks for Design Professionals and Contractors 105
- The Contractor—Builder and Designer 110
- Legal Documents 114
- Special Provisions for Risk Allocation and Breach Prevention in Contracts and Nonresidential Leases 116
- Dispute and Litigation Risks for Marketing Professionals 123
- Dispute and Litigation Risks for Property Managers 126

Chapter 6. Alternative Dispute Resolution (ADR) as a Business Strategy: From Setting the Stage to Making It Work 129

- What the ADR Strategy Requires 130
- The Goals of the ADR Strategy and Why It Works 130
- Why the ADR Strategy Is Good for the Client 131
- Why the ADR Strategy Is Good for the Lawyer 132
- Setting the Stage 132
- Basic Types and Features of ADR 133
- Making It Work 136
- Establish an ADR Strategy in Your Organization 143

Chapter 7. When the Ox Is in the Ditch: Managing the Claim, Managing the Legal Team, Controlling the Costs 149

- Effective Damage Control 151
- Some Strategic Suggestions 154
- A Word about Litigation Counsel 156

Chapter 8. Conclusion 159

Appendices

1. Checklist of Documents and Materials to be Retained by Developer 163

2. Builder Program Conceptual Plan   175

3. Disposition of Amenities—The Legal Issues   181

4. Protecting Your Assets While Dancing with a Gorilla: The Lender and the Master-Planned Community   205

5. Creating the Community—Senior Housing and the Fair Housing Act   239

6. Creating Community and Governance: A New Perspective   249

7. Operating a Community Association   275

8. Sample Provisions   279

9. Feasibility Checklist for Acquisition of Undeveloped Land   285

CHAPTER 1

Introduction

*You can dream, create, design, and build the most
wonderful place in the world, but it requires people
to make the dream a reality.*—Walt Disney

Protecting Your Assets: Strategies for Successful Business Operation in
a Litigious Society is a practical, "how-to" discussion of litigation
and how to avoid it and, when avoidance is not possible, how to
manage it. While theory is a necessary part of the discussion, the
book emphasizes the pragmatic and is designed to help avoid common mistakes, suggest new approaches, and outline techniques for
managing risk, costs, and lawyers.

The materials in the appendices to the book—articles, forms,
and other samples—are an essential component of the text. The
reader should make use of the materials even if they are not specifically referenced.

The book is designed to teach. Its purpose is to inform and assist
in the operation of your business by reducing the costs, stress, and
general level of "negatives" too often faced in today's business
world as a result of litigation. But this book is also designed to be
"user-friendly" so that nonlawyers will find it not only helpful but
understandable as well. The format is intended to assist in this
effort and to encourage the reader to make notes and annotations.
The occasional bits of humor, it is hoped, will also be welcome.

Following the introduction, the book proceeds with an overview
of the topics to be presented. The topics are arranged in both a
general and specific fashion. First, the overview discusses risk management and prevention as a general predicate for the book.

Second, several sections deal with the substantive causes of litigation and with specific strategies for avoiding litigation—for both residential and nonresidential developers and related real estate professionals. A third and extremely important component is the explanation of alternative dispute resolution techniques (ADR), from drafting the provision to making ADR work. The book concludes with a nuts-and-bolts discussion of how to manage litigation and litigators, how to control costs, and how to stay in control of the process.

Simply stated, the book's objectives are to develop an understanding of the substantive legal issues and principles that give rise to litigation and to offer tips and techniques for managing risk so that disputes are resolved without going to court. It also establishes some guidelines for making lawyers more "user-friendly." Given that this book is written by lawyers, it might be perceived as a "defense" of the way lawyers do their job. To the contrary, it is intended neither to bash nor defend lawyers; it is, however, structured to deal with lawyer issues frankly and thoroughly and to aid the client in doing so as well.

CHAPTER 2

Risk Management and Prevention: Basic Strategies For Avoiding Litigation

*[Litigation:] A machine you go into as a pig and
come out as a sausage.*—Ambrose Bierce

When they founded their law firm in 1973, the author and his
partner decided to practice *preventive law*. The philosophy
behind this approach asserts that it is better to avoid problems than
experience them and that it is less costly and less destructive to deal
with them before rather than after they spiral out of control. The
concept has worked, and for many companies and law firms it has
become a "mantra" for the 1990s. For the rest of us, it is merely a
simple idea with anything but simple consequences. It requires
avoiding a state of mind that accepts litigation as inevitable;
expending more time, talent, and resources in preparation for
peace than for war; understanding the tangible and intangible
causes of the litigation explosion; instituting practices and procedures for addressing these causes; and following a carefully structured plan for risk prevention and management.

Chapter 2 introduces the concept of preventive law and suggests
techniques to make the concept work for you. It is instructive to
point out why we start with this topic. Simply put, the goal is to set
the stage for more substantive discussions and to attempt to alter
the mind-set that "you get what you anticipate." Too much in the
litigation area is the result of a self-fulfilling prophecy that sees lit-

igation as the logical and natural outcome of certain types of business activities.

■ The Causes of Litigation

The causes of litigation in today's world are legion. Understanding the most common and relevant among them is vital to risk prevention. They include the following:

- *The "fear and greed" syndrome.* Those who fear what they either do not understand or cannot manage and control look to the courtroom and the lawyer for the promise of some ability to respond to whatever prevents the plaintiff from exercising control. The greed factor is so obvious that it needs no elaboration. Too many people see the litigation process as a means of realizing economic gain. Even though the process is often long, slow, costly, and devoid of significant reward, people still look to it. For example, many cases in the southern California courts are brought on behalf of community associations that have been assured that the cost of recovery will far exceed the "cost to cure." The implied premise is that the result will profit the association and its attorney.

- *Attitudes and expectations of homeowners.* The "Me Generation" has too often come to expect that real estate construction will be perfect and that the buyer will take delivery of the perfect house. When this does not happen, litigation can result along with an attitude of little tolerance.

- *Quality of workmanship.* The quality of workmanship does not always meet even the reasonable expectations of any generation.

- *Popularity of (major) recreational amenities.* The growing popularity of golf and country clubs and other major amenities as part of real estate developments has led to increased levels of consumer expectation and thus the opportunity for dispute, significantly expanding the areas of law potentially involved in a development's disputes, i.e., securities laws in club membership sales.

- *Popularity and power of homeowners' associations.* Associations play an important and positive role in today's real estate industry; however, they also provide a force for collective action that can result in collective dispute prosecution in contexts that would not lead to litigation if claims were handled individually. This fact has both a good and bad side as discussed in the next chapter.

- *Attitudes and practices of sellers and those affiliated with sellers.* Just as associations can have their negative consequences, sellers and those working in support of sellers often engage in practices that tend to mislead or raise the level of expectations.

- *Number, attitude, and practices of many attorneys.* It is a fact that some attorneys seek to capitalize on opportunities by doing more than just responding to legitimate needs. Too often, they actively solicit cases and clients through "seminars" and direct contact with management companies. This process can be characterized as not only business development but also as business creation.

- *Hard times.* Economic difficulties contribute to reliance on litigation as a way to deal with that which otherwise cannot be dealt with. In other words, economic hard times that are beyond the control of the individual sometimes cause people to sue over minor matters as a way of "getting theirs" or dealing with financial or other circumstances beyond their control.

- *Rising/unrealistic expectations of the public at large.* We all experience it; we all feel it. One example is the advertising pages of any newspaper's real estate section. The sales seminars that urge concentration on the "sizzle" rather than on the "steak" are also examples. The sales pitch is to embellish, to foster a mind-set and expectation of something very special. That is fine . . . if the product delivered actually meets the expectation. Too often it does not and, in fact, cannot.

Other influences that can increase the frequency of litigation include television. Both news programs and "entertainment" shows are full of situations in which individuals feel wronged because they have not obtained what they desire. They resort to the courtroom for redress. The process is made to appear more exciting and productive than it is. It encourages litigation just as *Perry Mason* and *LA Law* encouraged law school applications. Class action potential, increased jury awards, and contingency fees are still other causes behind the litigation explosion. The emergence of specialty practices over the last several years—in areas such as mold spores, polybutylene pipe, soils subsidence, fire-retardant plywood, amenity disposition, and electromagnetic fields—also fuels the number of lawsuits. Moreover, plaintiffs' own fear of a suit and attorneys' ability to capitalize on that fear drive litigious action. When someone is acting in a representative capacity, that person is susceptible to the argument that failure to take some legal action will lead to a suit for breach of duty. The result is escalation of the "fear and greed syndrome" and much litigation hardly understood by those ultimately responsible for it.

The underlying causes of litigation combine with innovations or evolutions in the *practice* of litigation to increase the probability of a lawsuit in any given business situation. Some of these factors are controllable and others are not. In each case, however, it is important that the industry not only be aware of the factors but also understand the subtleties and effects of each. Clearly, too many in the industry plan for litigation while failing to plan for ways to avoid it. Examples abound of developers who put aside funds from each unit sale as a litigation reserve. Few, however, spend any money on leadership training, association orientation and education, and preventive planning and practice. The immortal philosopher Pogo told us, "It's not what we know that hurts us, it's what we know that isn't so."

■ Some Counterapproaches

Some of the factors encouraging litigation are national forces that are not particular to the circumstances of an individual businessperson. It is, of course, difficult for an individual to control these forces or their effect.

Certain industry-level responses to national forces deserve brief mention and consideration. They include education and training at multiple levels, particularly for sales staffs, managers, and others as related to the risks of litigation, ways to manage or avoid risk, and how to react in the event of potential problems. Denial can be costly. If there is a construction defect problem, the builder should determine the scope of that problem and pay for it; the cost will never be less. Another example of an industry-level response has taken the form of legislative action as seen, for example, in the activities underway in 1995 in California to strike a better balance between the consumer and seller in the Uniform Common Interest Ownership Act, which includes warranty protections yet also deals with statutes of limitations and reserved developer rights. Finally, the conditioning of consumer expectations can influence the likelihood of litigation. We will return to this concept throughout the book, but the main point is that too often the marketing process raises the level of expectations—and unnecessarily.

The individual business must make preventive law part of its business practice by requiring a "litigation consciousness" in everyday business operation. The development of a litigation consciousness is based on the acknowledgment of some obvious and some not-so-obvious considerations as follows:

- Build it right. This sounds simple, even simplistic; however, it is neither. Too often a product is not built correctly.

- Build to budget. Not only does this make good business sense, it also makes sound risk management sense.

- Say what you will/will not do, and stick to it. The belief that a businessperson can make everyone happy is a myth. Establish a plan for responsiveness and follow it; do not deviate from a pre-determined approach.

One of the great sources of liability is the failure of reality to meet expectations. People have a right to rely on representations; in fact, they acquire "reliance rights" in the process. Each time a representation is made orally or by deed, the rights take on new meaning and a new level of expectations. Saying "no" in the appropriate manner may disappoint, but it most often will be accepted if it is delivered in accordance with an announced and consistent policy.

Examples of the expectation problem are numerous and range from the implied promise that the golf course will be given to the homeowners at buildout to the quality of the house and the nature of the surrounding open space. To manage expectations, you must document what you do/do not do. Preserve a record of the actions and the reasons for those actions. At the same time, it is equally important to review those records and to institute a records management program so that long-forgotten and no-longer-accurate records do not become unexplainable evidence. In addition, you need to develop and implement a genuine risk management plan. As with other forms of business plans, the risk management plan should reflect genuine business planning as well as discussions with the relevant businesspersons and professional people. After it is written, it should be periodically reviewed and updated. Perhaps most important, a senior manager should be in charge of it. Appendix 1 includes a handy checklist to aid the process of document retention and management.

The principles inherent in each of these considerations are applicable to all real estate-related businesses and, indeed, are so fundamental that they seem beyond mentioning. More often than not, however, they are violated. Instead, they need to become automatic and second nature.

Although this book deals with much more than just construction defect litigation, using that topic as a model for discussing some approaches to counter the litigation rush is appropriate. In fact, in almost every instance the approaches apply to nonconstruction situations as well.

Implementation of the ideas discussed above requires several specific steps. Using the construction business as an example, the steps are as follows:

- Project planning must include risk management planning structured around well-drafted documentation and a warranty certificate that both establishes rights and limits obligations without overreaching. The warranty certificate should include a written acknowledgment of receipt.

- Construction and marketing require active supervision and quality control.

- Responsiveness to problems must be timely and in accordance with an established procedure; problems only worsen if ignored.

- A program for the builders in a community should establish their responsibilities relating to buyers and to risk management. Appendix 2 provides a conceptual plan for such a program.

Any discussion of avoiding or managing construction defects must turn to marketing. The expectations created in the buyer's mind will have a profound effect on the consumer's satisfaction level, willingness to negotiate or sue, and, ultimately, impression of the developer/builder.

Marketing, of course, encompasses multiple activities but is inherent in most business interests of readers of this text. It is therefore relevant to add a few comments on the subject of marketing and how it becomes part of a risk management plan. Defensive tips on marketing should become the basis for your own preventive marketing plan.

- Choose your language carefully; you are creating expectations. What level of expectations do you *really* need to sell your product? Is your product a Cadillac or a Chevrolet? Each can be the best of its line, so why sell one while representing it to be the other?

- Train and *test* the sales staff. The sales staff is both the first line of defense and the first point of communication with the public . . . the potential plaintiff. Sales training should include liability issues as well as matters concerning the product, the association, the amenity plan, etc.

Too often, the sales staff is told what to sell but is not brought into the education and communication loops that condition consumer expectations. Therefore, testing the sales staff is vital and should take many forms. One approach calls for enlisting persons not known to the salespersons to go through the sales process and seek answers to the type of questions asked by a typical consumer. If you are the seller, you need to know what is said on your behalf. Testing at sales meetings by asking questions, through general conversation, and through other innovative, nonthreatening methods can and does work.

- Use the education and training of buyers as part of the selling process. This can and should take many forms. For example, well-drafted, readable community association documents can aid in the informing/training process, as can a well-structured warranty document. A readable newsletter can and should educate. The goal is to ensure that the buyer understands the product and all that it entails.

- Draft sales documents with risk management in mind, but remember that "overlawyering" is as bad as "underlawyering."

- Make selective but thorough use of disclosures and disclaimers. Do not fear saying what you will not do. In the long run, such candor is in everyone's best interest, and it will not cost sales or at least not cost a sale to someone you want in your project.

Marketing is merely the first step in dealing with the consumer. Whatever the product and whatever the nature of the consumer, a defensive marketing plan should be combined with a plan to deal with the consumer after sale. To be successful, such a program should include good owner relations and communications; active efforts to refute and reverse the "fear and greed" syndrome; the institution of *procedures* in sales or project documents that include rights to gain access, inspect individually and commonly owned property, correct defects, redesign as needed to cure defects, require notice to all owners before suit, require notice to and meeting with builders before filing suit, and require review of experts' reports before a representative may file; the establishment of practices and procedures for timely and thorough inspection of the property; and the employment of indemnification procedures as relevant and appropriate to reduce the "fear" factor.

Much of today's litigation in the real estate industry arises in the context of the master-planned community. Among the many reasons for this pattern—perhaps one of the most significant—is the coming together of the real estate interests and financial resources of a large group of owners. They command the resources to fund litigation. They have a group that can shield the individual. They have aggregated claims, making the potential recovery large. In the eyes of the potential plaintiff, the developer with both cash and insurance becomes an attractive target. The fact that both cash resources and the extent and availability of insurance are limited often remains overlooked.

In managing such risk, all the factors previously discussed and those in the next chapter apply. Before leaving this introductory chapter, however, two final and significant issues need to be addressed. What are the primary arguments used by the litigator, and how do you counter them? Briefly, the argruments include the fear and greed syndrome, the cost of recovery versus the cost to cure, fear that the insurance pool will run dry, concern that the defendant will run away, fear that the statute of limitations will expire, and the "duty-to-sue" myth to put pressure on boards of directors. Each argument has a persuasive counterargument that works only if you make it work. The remainder of this chapter discusses how to do that.

The first part of the question focuses on the already discussed fear and greed syndrome and the closely related duty-to-sue myth, which is a necessary component if the fear factor is to work. Simply stated, fear arises because the group representative—a condominium board president, for example—is told that if she does not file suit against the builder, she will be sued for breach of duty to sue to protect the condominium's interests. Sadly, too few laypersons know that courts have held that there is no duty to sue in a construction defect matter. The duty is to use the best business judgment to determine what is needed and how to achieve it. The business judgment rule empowers condominium boards to use judgment; it does not force them to file suit. In addition, the courts have held several times that the director or officer is no guarantor. In other words, the director has the right to be wrong so long as the decision is made in the right way.

The cost to cure is generally a dollar figure reasonably susceptible to determination. Despite genuine disputes as to what needs to be done and at what level, costs can be determined. The cost to recover can also be approximated and is an advisable approach as a rational response to the plaintiff's attorney who says that the cost to cure will be less. The costs of litigation to both sides include not only money but also time, opportunity, emotional duress, and other costs, all of which need to be included in the equation.

The insurance may run dry as it almost has in southern California, but insurance facts and figures are individual and need to be addressed in each case so that the potential plaintiff is not stampeded. The same applies to the rare tactic that the defendant will run away, which is simply an accusation that the seller will collapse and disappear. This is a factual argument that can and should be answered with factual responses.

The final argument is that the statute of limitations will expire. If the date for expiration of the statute is approaching, then both sides must make serious decisions about the strategic and tactical effect of its doing so. A simple tolling agreement, however, can prevent the expiration and give the parties time to continue to negotiate. The attorney who presents a lawsuit as the only option is simply not seeking to solve a problem but rather is gearing up for litigation.

The second of the two questions regarding a preventive initial strategy deals with project documentation. Project documents should contain several specially tailored provisions such as the procedural rights discussed above concerning rights of access, inspection, cure, etc., which should specify indemnification provisions, inspection programs, and other written procedures discussed under the topics dealing with community associations; alternative dispute resolution procedures as discussed in Chapter 6; a requirement for an association vote before the board's filing suit; a warranty responsibility chart and procedures; an explanation of what are and are not the duties of the board of directors; clear maintenance provisions with an adequate funding mechanism; and a section establishing the methodology to determine the need for and maintenance of truly adequate reserves. Most important, all documentation must be clear and understandable, and you and your team must understand *and follow it.*

Successful strategies for minimizing risk seek to balance the interests involved. Accordingly, documentation should be balanced and should not contain exculpatory language, waivers, and other provisions that usually do not work but also tend to inflame passions and defeat trust.

The last chapter of the book discusses what to do when "the ox is in the ditch." A major part of that discussion, which deals with managing the litigation problem when and if it arises, could be included here because the essential principles inherent in a risk management strategy apply both before and after problems arise. The context of that final chapter is important, however, and the discussion is tailored to a particular context. Nonetheless, Chapters 2 and 7 are companions.

Eight Steps to Less Litigation

1. Use a risk manager.
2. Supervise construction and marketing.
3. Uoo a wcll writtcn warranty.
4. Market at product level.
5. Disclose, disclose, disclose.
6. Build relationships.
7. Use defensive procedures when creating documents/operating an association.
8. Use innovative provisions in governing documents (alternative dispute resolution (ADR)/scope-of-business judgment/right to inspect, etc.).

Risk prevention techniques are workable only as they apply to a particular business. Accordingly, we now turn to discussions of specific business types and of thc spccific, substantive areas of potential liability they commonly face.

CHAPTER 3

Litigation Risk and Avoidance Strategies for the Residential Developer

Have you not learned great lessons from those who braced themselves against you?—Walt Whitman

There is always a tendency for lawyers to talk only about the law. That tendency certainly exists in a book about legal risk and liability; however, the goal of this volume is not to teach the law but rather to foster an understanding of both the legal issues of concern to the development industry and how to minimize the associated business risk. To do so, of course, some discussion of legal cases and concepts is necessary. Nonetheless, the text covers only major points and issues and is supplemented by appendix materials that, whether or not related to topics in the text, are complementary. In addition, the appendices include a table of cases and a bibliography for those either desiring more in-depth study or wishing to confound their lawyer.

■ What Business Are You Really In?

Liability arises in many contexts. Often, a problem stems from an activity that may not even be perceived as part of a business operation, especially among developers/builders who focus on building homes without realizing that they are also creating "governments" and raising expectations. To discern such activities requires a discussion of two important concepts: product and process. Obviously, developers/builders create a *product* in the shelter industry, but when that product triggers the need for some form of community association or joint ownership, it also involves a *process*. The process is the method by which owners share ownership and function to maintain and manage common property.

The concepts of product and process underlie the three major categories of developer/builder liability. When fully understood, the following three liability categories help answer the question of what business you are *really* in: marketing and representations, construction, or operation.

■ Marketing and Representations

Many different activities constitute "marketing," any of which can give rise to several different types of potential liability. In this discussion, there is a recurring theme: what has been represented? In other words, what has the seller represented to the buyer as to quality of construction, availability and nature of amenities, and other such issues? When the buyer can show these representations and reasonable reliance on them, a reliance right arises. The law gives effect to that right by requiring the seller to perform. As a natural part of marketing, the seller makes representations; for our purposes, it is important to understand that representations have multiple consequences, one of which may be legal liability. Liability can take the form of state law-related risks and several common federal law-related risks. Although land sales regulation is certainly related to marketing, it is treated as a separate topic later in this chapter.

The essential nature of the problem in the area of state law risk can be summed up as "can do," "cannot do," and "have to." These simple catch phrases mean that something that is said or done gives rises to an obligation. That obligation, which may be affirmative or negative, indicates an abridgement of property owners' rights to use their property. The abridgement may prohibit certain activities or require specific uses or activities.

Case: Sales Representations Create Rights, Even against Subsequent Owners

The master-planned community was about to be completely out of the developer's control. The last step in the process was to sell the large amenity package, including the golf course, clubhouse, and restaurant, to a large golf operator. The only problem was that the homeowners thought that they should have ownership. The home-owners alleged that during the sales process there had been representations that such would be the ultimate disposition of the property. The current developer was the third in the chain, and it had no such plan. In fact, it had a contract for a profitable sale.

The developer's problem was that sales personnel had made statements that the homeowners would have title to the property when the project was completed. In fact, the original developer had that intention, but his interests had long since ended in fore-closure. Nevertheless, the representations and the rights created by those representations remained.

Affidavits from the previous salespersons made the case, and the court ordered that there could be no sale to a third party. In the end, the developer transferred the property without any compensation other than a release to the homeowners.

The point was that what salespersons say creates rights, even against a subsequent landowner.

The legal issues are simple and certainly not new and may be said to touch and concern the land (a real estate principle that is required when a restriction runs with the land) and to give rise to benefit and burden. In a real-world context, these issues are manifest in many modern legal theories and include contracts, expressed and implied covenants, expressed and implied easements, implied negative reciprocal easements, fiduciary duty, fraud/misrepresentation, private dedication, and estoppel. Each of these is discussed in detail in Appendices 3 and 4 and in the section of this chapter dealing with transfer of amenities.

In seeking to establish one or more of these issues, a plaintiff's attorney looks to many sources of proof, *each of which the developer/builder controls initially and that can include* oral and written sales representations *of all types* (everything from billboards to brochures), master plans, recorded plats, sales contracts, deeds, zoning letters of intent, project documentation, land sales registrations (both state and federal, if applicable), minutes of meetings of both the association's board of directors and zoning and other government bodies, and statements made to the press and in public meetings. In each case, documents and other sources will be examined to see what was said both explicitly and implicitly as the plaintiff seeks to establish and prove a reliance right. This right is simply the buyer's right to realize the "benefit of the bargain" or to receive what was represented. It is a significant issue and is too often overlooked or not understood by the builder/seller.

If the goal is maximum development flexibility with minimum risk to that flexibility specifically and to the developer/builder generally, you need to do several things, which are part of the process of communicating to the public and formulating and preserving the development plan. First, disclose any reserved rights to alter the plan or change what is represented and disclose material facts that affect what is expected based on reasonable inferences from what has been represented. Disclosure of reserved rights or potential problems is vital to protecting all concerned. Second, assert control. Control the sales process by monitoring what is said, what is "represented," and thus what potential obligations are created. Control the building process to ensure that the product being sold is the one being produced. Also, control the customer relations process with risk prevention in mind, whether that is with the community association or simply a one-on-one process with buyers. Finally, test on a recurring basis all individuals who interact with the public. Be sure that they can explain the development plan and the representations and reservations.

Disclosing, controlling, and testing require developers/builders to review documents, development plans, and disclosures; preserve the right to alter and to amend; think about how language can be interpreted and remember that what people hear is not always what you said or more often what you thought you meant to say or said; develop a proactive plan for sales staff and merchant builders, underscoring once again the importance of training and testing the

Case: Sales Literature Creates Expectations

In the case of a development project in Arizona, the sales literature had promised a golf experience and made much of the fact
that the residential development was adjacent to a golf course.
The newspaper advertisements were full of enticements, but they
also made clear that the homeowners did not own the golf course.
When a subsequent developer sought to use the course for commercial development, the owners sued.

The court ruled for the homeowners, holding that it was not ownership that they sought or were entitled to but rather the benefit of
their bargain: the right to have a golf course as an integral part of
their community as promised in the advertisements. The issue was
neither the current developer's difficulty with water rights nor the
fact that the golf course was not as profitable as the proposed
commercial development would be. The issue was whether there
had been representations and reasonable reliance on them.
Finding affirmative answers to both questions, the court ruled that
the property had to remain a golf course.

sales staff; and appreciate consumer (litigation) hot buttons, which,
for purposes of this text, are arguments raised by the litigator. The
reader should compile a list of special concerns likely to arise in the
local area. Examples include soils problems, electromagnetic field
issues in areas adjacent to high-tension power lines, and most
everything in California. The potential for litigation and the risk
factors giving rise to it are as much a part of the business plan as
marketing hot buttons in making product decisions.

This does not mean that money should simply be allocated to a
litigation fund, which will ensure that you will have litigation.
Instead, it calls for seriously considering avoidance strategies and
how to interact with the consumer in order to avoid or minimize
risk. That is why the risk management plan is a major component
of the overall business plan and why it must be acted on at early
planning stages, not when "the ox is in the ditch." (See Chapter 7
for suggestions for dealing with such a calamity.)

Case: Reserving the Right to Change the Plan of Development

What if the developer reserves the right to change the plan of development and seeks to use that reserved right to make the type of change discussed in the previous case? The New Mexico courts addressed such an issue and held that the reserved right would be valid only if it were disclosed in language as clear and in type as large as the words that created the expectation in the first place.

To allow the "hidden" right to take away that which is given as a major inducement would, the supreme court held, violate public policy.

In addition, when developing with community associations, it is important to devise a *strategy* for the *general plan of development*. The strategy should include at least three parts: a creation and governance strategy; a disposition strategy dealing with common property and privately owned amenities; and an exit strategy. These will help frame how documents are drafted, how the association is run, and the declarant's relationship with the association. They should not be afterthoughts, but too often they are.

The strategies and the documents that memorialize and implement them should address a variety of issues, including what facilities will be in the project and the various governance relationships. Simply put, decisions are needed on the care, custody, and control of the development.

An example of a component of these strategies is the ultimate disposition of the amenities or other property. The plan of development's disposition strategy raises questions about the timing and methods of rational transfer of property but should not presuppose that a transfer is imminent. The business plan may in fact call for long-term retention of ownership and/or control. The important consideration is that ownership, control, governance, and other questions of responsibility are fully and properly addressed.

A vital part of any plan of development is flexibility to ensure that the plan can accommodate alterations in response to changed conditions, circumstances, and markets. The sales testing must guard against anything that could compromise that flexibility. The community documentation must meet the tests of flexibility, uniqueness, and realism and should reflect modern experience and methods to assist in creating not only a risk-averse development but also one that emphasizes the creation of community.

Statutory issues can give rise to marketing problems and liability. In addition to the more commonly understood state regulations and statutes, a key federal statute often remains overlooked by sellers. Specifically, the federal Fair Housing Act is a civil rights statute intended to end discrimination in residential housing on the basis of race, color, religion, sex, handicap, familial status, or national origin. To accomplish this objective, the act makes unlawful any form of advertising of residential property that indicates any discrimination or intent to discriminate on the basis of any of these factors.

Affirmative advertising and marketing should be part of everyone's business strategy. In general, marketing efforts should avoid indications of possible discriminatory intent as manifested by the content and form of advertising and the audience toward whom advertisements are directed. For example, all white models in advertisements convey the impression that the development is open only to white people. Catchwords such as "private," "restricted," and "integrated" are also impermissible for obvious reasons.

At the same, marketing efforts should not deny information to particular segments of the population by, for example, advertising in an English-language publication in an area with large populations of non–English speaking persons. Finally, marketing efforts should not cater to or indicate a preference for a particular group no matter how subtle the message. For example, it is illegal to give directions to a development by relying on landmarks that have particular reference to one group or that tend to discourage another.

Specifically, marketing efforts should comply with Equal Housing Opportunity guidelines, exercise great care when using human models in advertisements, employ an explicit nondiscrimination policy, provide training in fair housing practices to sales and administrative staff and ensure that senior staff are well versed in the fair housing law and its policy underpinnings, display a fair housing poster, focus on property rather than on people, and lead by example, which is the best advice for senior management.

The act's protections against discrimination on the basis of age or familial status embody protections for children. While draft regulations recently proposed by the U.S. Department of Housing and Urban Development (HUD) illustrate the vast scope of fair housing coverage, it is premature to deal with them. Appendix 5 includes a thorough article on the status of fair housing as of summer 1995.

Perhaps the most disconcerting aspect about marketing risks is that so many of them arise from the actions of others. Salespersons, advertising professionals, merchant builders and their salespersons, and many others are in a position to speak for you or *to appear* to be authorized to speak for you. Certainly, the law of unintended consequences comes into play. It also bears repeating that liability often arises not because of intentional misconduct and that innocence is usually not a justification, as is often true with state and federal claims. The keys to protection are *understanding, training, and testing.*

■ Construction

Construction would seem to be the one aspect of the residential development process that most easily lends itself to control: simply build it right. Sounds easy, does it not? Well, it is not so easy. The legal issues, the changing climate of the jury system and jurors, the heightened expectations of consumers, and—for a number of markets—the loss of liability insurance coverage all contribute to a high-risk environment in which developers/builders are rightfully concerned that building it right might not offer sufficient protection. The supplemental materials, particularly the texts listed in the bibliography, discuss in detail construction defect claims and how to prosecute and defend them.

The Two Basic Issues: Liability and Damages

Liability is the concept of being responsible for a problem; generally, it means that you are at fault, though in some circumstances you can be liable even without being at fault, especially in California with its concept of strict liability in construction defect litigation. There is no responsibility for damages, which also must be proven, unless there is liability. To resolve the threshold question of liability, six specific questions require answers.

- What is the problem (for example, cracked walls, leaking roofs, water in basement, etc.)?

- Where is the problem located (especially important in condominiums)?

- When did the problem first occur? When was it discovered?

- What caused the problem (as determined by *experts*, not by the developer's own employees)?

- Who caused the problem (for example, architect, general contractor, subcontractor)?

- Why is that party deemed the cause, i.e., what legal theories of liability apply?

This six-step analysis determines whether you are liable. If so, what is your exposure? Exposure relates to the calculation of damages, which can take the form of compensatory damages, punitive damages, and costs of litigation. Compensatory damages compensate for the wrong and may include the cost of repair, medical expenses, the cost of the new roof, etc. Punitive damages are imposed both to punish and to deter one from similar conduct in the future. Costs of litigation normally do not include attorney fees but rather are all of the hard costs of litigation that, for example, include witness fees, filing fees, expert costs, etc. Generally, punitive damages and litigation costs are not recoverable in a strict construction defect suit. For this reason, plaintiffs often combine "pure" construction claims with other causes of action that allow punitive damages, e.g., fraud, misrepresentation or breach of fiduciary duty.

A Word about Parties

The "who" in the threshold question of liability deserves elaboration. Many parties could potentially be tagged with responsibility for the problem. It is important to consider the ways potential parties can be involved in avoiding the risk and if they can accept some or all of the liability in the event of a suit. These parties may include the master developer—the person who conceives and creates the development; the declarant (may be different)—the person or entity that makes the project subject to a recorded declaration of condominium or a declaration of covenants creating some other form of community association; design professionals—the many types and kinds of professionals from land planner, architect, engineer, etc., who play a role in project design; lenders—the construction lenders, permanent lenders, and institutional and noninstitutional lenders who provide financial backing in the creation and sale of a development; attorneys—legal counsel professionally liable for advice given or not given and who may be part of litigation depending on their degree of participation in decision making; and builders—one or more builders may buy lots from or contract with the developer who has performed the entitlement work and land development and infrastructure construction.

Each step in the development and construction process gives rise to risks and areas of potential involvement in the defect suit by involving subcontractors—the crafts and trades responsible for specified components of the community and its dwellings; manufacturers and suppliers—those in the chain extending from manufacturer to supplier who become potential subjects for claims if any product is defective; building officials—code enforcement officials and the parties with a right to claim under the code; sales and marketing agents—the professionals charged with responsibility for representation; the community association—its officers, directors, employees, as discussed in detail in the next section of this chapter; property managers—the property manager as an agent of the community association is subject to the laws of contract; unit/homeowners—owners are the party ultimately responsible for the operation, maintenance, and administration of the development; consultants—the range of professionals involved in a particular consulting capacity who may become liable depending on their function; repair contractors—the individuals performing repair work are often on the scene even as new construction is ongoing, making it important to know exactly who did what and when; and insurance and bonding companies that often represent the final step in the chain of liability—it is crucial to know what their documents say and to be able to understand the language.

Theories of Liability

Liability most commonly arises from either contract or tort theory; in addition, some miscellaneous theories are noteworthy. This book briefly discusses each theory. At your leisure, you should review the various theories in detail and consider how they might apply in your business setting.

Tort theories involve wrongful conduct. Negligence or intentional misconduct may be at the root of tortious acts. The classic definition of negligence is a breach of a legal duty; the duty owed by one party to another is defined as the exercise of due care. Thus, the lack of due care in the design, construction, or supervision of a construction project that results in construction defects may give rise to a cause of action. Likewise, if defects are discovered during the construction phase of a project and the attempted repairs are negligently performed, the entity performing the repairs could be held responsible under a theory of negligent repair. Under principles of respondeat superior, both the individuals guilty of the tortious acts and the employers for whom they perform those tortious acts in the scope of their employment may be liable. These principles are important when the target of the construction claim is an individual with substantial assets rather than a judgment-proof corporation. In analyzing construction defect cases, it is important to determine whether any person or entity was negligent with respect to any portion of the project containing a construction defect.

The classic definition of fraud is the communication of false information to induce a person to act to his or her detriment in reasonable reliance on that information. An illustration of fraudulent conduct is the marketing and sale of dwelling units to homeowners when the builder is aware of the project's construction defects and has taken steps to cover up those defects before selling the units.

Breach of fiduciary duty involves the officers or directors of the community association who are charged with performing their duties in good faith in accordance with business judgment. Their duty is higher than due care. An intentional or negligent breach of that duty gives rise to a cause of action for breach of fiduciary duty. Individuals serving as officers or directors of the homeowners' association while the association is under control of the declarant (e.g., the developer) are particularly vulnerable to such charges because of the potential conflict of interest in attempting to serve both the declarant and the association.

Contract theories of liability revolve around contractual arrangements among parties. A contract specifies the standards against which performance is measured. The breach of those standards gives rise to a cause of action. Only contracting parties may be held liable for breach of contract. Thus, specific identification of the parties to all contracts is extremely important in the analysis of construction defect claims.

The usual operative document for the purchase and sale of real estate, including a unit in a community association project, is the sales agreement. The sales agreement is usually a lengthy and well-drafted document drawn up by the seller's attorney and is therefore designed to protect the seller. Nevertheless, a construction defect may in some instances constitute a breach of the sales agreement.

At the closing of the sale of a unit, it is not unusual for the seller to warrant the unit and common elements against defects in materials and workmanship for a specified period. Like the sales contract, the warranty usually is drafted by the seller's attorney with a view toward protecting the seller. The specific wording of the warranty is extremely important. A breach of the warranty by the seller gives rise to a cause of action for breach of warranty. The specific written warranty delivered at the time of closing is referred to as an express warranty. In some states, the seller also conveys an implied warranty with the deed. Implied warranties exist in these states as a matter of public policy and are recognized by the state's case law. The implied warranty arises because of a perceived inequality of bargaining power between buyer and seller.

The final category of warranty is the statutory warranty. As its name implies, a statutory warranty is created by state legislation and is an expression of public policy regarding minimum standards of construction. The federal Uniform Common Interest Ownership Act and the Uniform Condominium Act both contain statutory warranties of quality; the federal Moss-Magnuson Act may also apply to property inside the home.

Management companies may be hired to manage the affairs of the community association. During periods of declarant control, a management company may become aware of construction defects. Failure of the management company to fulfill scrupulously the duties for handling construction defects as described in its management contract may give rise to a cause of action on the part of the community association against the management company.

In some states, the concept of strict liability makes the builder/seller of real property absolutely responsible for any defects in materials and workmanship in the project without regard to fault. In a limited number of cases, other theories of liability may be applicable. For example, some courts have recognized a cause of action based on breach of building codes. Some bizarre situations may even give rise to a claim that concealment of construction defects is part of a scheme to pursue racketeering activity in violation of federal or state racketeering influence and corrupt organization acts.

Liability Prevention

Of course, developers/builders can take steps to minimize—if not entirely avoid—any type of liability by paying close attention to practical recommendations, project legal documents, sales documents, and general and specific disclosures. In terms of practical considerations, developers/builders often overlook some of the most obvious matters and, accordingly, find themselves the subject of litigation. Therefore, developers/builders should build it right and to budget, document everything, say what they will/will not do and stick to it, purchase liability insurance, require and verify that subcontractors purchase adequate liability insurance that names the affected developer/builder as an insured, and supervise and control quality. Much can be done and said on this topic, although it is worth noting that the developer/builder or representative must supervise the supervisors as part of the training and testing program. Supervisory responsibility should be specified in the job description of the person responsible for the risk management program. The obligation to supervise extends to supervision not over only construction but also over marketing. Indeed, the person responsible for overall supervision of both the construction and marketing operations should ensure that the risk plan and each person's place in it is understood, thereby reducing the "us versus them" syndrome that can arise as someone seeks to fix blame.

The process of supervision should include a considerable amount of risk management. For example, developers/builders should spell out changes, maintain records to show the reasons for deviations from the original plans and specifications, and periodically videotape and photograph various steps in the construction process. When someone later alleges that footings were improperly poured, the video will be the best evidence that the assertion is incorrect. Not all construction must be videotaped, but examples of various steps in the process should be recorded in the ordinary course of business.

Other practical considerations call for the developer/builder to remain responsive to customer needs during both the pre- and postsales periods by charging an employee with full-time responsibility for responding to complaints and maintaining a log of actions taken. The employee should be someone with considerable people skills who knows how to keep a decision moving.

The developer/builder should also establish and enforce procedures/requirements regarding subcontractors. In one way or another, the developer/builder must answer for the actions taken or not taken by subcontractors. It is essential, therefore, to bring the subcontractors into the risk management program as noted in the earlier discussion of the builder program and in Appendix 2. Finally, practical considerations dictate the provision of a written warranty whose words include disclaim, disclose, balance, mutual protection, and follow-through.

As to marketing, the developer/builder must exercise care with respect to language in order not to misrepresent the product, train and test the sales staff to ensure that the product for sale is the product delivered at closing, and focus expectations so that buyers do not develop an unrealistic and inaccurate perception of the final product.

In terms of business operation and management, the astute developer/builder must institute ongoing inspections, remain aware and wary of technology and code changes, and require errors and omissions insurance for design professionals, engineers, and other consultants and other appropriate forms of insurance for everyone who is part of the development team. In addition, the developer/builder should probably form a separate corporation for each project. The new limited-liability company offers several advantages but requires sound tax and legal advice for its creation, assuming that it fits the business's overall needs and circumstances. Finally, developers/builders must be willing to sue subcontractors for loss of reputation and notify them that legal action is not out of the question if circumstances dictate. It is a straightforward reminder that subcontractors, general contractors, builders, developers, and sellers are all working toward a common end. Each has responsibilities to the other, and it is simply wrong for some to believe that others will take the fall.

Legal Management Documents

Building in a condominium or master-planned community means that many provisions can and should be included in the project's covenants, conditions, and restrictions (CCRs) and bylaws. Although a few states, California primarily, may limit or restrict some CCRs, none of the following provisions is overreaching or designed unfairly to limit homeowner rights. Experience has shown that the provisions can benefit everyone. Such provisions reserve the right for builders to *enter and inspect* property to *correct* problems, etc.; reserve the right for builders to *redesign* property as needed to cure a problem; require the board to give *notice* to all homeowners before filing a lawsuit, thereby providing those ultimately responsible—the owners—with the right to know what is being done in their name and at their expense without compromising the litigation strategy; require that notice be given to the builder and that a meeting be held before filing a lawsuit and *before* experts write up their reports, thus providing an opportunity to talk a solution through before a suit is filed; and require a vote of a minimum percentage of homeowners before a lawsuit is filed. The minimum percentage requirement recognizes that there is neither any assurance of victory nor any immunity to the homeowners' association from cross-complaint. Further, after a complaint is filed, existing homeowners must disclose all allegations when they resell their homes. Finally, if the attorney receives 30 to 40 percent of the settlement or award, the funds remaining for remedial work might prove insufficient.

Reasonable and highly professional attorneys who represent community associations as both advisers and litigators take exception to the suggestion about public disclosure. Their counterargument holds that it costs the element of confidentiality, reveals the strengths and weaknesses of the case in a forum that includes developer representatives, and otherwise weakens the confidential nature of the attorney/client relationship. They argue, too, that the defense operates under no such restraints and thus can further compromise the balance between the parties.

There is some validity to these arguments, but it relates not to the disclosure requirement in theory but rather to how it might be used and applied in practice. In other words, the goal is not to give developers and their attorney a "free look"; instead, members of the community association should be legitimately assured and agree, at least in some meaningful percentage, that litigation is appropriate. Moreover, a talented and experienced attorney knows how to hold an open meeting that discloses a certain level of information and a closed meeting that deals with more sensitive matters. Even when the developer is still a member of the association, an appropriate level of information can be disclosed with enough thought and planning. The point is that the developer should not have a free look and should not be able to participate in such a meeting other than as an invited guest. At the same time, attorneys who argue that if they had to comply with such a provision, they "would not be able to convince [their] client to sue" should not be able to enjoy such a free ride either. As has been observed several times, documents need to be drafted to reflect a *balance of interests.*

Other CCR provisions call for adopting a homeowners' bill of rights that would allow greater protection for the individual while giving the association and its board greater ability to "govern" and reinforcing the desire to create communities even as governance processes evolve; establishing a thoughtful and balanced limit on the use of assessments; indemnifying the officers and directors of the homeowners' association; requiring binding arbitration or mediation for all disputes (see Chapter 6); creating and following a warranty chart and procedures to inform the association and its members of who is responsible for what and to help defuse disputes; defining board duties and nonduties to make clear that the board has the power both to exercise business judgment and to refrain from taking an action if it determines that to be the best course of action; and specifying a broad, well-funded maintenance provision.

Sales Documents

Among their several functions, sales documents teach, condition expectations, and create *and* limit rights. In other words, they are much more than boilerplate documents. Sales documents should therefore include language dealing with alternative dispute resolution techniques and provisions for a waiver of jury trial, site access and inspection rights, express warranties, walk-through procedures that establish the procedures by which buyer and seller see and agree on the condition of the property or at least agree on the nature and extent of the areas of disagreement, customer service provisions, and the rescission right of the buyer.

In the course of good business practice, the seller's attorney should review the marketing materials, including the contract and other legal documents, as well as collateral marketing materials, advertisements, and the other forms of communication that will "sell" the public on the development. This examination should cover all of the topics and pitfalls discussed in this book and should acknowledge that the first contact with the prospect is often the point at which the desire to buy is created and the nature of the ultimate relationship established.

The attorney or risk manager should also determine if any materials remaining on file with local government are inconsistent with the development plan. The team dealing with permit approvals probably should perform this check. If any submissions on file are found to be inconsistent, steps need to be taken to resolve the ambiguity in order to avoid the public's reliance on the wrong information.

Finally, a briefing should be held for all salespeople on the documentation. If properly written, disclaimers and disclosures in the sales documents do not chill sales; they may, in fact, enhance them. Such disclaimers can cover issues from errant golf balls to security; from soils, slabs, and electromagnetic fields to wildlife. They can and should extend from the general reservation of the possibility of changes to site-specific issues.

It is important that the developer/builder obtain from the purchaser a written receipt and acknowledgment of the sales contract/disclosure package. In some states, the acknowledgment is required as proof of the public offering statement process. In any case, it makes good business sense and protects all concerned.

■ Operation of Community Associations

Not all residential developments organize community associations, but an increasing number do. As a result, many developers experience the challenge of structuring and operating a community association. Out of innocence and inexperience, some may well ask, "So what's the big deal about associations?" The big deal is that associations give rise to some of the most emotional, difficult-to-resolve litigation among all of the areas of risk under discussion. Three introductory articles in Appendices 6, 7, and 8 provide an in-depth analysis of some of the technical and operational issues in the creation and operation of an association. This is an appropriate point to restate the fact that the developer of master-planned communities is creating not only a *product* but a *process* as well. The following threshold questions about community associations require thoughtful attention:

- Why is so little attention paid to something so important?

- What is the developer/declarant *really* creating?

- What is the community association and what is the declarant's relationship to it?

The answers to these questions are interrelated and form the basis for the legal issues involved in this chapter. What is actually created and the declarant's relationship to it come together in certain additional issues such as when the association comes into existence, the existence of the association separate from the developer/declarant who creates it, and how the declarant exercises control over the association.

A community association is an entity separate and apart from the developer. It has an independent existence and exists from the time that the creating documents are recorded. Although the declarant or its representatives have the power to control the actions of the association for a specified period, that power is limited by the fact that those in control have the obligations of fiduciaries and thus must act in accordance with the rules of law applicable to fiduciaries. In addition, the association operates in accordance with its own business and operation plan.

Three critical elements set community associations apart from other forms of business organizations.

- *Mandatory membership.* Anyone who takes title to property subject to the association's recorded documents automatically becomes a member of the association and is bound by the rights and obligations spelled out in the documents. Members do not have to be active, but they must comply with the regulations.

- *The power to control property.* The community association has unusually broad power to regulate the use and enjoyment of both commonly and privately owned property. This power derives from both state law and, more particularly, the governing documents of the association itself. The power contributes to the special roles associations play and the treatment they receive in accordance with community association law.

- *The power to "tax."* The obligatory assessment leveled by the association is not strictly speaking a tax but is analogous to a tax. The power to impose such charges singles out the community association from other nongovernment organizations. This power also gives rise to special roles and legal treatment.

Unique Character of the Association

The truly unique character of the community association rests with the special roles or functions it performs in the operation and administration of the project. These roles, which courts have recognized in cases throughout the country, have significant legal consequences.

The Association as a Business

The association is a business because of what it does and because it performs businesslike tasks. It is a service-oriented, cooperative business that provides maintenance, upkeep, and other services to those who "own" it. The powers and duties set out in the documents that created the association define the nature of the association's business role. As in any business, the association operates by

Case: Developer-Controlled Board Acted with Conflict of Interest

When the developer of a townhouse project turned over control of the homeowners' association to the owners, the owners discovered that no reserve account had been established. This occurred despite the fact that the developer knew that exposure to severe wind and salt spray created problems with the paint and exterior trim to the townhouses. The court ruled that since the original directors (who were owners of the development company and its employees) failed to exercise their responsibility to assess each unit for an adequate reserve fund and acted with a conflict of interest, they abdicated their obligation as initial directors.

The conflict arose when the directors kept the assessment low in order to make it easier for the buyers to qualify for mortgages. The court found that the initial directors were liable for breach of fiduciary duty and ordered them to pay the cost of remedying the defects.

---

and through its officers and directors. As with any officer or director, those on homeowners' association boards are subject to the fiduciary and other legal responsibilities applicable to the exercise of their duties. Consequently, there are limits to their power as well as inherent risks. Generally, the senior person on the development team responsible for the project should not serve on the board. That person should not be in a position in which he or she must speak as the developer in the context of a board meeting.

As to the nature of duty, three considerations apply. First, the courts have long explained fiduciary duties and their nature. A fiduciary relationship "exists where there is a special confidence reposed in one who in equity and good conscience is bound to act in good faith with due regard to the interests of others." A different court explained that "the duty of undivided loyalty applies when the board of directors of the association considers maintenance and repair contracts, the operating budget, creation of reserves, etc. The board may not make decisions for the association that benefit their own interests at the expense of the association and its mem-

Case: Failure to Levy Assessments

The initial developer-appointed directors of an association failed to levy assessments against the unsold units owned by the developer. In court, the directors argued that they could not be held personally liable for the corporate developer's failure to pay assessments because officers or directors of a corporation are generally not liable for corporate acts simply by reason of their official relation to the corporation. The court said that the directors clearly had a duty of loyalty and good faith to their employer, the developer. However, when they were appointed to the board of directors of the association, taking on the role of fiduciaries of the association made them liable for failing to enforce against their employer the requirement to pay assessments.

bers." The main point is that the fiduciary is charged with high-level responsibility and must avoid self-dealing and conflicting interests while making proper disclosures and taking appropriate action when conflicts arise. Not every apparent "conflict," however, is fatal. Accordingly, the fiduciary must demonstrate sensitivity to and clarity of understanding of the consequences.

The second consideration asks to whom duty is owed. Simply put, it is owed to the association and to the members of the association. The third consideration involves the business judgment rule, which requires the exercise of ordinary and reasonable care in the discharge of the directors' duties. It requires supervision, imposes limits on the ability to delegate, and requires good faith, diligence, care, and skill. What it does not require is that the director always be right. It allows for error as long as the director acted in good faith and in accordance with the basic authority set out in the governing documents.

Several common activities that cause difficulty for a developer-controlled board of directors are business activities in which the association generally is or should be involved. They do not, however, present stark conflict-of-interest problems. They include entering into a long-term contract in violation of provisions of the association's declaration or bylaws where the contract turns out not to be in the best interest of the association (for example, a contract with a management agent); failing to observe the required corporate formalities such as holding regular meetings, keeping a corporate minutes book, and properly authorizing as well as documenting all board actions; failing to purchase adequate insurance or failing to renew an insurance policy; entering a dwelling unit without proper authorization; failing to require the developer to complete (and convey to the association as necessary) the common areas in a timely manner, failing to order an impartial inspection of the common areas by the association, and failing to maintain the common areas adequately or to have sound business reasons for the decision not to do so; failing to collect assessments as described in the declaration and to increase assessments as necessary to maintain an acceptable level of services; failing to enforce the declaration's architectural control provisions; failing to review the association budget and evaluate the association's reserve funds policy; failing to prepare quarterly and annual reports in accordance with association documents; failing to file a lawsuit before expiration of the statute of limitations or failing to toll the statute or to take some other appropriate action to protect the rights of the association from improper termination; failing to use due care in the hiring, supervision, and discharge of personnel; failing to give notice of an increase in assessments as may be required by the governing documents; failing to file tax returns and other required forms with the state and the Internal Revenue Service; and discriminating in violation of civil rights statutes. It is worth noting that in some situations the association becomes the "housing provider" and is liable for violations of the law even if the original marketing plan was created by some other entity.

In addition to the above, other association activities are fraught with potential real or perceived conflicts of interest. Such activities involve developer/declarant representatives on the board of directors, who, caught in a potentially untenable situation, wrong someone no matter how they decide an issue. Accordingly, the activities require sensitive and careful handling. They include contracts and leases that involve the developer/declarant or related entities and the association; assessments and the various financial issues inherent in the assessment process such as amounts, shortfalls, payment or nonpayment to the developer, collections from delinquent owners, reserves, and a host of other issues; acceptance of common

Case: Courts Treat Association Design Committees Like Zoning Boards

A property owner had paid a premium for a lot with a spectacular view, spent $37,000 on improvements to the backyard in order to enhance the view, and obtained approval from the association's architectural committee to build a fence, which included a solid two-foot base topped with wrought iron. When a neighbor received approval from the architectural committee to construct a solid fence across the back of his lot, the first owner objected on the grounds that the fence would materially obstruct his view.

The first owner eventually sued his neighbor, the association, and the developer. The court noted that the central question in this case was whether the association had a duty to act in good faith and avoid arbitrary decisions in approving plans for construction of a fence on a codefendant's property. The court ruled that decisions made concerning the approval or disapproval of an individual homeowner's construction and/or improvement plans must be made in good faith and must not be exercised capriciously or arbitrarily.

The court treated the architectural committee as it would treat a zoning board in the granting of a variance and held it to a standard to protect the rights of the people living in the community who relied on the design system in place.

areas along with settlements for any defects in those areas; determining if defects are related to maintenance or construction and who pays; businesslike bookkeeping and recordkeeping; understanding community association insurance needs and costs and potential areas of dispute; enforcing the declarant's own obligations and recognizing the difficulty associated with suing the declarant for failure to comply with the rules and procedures of the association; enforcing rules when the development office believes that tolerating violations is better for sales than enforcement litigation; failing to understand the taxes that the association must pay and the legal issues involved; and problems with sales and the operation of a sales facility on community property if the right to them was not properly reserved in the community association documents.

The Association as a Government

Many people have difficulty seeing a community association as a government. Nonetheless, the association's governance functions are real and have legal consequences. The association is essentially a private government delivering public or quasi-public services. The association's characterization as a private government arises from the powers and duties discussed earlier. It is neither the state nor an instrumentality of the state. When the U.S. Supreme Court says that a city may not prohibit signs, for example, that stricture does not apply to Heavenly Acres Condominium just because the latter is a regulating private government. The consequences of the association's characterization as a government are many and generally require the association to meet certain standards of operation. The most significant consideration is that actions need to be taken in compliance with the rule of reasonableness.

How to Create a Community Association to Minimize Risk

The first step in the process of making the operation of associations more user-friendly is to structure the association and its documents so that they "work." In other words, the documents and the association plan should function during the sales period, the transition period, and the period of ongoing operation by meeting the objectives of sound legal documentation. Many different approaches are available for structuring an association. The most obvious is not necessarily the best way to meet a particular development's needs. Whatever the chosen structure, the objectives of the documents fall into two categories: general or theoretical and specific, legal. In the first case, documents must fit the project, be certain in their application and enforcement, and embody or become the "law of the project." In the second case, for the community to be properly formed and empowered, the specific objectives must define who owns what, establish interlocking relationships among the owners, set forth standards and restrictions, create the administrative vehicle to operate the property, provide for project operation and finance, outline a transition process, and specify and preserve appropriate declarant rights.

Balancing the interests within the association context is vital not only for risk reduction but also for ensuring that the governance process works. Balancing the interests means not that association documents are protective of the developer/declarant at the expense of the association and its members but that they protect and enhance the interests of both parties. Further, the documents should not be overlawyered; instead, they should reflect experience and common sense.

In creating a community association, it is important to understand the basics of community association law and operation; ensure that the selected structure fits the property and satisfies the needs of the community; use a development team, formulate good checklists, and develop a realistic timetable; understand the project and its peculiarities, including geography, demographics, amenities, etc.; remain flexible and realistic; and protect the project's plan of development in both documentation and practices and procedures.

How to Operate a
Community Association to Minimize Risk

"How do I avoid these problems?" is the question most often asked after the problems have surfaced. The most important factor in problem avoidance is initiating the avoidance process *at the outset.*

• Understand and become familiar with the community association documents, especially if you are the declarant or a member of the development team. The documentation package is an essential part of the project.

• Understand the structure of the association. Not all associations are set up the same way, and how the process works *for you and your project* is something that all members of the team need to comprehend.

• Be certain from the beginning that the association structure is adequate to do the stated job, fitted properly to the particular

Case: Association Decisions Must Be Reasonable

When the owners of a condominium unit were transferred and could not find a buyer for their unit, they arranged to assign three one-quarter interests in the unit to three other couples and retain a one-quarter interest for themselves. The transfers were made, and the association sued to have the transfers declared void, arguing that the project was to be "single-family."

The court determined that the issue in this case was whether the association's refusal to approve the transfer was reasonable. The court noted that there are two criteria for testing reasonableness: whether a decision is rationally related to the protection, preservation, or proper operation of the property and the purposes of the association's governing documents, and whether the power was exercised in a fair and nondiscriminatory manner. The court ruled that the association's decision was unreasonable and allowed the transfers of four interests in the unit to stand.

---

facts and circumstances of your development, and in place and operational at the outset of the sales and marketing process.

- Always keeps in mind *the obligation to act*, which falls on those running the association; *who may act*, which may be the developer/declarant, the board, one or more officers, or the association membership by some majority or greater vote; and *how to act*, which once again presents the issues of duty and the rule of reasonableness.

- In addition, do not try to do it all yourself. Document whatever you or the association does, remain flexible and willing to "spread the risk," and never underestimate the role of the association manager.

Actions the Board Should Take

The board should follow some basic business steps that often double as sound risk management practices. For example, the board should select and work with an attorney as necessary; employ a management agent, independent contractors, or employees as necessary and prescribe and supervise their duties; appoint committees involving owners/association members if necessary, cooperate with them in their work, and ensure that such work contributes to the association; oversee the development of recreational, social, cultural, and educational programs to meet the needs and interests of the members based, to the extent possible, on member input; and advise owners of their responsibilities and opportunities and serve as the catalyst for communication within the association.

Recommended Basic Practices for Directors and Officers of Associations

To ensure the faithful, effective, and active performance of the duties of a director or officer in accordance with the legal standards discussed above, each director and officer should continuously strive to use due diligence in supervising the actions of employees, agents, and consultants; keep abreast of the association's business; attend and participate in relevant meetings and follow standard practices for absences and acceptance of minutes; vote against actions taken or resolutions adopted by the board as circumstances dictate and ensure that the minutes reflect dissent; become knowledgeable of the legal documents governing the affairs of the association; exercise reasonable diligence in carrying out and following through on responsibilities assumed or assigned; perform all duties required by law or the association documents in a reasonable and responsible manner; and make every effort to document fully in the association's records the basis, process, background, and any other relevant facts for making decisions.

In summary, a prudent director or officer must perform his or her duties in good faith and exercise such care as an ordinarily prudent person in a like position would do under similar circumstances. He or she must use information, opinions, reports, and financial statements furnished by persons, firms, or committees that are reliable, competent, and expert and merit confidence. If, after conducting this reasonable inquiry, you take or refrain from taking a particular action, you should be effectively insulated from liability on the basis of claims that you failed to discharge your obligations properly.

■ Amenity Ownership, Operation, and Disposition

Developers of projects with amenities eventually face the question of what to do about the amenities. Own and operate them forever? Sell them to the homeowners? the members? the users? a third-party operator? These and many other questions arise in the normal course of business, and each can trigger litigation. This section discusses a number of practical and legal issues involved in amenity disposition and explores some of the creative options used by today's developers.

The primary sources of amenity disposition problems are poor planning, poor project documentation, inadequate disclosure, and overly aggressive marketing. Project amenities are major assets, and while developers need the flexibility to be able to deal with them in various ways, the homeowner or member has a right to rely on the development plan as originally disclosed. Therefore, the plan and its disclosure must provide for flexibility, specific options for the developer, and some protections for the purchaser.

What Are You Selling?

A discussion of mistakes made and lessons learned is incomplete without acknowledging that a recurring, threshold mistake is the failure to perceive that today's large-scale residential projects embody not one but rather two major asset bases, each of which is independently subject to disposition. Those asset bases are the dwelling units *and* their lots and all project amenities.

A basic assumption is that the developer is not in the business of primarily developing and operating the amenity package. Rather, the assumption is that the amenities are constructed as an adjunct to the primary business of the development and sale of land. Thus,

Amenity Trends

[M]ost developers just don't want to be in the business of developing golf clubs.—Robin Baker

Most new members want turnkey clubs that are managed professionally.—Dennis Hillier

We're seeing a trend toward semiprivate or public golf courses within planned communities, simply to spread the costs of a club among a greater number of users.—Judith H. Reagan

If you factor in some public play at the golf course, it builds community support for the project.—Wayne Hyatt

Source: From David Salvesen, "Emerging Trends in Amenity Clubs," *Urban Land*, August 1994, pp. 55–58.

the price of the parcel or the housing unit increases with the amenity's increase in value.

Too often, however, the developer/builder does not recognize the significant intrinsic value in the amenity itself and, assuming a decline in value of the amenity upon sale, decides to leave money on the table. When the development plan does not include a means for realizing the value of the amenity through the disposition process, the developer/builder loses money.

To realize the amenity's intrinsic value, it is important to recognize that the amenity, as a separate part of the development, has great value to the homeowners both individually and collectively. In all probability, the sales prices of the parcels and housing units have partially or fully paid for the amenities, which have been and can continue to be operated by fees and assessments generated from property owners and nonresident users. In other words, with proper planning, an asset with significant intrinsic value can be made available for disposition on a debt-free basis.

The Lesson Learned: Planning

In a large-scale planned community with substantial amenities, the development team and the development plan must carefully and thoroughly address an amenity strategy. In addition, four key considerations must be included on the planning checklist. The first concerns the care, custody, and control of the amenity package itself. Planning should address these issues not only for the period of development and sale, but also for the posttransition period. The objective is to plan and prepare the project documentation in such a way as to permit development needs to be met properly without regard to the issue of ownership and management authority.

The second key area of planning deals with the method for rational transfer. A decision as to how the amenities will ultimately be held or conveyed is not important at this stage, but it is vital that the developer/builder is accorded the right to options in this regard. For example, it is entirely appropriate for the documents creating the planned community to specify that the developer/builder may convey the amenities to a third party, hold the amenities and operate them as a for-profit component of his or her own business, convey the amenities as an equity club, convey the amenities to the homeowners' association as common area, or use some combination of these or take another approach. If carefully drafted, such document provisions do not create significant buyer resistance. In fact, the secondary mortgage market and the regulators of various states have accepted the provisions. The goal is to satisfy the third key planning objective: flexibility.

Flexibility must be created, for it will not emerge on its own. It can be and often is lost when the developer/builder takes actions inconsistent with project planning or project documentation and representations. A program that monitors the sales process can help guard against inconsistent representations that could ultimately result in an abrogation of the flexibility built into the development plan and amenity strategy.

The fourth key planning area concerns timing of the ultimate transfer of the amenities. As with most business decisions, there is little certainty on this topic. It is a given that planning should be completed early, yet the best time for the execution of the plan—

whether early in the project's life, at mid-life, or late in the build-out stage—is a matter of judgment.

A Significant Lesson Learned: The Effect of Representations

Salespersons usually do not lie; therefore, buyers usually do not win misrepresentation lawsuits. But misrepresentation lawsuits do not go away easily, and they do not go away early. Misrepresentation cases are generally factual disputes that make summary disposition at the motions level inappropriate. The result is that cases are often concluded at or just before trial and thus are expensive in terms of time, money, and lost opportunities.

Monitoring representations is extremely important and is heightened by the fact that while misrepresentation cases often are resolved in favor of the builder/seller, the property owner/plaintiff often wins representation cases in which the salesperson has made affirmative statements inconsistent with an ultimate development. It is here that the innocent answers of the salespersons that run counter to the flexibility of the development plan take over and become the controlling factor in what a developer/builder may ultimately do. Vital to the preservation of disposition flexibility and a reduction in potential liability is a sales staff that is trained in the legal and development issues specified in the development plan and amenity strategy and whose work is regulated and periodically tested.

A survey of mistakes made and lessons learned helps identify several key areas of concern related to representations. For example, one major consideration is the type of facilities to be constructed both at the outset of the development and in the future. (Misconceptions could arise from explaining what is believed to be the development plan or from applying adjectives to the project that are not believed to carry legal weight.) Other considerations include levels of maintenance, the cost of facility maintenance and operation to be borne by unit owners, the date the facilities will be available for use (the developer/builder/seller should exercise considerable caution and realize that the buying public will more readily accept a promise of a lengthy delay when that delay is explained upfront.), the nature and extent of nonowner/nonresident involvement in the facilities, the natural divisiveness that results from the varying interests of different

Representations: Words to Think About

All of these examples come out of the Sunday real estate section of the *Atlanta Journal-Constitution.* All create rights and expectations. None was anticipated or intended.

- "Value."

- "Your home comes with a $5,000,000 recreation facility."

- "Mr. Smith just bought his wife a house and an Olympic-size pool." (Do you know how large an Olympic-size pool is?)

- "Always"; "Fixed cost"; "Annual."

- "World class."

- "Championship." (Do you know what a championship golf course is. . . and what the buying public thinks it is?)

- "Your lot will appreciate because of the availability of the amenities. . . ."

- "The lot value reflects a premium, because. . . ."

classes of users within a large-scale resort community, and the extent to which owners acquire some legally enforceable interest in the amenities themselves. (This interest could range from simply some right of use to an ownership right.) These problems can be avoided by the careful drafting of basic community association and club documents in conjunction with carefully structured sales and disclosure materials.

Throughout the sales process, it is important to recall that words convey different shades of meaning to different segments of the buying public. Marketing materials must reflect thoughtfulness and care when using terms such as

- "planned" versus "proposed" (if something is planned, buyers believe they have a right to see it);

- "championship" golf course (most people do not know that this term deals with length of the course, not with the caliber of players);

- "world class" (does anyone know what this means?);

- "first class" and "highest quality" (these terms inflate expectations);

- "Olympic" pool (Olympic-size pools are enormous and few communities build them, although many advertise as if they do);

- "your home comes with . . ." (many advertisements promise amenities and create expectations of ownership, which often trigger legal consequences);

- "always" (that is a long time; is it what you really mean?);

- "premium" (what does it mean?);

- "fair" (one person's fairness is potentially another's most egregious unfairness); and

- "value" (it is sufficient to note at this point that "value," especially when used with "appreciate," can quickly give rise to serious problems).

These and other loaded words and phrases are major sources of risk. You should review your marketing materials to see whether you have used any terms in a manner that could produce unintended consequences.

Amenity Disposition

The successful amenity disposition plan should give considerable weight to homeowner concerns and specify what will be done in the areas of greatest concern in order to maximize the plan's attractiveness and acceptability. At the same time, the plan should minimize the potential for dispute and litigation.

Among the significant concerns of property owners are the maximum number of units; the maximum number of members available to use the facilities; membership transferability (representations that a membership will be transferable at the sale of the purchaser's home or lot can present a variety of subsequent problems, including the creation of claims that may bar a subsequent equity conversion if a "membership" was granted at the original time of home or lot purchase and purports to be perpetual and transferable); whether the amount of permitted cost increases that can be passed on to members can be capped; use of facilities for some other future purpose, e.g., rental, commercial, convention, or simply a change from a recreational amenity to residential or commercial; membership, initiation, and user fees both now and in the future (guarantees of any economic charges for more than a relatively brief period are somewhat foolhardy; the buying public will look for such guarantees, and the developer/builder must resist giving them unless they are carefully researched); the rights of nonresidents or nonowners in the facilities (if nonowners have acquired membership rights, prospective purchasers will want to know if nonowner or nonresident membership rights phase out so as to permit future purchasers of housing units to be able to acquire them); whether the membership offering is a security and, if so, how it is to be handled; whether the amenities were "bought and paid for" in the price of the housing unit (the developer/builder and the development team must realize that this question must be dealt with forthrightly, correctly, and with sufficient factual foundation to support the legal argument when the answer is "no"); and the nature, number, and extent of amenities.

The Substantive Law Issues

The disposition of amenities can involve several distinct and significant areas of substantive law. In one form or another, each leads to the potential creation of certain property interests or other rights of property owners to use and enjoy the amenities—interests that the developer must inevitably address. The various legal theories that may be used to establish these property interests or rights include express or implied easements, implied covenants, estoppel, breach of fiduciary duty, breach of contract, and fraud.

Theories of express or implied easements, including negative easements, may be used to assert that purchasers of lots obtained an express or implied easement for access and use of the amenities under certain terms and conditions. These property rights run with the lot and cannot be subsequently modified or taken away. The theory of negative restrictions simply asserts that certain property may not be used for any purpose other than that specifically represented at the time of sale and conveyance of the unit or lot. For example, an area on a recorded plat that includes parcels marked "open space" or "golf course" and that is referenced or incorporated into a deed of conveyance of an individual lot creates a negative easement restricting the use of that land to "open space" or "golf course." Future use of that parcel for any other purpose is precluded.

The theory of implied covenants is similar to the theory of implied easements; in fact, the two are often used interchangeably. The difference, however, is that implied covenants may include affirmative obligations to perform certain acts or duties while implied easements generally are permissive or restrictive and do not require any affirmative action by the owner of the property burdened with the easement. An implied covenant may include the affirmative obligation on the part of the developer to perform certain maintenance duties on amenities and facilities.

The best-known case applying the theory of implied covenants is *Shalimar Association* v. *D.O.C. Enterprises, Ltd.*, 688 P.2d 682 (Ariz. 1984). The case provides a virtual checklist of developer actions that may conspire to create an implied covenant in favor of lot purchasers. The developer showed potential lot buyers a plat of the proposed Shalimar Estates development, which included a golf course; subsequently, the plat was recorded in the county land records. Use restrictions for Shalimar Estates, which referenced the tract of land on which the golf course would be constructed, also were recorded in the county land records. The recorded plat showed an easement for a golf cart path. The developer placed brochures and sales material depicting the golf course on file with the state department of real estate. Throughout the sales period, purchasers were told that the golf course and the recorded use restrictions on the residential lots would be maintained until the year 2000, with provision for an extension of 25 years. The court applied the theory of implied covenants and held that the developer's actions had created a covenant restricting the use of the land to a golf course. That covenant now binds the current owner of the golf course and all subsequent owners until the year 2025.

Estoppel is a claim based on equitable arguments rather than on express legal obligations. Homeowners may assert estoppel if the developer made certain promises or representations that homeowners relied on to their detriment. In such event, the developer might be precluded from later denying those representations or acting in a manner inconsistent with them to the detriment of homeowners who relied on the representations. If a developer represents that certain property will be maintained as a golf course or other recreational facility and homeowners rely on those representations in improving their property or purchasing houses, the developer may be estopped from making other arrangements for the use of that property or from abrogating maintenance responsibility. Estoppel, however, generally applies only where the affected land is well defined and the restrictions on it are clear.

A good example of the application of estoppel principles is *Oceanside Community Association* v. *Oceanside Land Company*, 195 Cal. Rptr. 320, 522 P.2d 427 (1983). In that case, a developer recorded a declaration of covenants, conditions, and restrictions limiting certain property adjacent to the community to use as a golf course for 99 years. The declaration stated that the covenant was to run with the land. The developer built the golf course and operated it for several years. A reference to the declaration was included in the deeds of all purchasers who bought in the planned community. The court held that a successor developer could not deny the existence of the covenant to maintain the property as a golf course or the fact that the covenant ran with the land and bound successor purchasers of the golf course. The court imposed an equitable lien against the golf course that could be foreclosed by the lot owners whenever the developer was not in the process of renovating and maintaining the golf course. In this case, the developer clearly defined both the tract of land and the restriction to be imposed.

Breach of fiduciary duty may be applicable if the developer places him- or herself in a position of trust and confidence of the homeowners. The position of trust and confidence gives rise to certain duties on the part of the developer. Fiduciaries who handle property or operate a business on behalf of others must do so as if the property or business were their own. Breach of these duties by a developer may be the subject of a lawsuit by homeowners. Fiduciary duties arise in at least two situations. First, the developer is in a position of total control of an existing recreational club on behalf of the homeowners. Second, the developer has undertaken to perform services for a recreational club on behalf of the homeowners. In such situations, the developer is in a no-win position in that he or she must evaluate any amenity disposition plan from the viewpoint of the homeowners. Self-dealing in the form of a "sweetheart" deal for the sale of the amenities or simply a disposition contrary to the interests of the homeowners may lead to substantial liability against the developer and sometimes personal liability against those persons in the decision-making role.

Again, it should be emphasized that fiduciary responsibilities are not created out of thin air. The developer creates such responsibilities by placing him- or herself in a position of control over activities conducted for the benefit of the homeowners. The developer sometimes takes on fiduciary responsibilities simply to demonstrate that he or she operates in good faith. Nonetheless, the developer can avoid the pitfalls associated with a fiduciary responsibility by paying careful attention to issues of ownership, control, and expectations regarding the amenity package. It has been our experience that homeowners will accept virtually any reasonable plan for the operation and eventual disposition of amenities as long as they are aware of the situation and the possibilities from the outset.

A contract between the lot owner and club may exist if the developer, as owner of the amenities, establishes a club that lot purchasers can join and represents that certain rights will be granted in exchange for payment of initiation fees and periodic dues. Changing the terms of the contract in an amenities disposition deal, after payment of initiation fees and dues, may constitute a breach of contract. The key is the extent to which the developer has protected him- or herself by retaining the right to modify unilaterally the terms, fees, and rules of the club. If in the process of accepting lot owners as members in a club the developer makes oral or written representations that the club will be transferred to a homeowners' association, such a representation becomes part of the basis of the bargain of membership in the club. Without the express right to modify the plan for disposition, the developer can be held liable for breach of contractual obligation. Homeowners may recover damages for the breach or force the developer to perform his or her obligation to convey the facilities.

The final theory is that of fraud. Fraud is extremely difficult to prove since the state of mind and intentions of the persons making representations are at issue. The key elements of fraud are an intentional misstatement or misrepresentation, knowledge on the part of the developer that the statement is false, and justifiable reliance by the buyer. Statements of opinion, hopes, and expectations or normal sales puffery as distinguished from intentional misstatements of fact do not suffice as a basis for determining fraud. Developers often represent that certain amenities will be transferred to a homeowners' association after a certain period. If the developer, at the time he or she makes such a representation, does not have any such intention, homeowners may be able to force a transfer of the amenities free of charge based on a successful allegation of fraud.

In each theory discussed above, it is implicit that the developer must "do something" in order to create rights in homeowners. Determining whether the developer has created rights in homeowners is fact-intensive and can cover virtually every aspect of a project's development from initial planning to marketing. Any one of the following considerations can be critical in determining whether the developer has created irrevocable rights in homeowners to use or own the facilities and amenities: state and U.S. Department of Housing and Urban Development property reports; project covenants; the project master plan, including all revisions; recorded plats; written advertising materials, sales brochures, and sales handouts; oral and written representations of sales agents regarding the amenities; documentation for the country club or other amenity, including application forms and related materials; and sales contracts for the lots in the project to determine the nature and extent of any representations regarding the amenities.

This list is not exhaustive. The point is that the developer must exercise great care in *all* aspects of the development process from the inception of development. He or she will spend much time and money to create high-quality amenities and must use caution not to lay the foundation for later claims that he or she has given away those amenities.

Applicable Cases

Atlanta Association of Baptist Churches v. *Cowan*, 183 Ga. 187, 188 S.E. 21 (1936), *on remand*, 186 Ga. 10, 96 S.E. 780 (1938). Sales personnel remarks that an area on a recorded plat marked "reserved" for developing a park created an obligation that the area could be used only for a park.

Case v. *Morrisette*, 475 F.2d. 1300 (D.C. Cir. 1973). A recorded plat designated that a particular parcel was to be used for parking. When the successor developer conveyed the parcel, the new owner proposed developing it for parking for an adjacent apartment complex. The court ruled that the parcel could not be used for a new purpose.

Hendley v. *Overstreet*, 253 Ga. 136 (1984). The court held that where a declaration of restrictive covenants described a park or lake for the use of lot owners, the sale of lots by deeds referencing the declaration created an irrevocable easement in such an area for the lot owners.

Old Port Cove Property Owners v. *Ecclestone*, 500 So.2d 331 (Fla. Dist. Ct. App. 1986). The developer of a large-scale homeowners' association did not breach his fiduciary duty to the association when he sold the project's entire road system to the property owners' association and retained for himself a rent-free easement in the road system to allow access to the commercial areas.

Piechowski v. *Case*, 255 N.W.2d 72 (S.D. 1977). The court found that a covenant designating a parcel on a plat as a park and commercial area was an added inducement that influenced potential owners to purchase lots.

Walker v. *Duncan*, 236 Ga. 331 (1976). A court stated that where a developer sells lots according to a recorded plat, the buyers acquire an easement in any areas set apart for their use. An easement acquired in this manner is considered an express grant and is an irrevocable property right.

Amenities Documents and Issues Checklist

The following is a checklist of documents to review and issues to address with regard to amenity ownership, operation, and disposition:

Documents

- Zoning letters of intent;

- All written (and oral) representations of sales agents regarding access to and availability of amenities;

- Original project master plan and all revisions through the current master plan;

- Recorded plats referencing or showing amenities;

- Restrictive covenants or declaration of covenants, conditions, and restrictions;

- Federal (HUD) and state property reports from the original to the most recent;

- Minutes of developer-controlled homeowners' association meetings regarding amenities;

- Country club documents and related materials, including articles of incorporation, bylaws, minutes, rules, and application forms;

- Sales contract regarding written representations and references to the amenities; and

- Written advertising materials, sales brochures, maps, and drawings involving the amenities.

Issues

- Restrictions on the transferability of the amenities or country club property;

- Representation that homeowners' association members will not pay an additional lump-sum charge upon sale of amenities to a third party;

- Transfer of amenities at the option of the developer or association members;

- Transferability to a homeowners' association, including compensation of existing association members, accommodation of nonowner association members, and option or right of first refusal of members to purchase amenities from developer;

- Obligation of homeowners' association to accept the facilities;

- Restrictions on future use of amenity property;

- Transferability of memberships, including ability to transfer to grantee of lot and potential for profit to member upon transfer;

- Presence of disclaimers informing the association and its members that they acquire no proprietary or other interest in the amenities;

- Maximum number of members;

- Membership qualifications, including residency in development or membership in association and membership requirement if resident or association member;

- Priority of certain persons, especially residents in development or association members, to obtain memberships in club;

- Nature, type, and extent of voting and/or management rights and obligations of homeowners' association members;

- Representation that purchase of lot or membership in association entitles owner to membership in club or right to use the amenities;

- Existence of special privilege memberships or special categories of membership;

- Advertising regarding extent of availability of amenities or use rights in amenities; and

- Applicability of restrictive covenants to amenity property.

A few final words about amenity disposition and operation are in order. First, there are several different ways to develop amenities and, upon completion, several different ways to structure them (see Appendix 3). Second, after reviewing and considering the options, the developer/builder needs to "think outside the box." Following the same approach in Boise as in Boca Raton is usually a prescription for multiple problems. Third, in dealing with amenities and homeowners' associations, it is instructive to recall the words of Charles Fraser, the dean of the recreational development industry. He warned of the "power loss stress syndrome," which affects retirees who think that the operation of the amenity requires the benefit of their corporate experience. By the same token, developers/builders should never underestimate property owners in terms of the issues they are likely to raise and their capacity for problem solving. The latter is far greater than might be expected.

■ State and Federal Land Sales Regulation

Sales and marketing issues were discussed in the context of expectations and representations. In that discussion, the ultimate concern related to monetary damages and the loss of flexibility in the use of land. Sales and marketing issues also arise in another context: the regulation of land sales. Here the risks range from loss of the ability to market to civil or even criminal sanctions.

The scope of regulation is broad. Although not every state has created a regulatory web, most have enacted at least some statutes that govern land sales. In addition, the complex system of regulation at the federal level may apply to land sales depending on the product offered, the method of sale, the type of financing, etc.

While the appendices contain an in-depth discussion of regulation, it is appropriate to note several commonly encountered federal and state statutes that give rise to regulatory compliance considerations.

At the federal level, the developer/builder must consider the Interstate Land Sales Full Disclosure Act (ILSFDA), the Real Estate Settlement Procedures Act (RESPA), Truth-in-Lending Regulation Z, the Federal Trade Commission Act, the Federal Securities Acts, and the Fair Housing Act. At the state level, the developer/builder must consider the Uniform Land Sales Practices Acts, subdivision laws, the Condominium, Timeshare, and Uniform Common Interest Ownership Acts, securities laws, consumer protection laws, and broker licensing laws.

Marketers in particular must be careful not to overlook the federal ILSFDA and its requirements, under which HUD has jurisdiction over any means of interstate commerce used in marketing even if the sales process is not directed outside the developer's/builder's state. Means or instrumentalities of interstate commerce include mail, telephone, facsimile over telephone lines, and advertising in any media with interstate circulation.

If the ILSFDA applies, it prohibits the sale of subdivided land unless the property has been registered with HUD or is exempt from registration. Several points must be noted about exemptions. First, many exemptions are considered self-determining; in other words, no filing is required to take advantage of them. However, the developer is responsible for retaining the documentation necessary to establish eligibility for the exemption. Second, even if a property qualifies for an exemption, the antifraud provisions of the ILSFDA may still apply. The provisions prohibit anyone from making representations to purchasers that infrastructure or amenities will be provided unless the developer is contractually obligated to provide them. Finally, all lots in the development need not qualify for the same exemption. Certain exemptions may be combined while others may stand alone.

The primary exemptions from HUD registration and the basic requirements to qualify for the exemptions are the 25-lot exemption, under which no more than 25 lots may be sold under a "common promotional plan"; the improved-lot exemption, under which the lot must be improved with a building or sold under a contract that obligates the seller to construct a building on the lot within two years; the builder exemption, under which the lot must be sold to a person engaged in the business of constructing buildings for resale and who acquires the lot for that purpose; the 100-lot exemption, under which fewer than 100 lots for sale under a common promotional plan are not exempt under one of the previous exemptions or certain other exemptions; the intrastate exemption, under which all lots not sold under certain other specified exemptions must be sold to purchasers who reside in the state where the project is located; and the single-family exemption, under which the lot and subdivision must satisfy various technical requirements.

According to the ILSFDA single-family exemption, the first requirement holds that the lot must be located in a county or municipality that specifies minimum development standards in a number of designated areas while the subdivision must meet all local codes and standards. Second, the lot must be located on a paved street built to state or local government standards for dedication (if construction is not complete, the developer must post a performance bond or other surety with the municipality or county in the full amount of the cost of completion). Third, the local government or a homeowners' association must be obligated to maintain streets. In the case of a homeowners' association, the developer must provide each purchaser—before the purchaser's signing a contract—with a written good faith estimate of the cost of maintaining the streets for the first ten years of the community's life. Fourth, potable water, sewer service, and electricity must be extended to the lot at the time of closing (or the local government must be contractually obligated to install such services within 180 days). Fifth, a warranty deed conveying title free of all monetary liens and encumbrances must be given to the purchaser within 180 days of signing the purchase contract. Sixth, a title insurance binder or title opinion must be given to each purchaser at closing to show marketable title subject only to exceptions approved in writing by the purchaser. Seventh, the purchaser or the purchaser's spouse must conduct a personal inspection before signing the contract. Last, no offers of gifts, trips, dinners, or similar promotions shall have been used since June 13, 1980, to induce prospective purchasers to visit the subdivision or purchase any lot in the subdivision (including lots sold under other exemptions).

In addition to the above ILSFDA requirements, many states regulate the sale of subdivided land. State approaches differ as to the types of activities that trigger jurisdiction under their acts and the types of legal requirements. Some states require disclosure only while others require disclosure and impose substantive requirements for the legal documents, the terms of the offering, and project development.

A particular state's statute may be inadvertently triggered by certain types of contacts with residents of the state, even if the developer/builder does not advertise or maintain a physical presence in the state. It is essential to deal with the issue of registration or qualification for exemption before making any contact with purchasers from another state. In some cases, once contact is made, the "pool is poisoned"—sometimes irrevocably.

The least restrictive states do not attempt to assert their jurisdiction unless salespersons are physically present in the state to conduct promotional activities. Other states permit advertising in publications with nationwide circulation but prohibit direct mail or telephone contact with prospective purchasers who reside in their state, even in response to unsolicited inquiries from the resident. Still other states prohibit any contact with residents unless and until the project is registered. In some cases, a state may hold the developer/builder responsible for actions of third-party "agents" who distribute the developer's/builder's marketing materials in their state without the developer's/builder's specific knowledge or authorization. State registration requirements and the availability of exemptions vary widely. Charts and checklists in the appendices describe many of the requirements and exemptions.

One word of caution based on experience. Work with regulators, not against them. Argue your point, but do not cut corners and do not try to "pull the wool over their eyes." They have seen it all and quickly recognize those with honest positions to argue and those who simply are pushing to see if they can get by. You may get by once, but it is a long process, a long life.

CHAPTER 4

Litigation Risk and Avoidance Strategies for the Nonresidential Developer

*Seeking balance has become more difficult because we
have misplaced the vocabulary of accommodation.—*
Philip Howard, *from The Death of Common Sense*

T his chapter addresses litigation risk and avoidance strategies for the nonresidential developer. First, it focuses on certain situations that often generate disputes: acquiring property, borrowing money, investing with others, leasing, and operating/ managing property. Then, it provides both general and specific strategies for minimizing risks and avoiding litigation.

■ Definition of the Nonresidential Developer

The nonresidential developer is a person or entity that develops any type of property other than residential property for sale to consumers. Properties may include office buildings, shopping centers, apartment buildings, warehouses, industrial and research parks and buildings, special-purpose buildings, hotels, motels, office parks, or mixed-use projects that combine these and other types of uses. The customer of the nonresidential developer is a tenant or an owner/user.

In terms of litigation risk and avoidance strategies, the differences between residential and nonresidential developers are dramatic. The nonresidential developer deals with a different customer, generates a different kind of citizen opposition, and experiences more difficulty than the residential developer in meeting land use and infrastructure requirements and obtaining the associated approvals.

The nonresidential developer's customer is a businessperson with some experience in commercial real estate and should be, but is not always, sophisticated. In addition, the customer makes decisions based on economics, not emotions, and is motivated primarily by profit. The customer does not join in the "mob mentality" of homeowners' associations or neighborhoods.

The customer is not protected by or subject to consumer protection laws. The courts and legislatures have, however, substantially relaxed the doctrine of caveat emptor (let the buyer beware) and, in some cases, have imposed disclosure requirements that afford access to adverse information otherwise not available.

The citizen opposition faced by the nonresidential developer is often based on the "NIMBY" (Not In My Back Yard) syndrome. Citizens often raise "quality-of-life" issues in opposition to what they perceive as "blatant commercial profiteering." Since citizens, not the nonresidential developer, elect local officials, citizen opposition makes government consents and approvals more difficult, time-consuming, and expensive to obtain.

For several reasons, the nonresidential developer experiences more difficulty than the residential developer in satisfying land use and infrastructure requirements and securing the related approvals. To begin, the ability to obtain the necessary approvals may depend on traffic, wetlands, and/or environmental studies. These studies are highly conjectural; even experts often arrive at widely varying conclusions. Citizen groups can always find an expert who is sympathetic to their point of view and willing to issue a report with conclusions that differ materially from those of the nonresidential developer's expert. To complicate matters, multiple and overlapping government authorities usually must approve development proposals. State, county, and city/town/village governments control different pieces of the puzzle and do not necessarily coordinate their efforts. Many times, their competitiveness and "turf wars" actually impede the review, permitting, and approval process. Finally, government authorities may impose additional requirements on the nonresidential developer to redress the government's past mistakes, usually at the developer's expense. The imposition of additional requirements is the product of government's inability to predict the location of future demand, sometimes poor planning, and/or politically driven agendas.

Despite their several differences, residential and nonresidential developers share many similarities with respect to litigation risk and avoidance strategies. For example, both developer types must deal with disclosures, risk allocations, mistakes, unanticipated facts, design defects, construction defects, difficult lenders, disgruntled investors, market changes, etc. In addition, the development process is similar for both developer types. They must deal with conceiving the project, planning, design, government approvals, financing, construction, leasing or sales, etc. Finally, the results of litigation are equally devastating for residential and nonresidential developers. Litigation usually stops further loan advances, stops refinancings, stops sales, and sometimes stops leasing when the tenant wants a recorded lease or nondisturbance agreements from all parties with liens ahead of the tenant's lease. Title insurance does not cure most of these problems because the title company commits to reimburse the losing party only after the real property or lease is irrevocably lost. Except with respect to mechanics' liens, bonding against a court's adverse decision is typically not possible because either no statutory procedure exists for prejudgment bonding or, if it does exist, it is too expensive. Further, bonding encourages the other side to continue the litigation by ensuring a source of recovery. Many developers forget these effects and find themselves suddenly in financial duress. Moreover, litigation seldom provides for either full restitution to the aggrieved party or adequate penalties on the perpetrator of the harm. The costs of real property litigation, including attorney fees, typically are not recoverable and often diminish the award to the prevailing party to the point where the "lost opportunities" caused by the time and effort spent on the litigation outweigh the net award. In any event, once litigation commences, both sides have "lost" whether or not they know it. Most developers learn the hard way.

■ Risk Situations That Often Generate Disputes

Nonresidential development is a high-risk profession. Almost every aspect of the developer's work involves risk situations that quickly generate disputes. This section reviews some of the developer's typical activities to identify circumstances often associated with high risk and to suggest ways of mitigating those risks.

Acquisitions by the Nonresidential Developer

No activity is more critical to the nonresidential developer than the acquisition of property. It is the sine qua non (indispensable requisite) of the business. Therefore, the pressures on the developer to acquire property at the best price and on the best terms are enormous. The acquisition process is a delicate one involving many objective and subjective factors. A single mistake can cause huge problems with expensive ramifications. The following is a review of the acquisition process and situations that often generate risks, disputes, and litigation.

Negotiations

Getting the seller to the negotiating table is sometimes the hardest challenge, especially if he or she was recently "burned" by a prospective purchaser. Once the seller agrees to come to the table, however, the prospective purchaser must exercise self-discipline and know when to *stop* talking. Most developers love to talk, sometimes to the point of hurting their own interests. They sometimes make an untrue statement or promise something they cannot deliver. In acquisition negotiations, if you have won, compromised, or conceded a point, stop talking about it. Move on to the next issue.

Here is an example of a common mistake made by nonresidential developers. Brokerage commissions are typically paid by the seller with a commensurate increase in the purchase price. When listing brokers or nonlisting brokers are the "procuring cause" of the sale, i.e., the event that brought the buyer and seller together, developers often ignore them with the expectation that they can avoid paying the brokers a commission. Curiously, brokers have a habit of resurfacing at the most inconvenient times, such as at closing. Litigation with a broker may "cloud" title to the real property, thereby stopping the acquisition or further loan advances, refinancing, and sales. Several states have enacted laws that protect brokers and impose a lien on the property during such litigation.

If a broker is the procuring cause of the sale, the seller and/or buyer is obligated to pay the broker a commission. However, if a broker or a "finder" is not the procuring cause of the sale but tries to extort a commission or fee, ignoring the claim seldom improves the situation. Therefore, you need to keep in mind that the longer you ignore the claim, the more facts the broker can manufacture against you. Telephone logs are a good example. Unless you log every call, you cannot prove that you did not talk with the broker. However, a broker's telephone log may be used to prove the broker talked with you about the real property. In addition, brokers with commission claims often have "relationships" with the seller. Understand the relationships before you respond to a claim. It can be detrimental to your efforts if the broker is a close friend or brother-in-law of the seller. In some states, "finders," i.e., persons who act as brokers but are not licensed, are not protected; the courts will not enforce their commission claims. In those states, it may be possible to defeat their claims. If a "finder" provides you with services that you could have performed yourself, a court may hold you liable for the value of the services under the doctrines of "unjust enrichment" or quantum merit (as much as deserved). Even where a court does not enforce the finder's claim for a sales commission, it may create the same result by awarding compensation for services.

Drafting of Purchase Agreements

The process of negotiating and entering into a purchase agreement presents the best opportunity for building a relationship with the seller to minimize the risk of litigation when subsequent disputes and difficulties arise. They always do! Remember, you are not trying to make the seller your friend, but you are trying to win the seller's trust, respect, and cooperation.

Do not be a "tiger" or a "pushover" during negotiations. If something is important to you, state your reasons, test the seller's sensitivity on the issue, and fight for it. If something is not important, do not try to win every point. Everyone needs to finish the negotiations with some dignity and sense of accomplishment. One of the least productive practices is to keep a numeric score on your wins and losses in negotiating issues in the purchase agreement. You may have many or only a few. The circumstances you find yourself in control how many issues you must negotiate and change. If the other side is fair and rational, it may be only a few issues. If the other side is overreaching and irrational, it may be most of the issues in the purchase agreement.

Be sure you understand the seller's perspective on an issue before you respond. Negotiating parties have a tendency to overstate their concerns and to suggest excessively broad terms that provide more protection than the party needs. Often, the seller is concerned with only a single aspect of a larger issue. It may be possible to address the seller's concern while still satisfying your needs. Turning a potential "head-on collision" into a "near miss" is a skill that many developers, brokers, and attorneys need to develop.

Traditionally, the purchaser's attorney drafts the purchase agreement unless the property is part of a larger development, whereupon the seller's attorney drafts the agreement. Any cost savings realized by relying on the seller's drafting of the agreement will be offset by the extra time you and your attorney must spend in reviewing the document. First, you must determine if any provisions were omitted. It is both risky and difficult to review a purchase agreement for missing provisions. Use of extensive checklists and detailed analyses of important issues are the only means of protecting yourself. Second, you must determine how to insert the provisions you need and/or to which you are entitled. The other side will argue that it already included those provisions that are reasonable and necessary, thus implying that your requests are unreasonable and unnecessary. Finally, the person drafting the agreement has the advantage of initially specifying the risk and cost allocations in the drafting party's favor. You must determine how to rebalance those provisions that place an unfair or unacceptable economic burden on you.

The above is not intended to suggest that the developer should control the drafting in order to "trick" the seller or build "traps" into the purchase agreement. Any nonresidential developer who approaches contracting dishonorably is virtually assured of litigation. Judges and juries do not like tricks or traps. They often find ways around them. A court of equity has broad discretion to achieve equitable results. We therefore suggest the following three-step approach to negotiating and drafting purchase agreements:

- Negotiate with the other party as to the purchase agreement's terms and provisions.

- Carefully draft the purchase agreement and meticulously follow the negotiated terms or clearly indicate those that changed.

- Show the other party exactly what you drafted or changed, especially if it varies from earlier discussions.

With today's word processing capabilities, attorneys can regularly provide computer-generated "redlines" of each draft, showing all changes since the last draft. The availability of word processing speeds up the contracting process and virtually eliminates the complaint and risk that the drafting party made a change to the purchase agreement without telling the other side. The risk of disputes and litigation is thus reduced while trust, respect, and cooperation are fostered.

The best purchase agreements are those that are clear and understandable. For example, developers who use a formula for setting the price or some other variable should attach a sample calculation to the purchase agreement as an exhibit but should never agree to a formula until they have mathematically tested it under all conceivable circumstances. The developer who knowingly creates or accepts an imprecise or incomplete formula with the intent of later modifying or clarifying it to his or her advantage may ultimately lose. Contract interpretation generally goes against the party that wrote the purchase agreement. In the case of two possible interpretations of a disputed clause, the court favors an interpretation suggested by the nondrafting party. In addition, if the parties failed to agree on a material issue due to a mutual mistake, the purchase agreement may be unenforceable and void, forcing a repeat of the drafting process with two parties that no longer trust one another.

In the case of litigation over the purchase agreement, the judge and jury must read and interpret the purchase agreement. Judges and juries often have limited experience in and understanding of nonresidential real estate transactions, frequently do not understand complex real estate concepts and issues, and tend to oversimplify their analysis. Therefore, it is incorrect to assume that everyone will recognize the parties' intent. Further, it is difficult to prove "custom and practice" in purchase agreement provisions because expert witnesses tend to be advocates rather than impartial experts. Judges and juries also tend to focus on the conduct of the parties rather than on the terms of the purchase agreement. Even when they do not understand the issues, they can make a judgment based on someone's character.

Representations and Warranties

If the seller will not provide any facts and the developer wants every fact represented and warranted in the purchase agreement on an absolute basis, the sale will never materialize. Clearly, the parties need to compromise. Contracts usually distinguish between two different types of fact: those the developer cannot discover without the seller providing information and those the developer can research independently of the seller.

Each party should represent and warrant certain facts on an absolute basis primarily because the other side does not know and cannot learn about such facts. For example, each party requires assurance of the due organization, existence, capacity, authority, etc., of the other party, which usually involves the provision of organizational documents; certificates of good standing; certified copies of resolutions; incumbency certificates; consents to the sale from limited partners, members, trustees, and shareholders, etc. Such documentation is important because an entity that fails these documentary requirements usually lacks the capacity to contract. In that case, the purchase agreement is *void*.

Both parties also need to ensure that no conflict with or breach of other agreements will affect either the seller or developer. Examples would be a right of first refusal or right of first offer to a tenant or another party, a "due on sale" clause in loan documents the developer contracts to assume or "take subject to," and a prohibition in the business owners' association documents or land use agreements/restrictions with a government authority against the developer's planned use.

Other required information includes what constitutes the loan documents, contracts, and/or leases being assumed by the developer; whether they have been amended by the seller; and whether the other party has fully performed under them. If the full agreements are not recorded in the public records, the developer has no means of finding out what is being assumed or "taken subject to" unless the seller provides the information.

From the developer's perspective, it is imperative to determine whether the seller is a party to any pending litigation or has been served with any government notices. If the seller is involved in litigation that results in a judgment before the closing, the judgment lien will attach to the real property when it is domesticated in the county or city where the property is located. The judgment lien may eliminate the seller's ability to close. As for government notices, they usually involve some physical defect or violation at the property and attach to the property regardless of ownership. If the developer has to cure some defect, deficiency, or noncompliance at the property immediately after the acquisition, he or she may not have the resources to do so. Further, the developer will end up paying more for the property than was expected.

Generally speaking, the seller should warrant, to the extent of his or her knowledge, those facts that are within his or her knowledge. In a related matter, the seller should insist on a written definition of what will satisfy a standard of "to the extent of its knowledge" or "to its best knowledge." The seller should also consider specifying which current employees will be questioned and what files will be reviewed. If the seller has downsized during the last few years, the developer should consider whether to talk with former employees who worked on the project under consideration for sale.

More specifically, purchase agreements often require the seller to review and/or deliver everything "in its possession or control." The seller should clarify which files and records must be reviewed and what it means to be "in the control" of the seller. For example, must the seller review his or her architect's, engineer's, accountant's, and attorney's files just because he or she can control them? That is not practical. In some cases, however, the developer may have a legitimate need to review specific files. The developer should talk with the seller about the latter's files and create a definition that balances the search-and-review difficulty against the developer's legitimate need to know.

Many facts and concerns about the property can be covered in the seller's "to the extent of its knowledge" warranties. The seller's only duty is to follow with care the agreed-upon procedure for determining and reporting what is in his or her knowledge. If the seller does not know, then he or she has no liability. From the developer's perspective, the representations and warranties given "to the extent of seller's knowledge" provide much-needed information that the developer can use as a starting point for his or her due diligence investigations, thus permitting the seller to require a shorter "free look" at the property while it is off the market; assurance that the seller is not holding back some negative information on the property; and a reduction in the risk of a subsequent dispute and litigation, especially when the seller has provided carryback financing. The drafting of representations and warranties in purchase agreements must address three kinds of problems: those known only to the seller; those known only to the developer; and those unknown to both the seller and developer. Representations and warranties limited to the seller's knowledge make the seller liable only for those problems of which he or she knows. Accordingly, the developer assumes the risk of the unknown problems and should factor such risk into the purchase price.

In negotiating representations and warranties, the parties must also consider the nature of the parties. The willingness of a party to make representations and warranties generally is inversely proportional to its net worth. If the seller is an institution that exclusively uses asset and/or property managers to run the property, its knowledge about the property may be limited. In this case, it may be reasonable to ask the property manager to provide the representations and warranties. However, the seller may not be willing to assume liability for the manager's representations and warranties while the property manager may not command sufficient net worth to give the developer any level of protection.

A typical example of how the seller's ownership structure creates a problem occurs when the seller is a single-asset limited partnership with a corporate general partner or a limited-liability company. If the seller's outside debt equals or exceeds the sales price, it lacks any net worth backing the representations and warranties. One solution is to adjust the purchase price to account for the risk assumed by the developer. Another solution is to convince the seller's principals to be personally liable for the representations and warranties, if such principals are deemed creditworthy.

The developer should also consider statutory provisions that can protect certain types of ownership entities. In many states, the limited partners of a limited partnership are obligated to return liquidating distributions for only one year. Claims that arise after that year affect only the general partners and thus must be raised promptly. Many states shield from personal liability directors, officers, and employees of nonprofit corporations as long as their conduct was not criminal, fraudulent, or intentionally wrongful.

In addition, if the seller is willing to accept carryback financing on the property, the developer should make sure that a breach of the representations or warranties can be set off against the seller's loan. In that situation, the seller cannot escape liability.

Assuming that the representations and warranties are not merged into the deed and that, at some point, the party giving the representations and warranties should be able to delete them as a contingent liability, the parties should negotiate and include a "sunset" provision for the representations and warranties. State law generally cuts off liability after one to three years for unsealed contracts and after a much longer period for sealed contracts. In most cases, these time periods are excessive. A few representations and warranties are so important (if a breach voids the transaction), however, that they should continue forever. Fortunately, most of the associated risks can be insured with title insurance.

Due Diligence Investigations

In acquisitions, thorough due diligence investigations are the best way to reduce dispute and litigation risks. Three types of due diligence apply. Business feasibility due diligence requires the review of the overall economics of the project and the specific economics of each material component. The review may extend to appraisals, feasibility studies, market studies, reviews of existing leases, availability of financing, availability of equity funding, and detailed projections of each material item of income and expense with each material assumption clearly identified to enable others to understand the projections. Physical due diligence requires the physical review of the property, including its development limitations and potential, and may include boundary and topographic surveys, review of highway maps and plans, geotechnical (i.e., soils) studies, environmental studies, environmental impact reviews, stormwater management studies, traffic studies, a report on the availability of public water and sewer, calculations of available densities and bulk on the property, preliminary master plans for large projects, conceptual planning for building development, and other reports relating to the physical condition of the property. Legal due diligence requires the review of legal issues affecting the project and may include a title report, easements and other recorded title matters, leases, master plan and zoning studies, the existence of government notices of violations or noncompliance, the status of taxes affecting the property (i.e., assessments and real property, transfer, recording, documentary, intangible, and other taxes), and a review of the impact of certain laws on the planned development. With regard to due diligence investigations, the developer should not start from scratch. The seller should provide copies of information available in his or her files. A Feasibility Checklist for Acquisition of Undeveloped Land is contained in Appendix 9.

The existence (or absence) of government, zoning, and land use approvals and entitlements significantly affects the degree of risk involved in any acquisition. Given that the property's purchase price often assumes the existence of these approvals and entitlements, the developer must verify their continued availability and enforceability. In addition, compliance with building laws is a significant issue in the purchase of any developed property. The laws may have changed since the project was built, possibly with a "grandfathering" of preexisting conditions. However, the grandfathering is often voided if the building becomes vacant or a major casualty loss occurs.

Sometimes the building cannot be rebuilt after a casualty loss because of downzoning or additional parking or greenspace requirements. The standard "replacement cost" rider to hazard insurance policies does not cover such a loss. Collection of the full replacement cost requires rebuilding of the structure. While a specific rider to hazard insurance policies purports to cover this risk, the standard rider provides little protection; in fact, many insurance companies do not offer it or otherwise modify its terms.

Some laws involving life-safety and/or building code compliance issues prohibit grandfathering and must be complied with over time. A good example is the retrofitting of sprinkler systems into existing buildings. In some jurisdictions, the owner can delay the obligation to sprinkler a building by agreeing to a specific installation schedule. The fire marshal or other local government official determines the installation schedule, which often requires immediate sprinkler installation in stairwells and public hallways. Moreover, laws such as the Americans with Disabilities Act (ADA) or the Uniform Federal Accessibility Standards (applicable to all federally leased buildings) provide little or no phase-in and require immediate developer compliance. If any major renovation or tenant buildout is planned, the level of alterations required to meet the ADA requirements can be much greater.

It is imperative for nonresidential developers to confirm the nonexistence of every state and local "super lien" that applies to the property. Nuisance, abatement, sidewalk, etc., assessments may not show up in a title report or tax certificate but may still constitute a lien on the property superior to all mortgages. Standard title insurance does not protect the developer or the lender from such assessments.

If the property for sale already is developed, the developer must determine that the seller has both obtained all required licenses to operate the property and paid all expenses that can become liens on the property. For example, even though the developer may not be liable for the seller's unpaid sales taxes, the local government may file a lien or claim against the developer in an attempt to put pressure on everyone to get the back taxes paid.

Environmental Due Diligence

Liability under federal and state environmental laws for hazardous materials takes the form of "strict" liability; in other words, the mere holding of title makes the owner liable. In addition, environmental liability ignores the ownership structure. No matter what the entity, each individual "operator" can be held personally liable. Moreover, certain exceptions or defenses (for example, the innocent landowner defense) are difficult to prove and too uncertain. The only way to protect yourself is to determine and understand every environmental liability before you purchase a parcel of land.

Given that the standards for certain hazardous materials may vary between federal and state laws, the developer must review the full range of regulations governing permitted levels of hazardous materials. Federal and state testing and reporting requirements can also vary, and obtaining a specific, clear, and timely response is neither simple nor inexpensive.

With regard to environmental due diligence, it is critical to determine as early as possible who will perform the assessment, what level of investigation will be pursued, who must receive the information and when, and how to protect the information discovered during the investigation. Before engaging the environmental firm, the developer should clear the firm's credentials and the description of the services it will perform with every person who will receive and approve the environmental assessment: the appropriate government agencies, the lender, joint venture partner(s), major tenant(s), and the seller. Such clearance is an important element in risk reduction.

The American Society of Testing and Materials has promulgated a uniform standard for a Phase I environmental evaluation. It should be noted, however, that many environmental firms offer fewer services than are required under the new standard. Unless the developer carefully reviews the environmental firm's engagement letter and insists on a full evaluation, the resulting environmental evaluation may prove unusable. Further, some institutional lenders impose additional environmental requirements, which are easy to satisfy by including them in the initial engagement.

In addition to providing fewer services than the new standard requires, many environmental firms lack the knowledge and experience to recognize an environmental problem and advise the developer on how to deal with it cost effectively and in the least risky manner. Environmental firms typically use the engagement letter to limit their liability for improper or inadequate work. Though they are tenacious about protecting themselves, they often command little net worth. Thus, the developer accepts the risk of an error on the part of the environmental firm. Accordingly, the developer needs to make sure that the environmental firm is capable of seeing a complex issue through to completion in accordance with government regulations and that the firm can formulate a remediation program that will be approved by the appropriate government agencies, the lender, the institutional investor, etc.

Phase II environmental evaluations are expensive and time-consuming and should not be considered unless circumstances are compelling. The developer might even decide to walk away from a prospective deal before absorbing the related opportunity cost. In any case, the decision to undertake Phase II study should trigger notification to all parties to the transaction that they will have to await the study results.

On occasion, the seller may consider the commissioning of an environmental study before contracting to sell. Such a decision, however, may give rise to more risk than performing the study. If the study reveals the presence of hazardous materials, the seller must usually remediate them before any sale. If the property is undeveloped and the seller is not sure what type of development is likely to occur, the seller may not know what type of remediation program to undertake. The time and cost of remediation programs can vary widely.

The developer who finds him- or herself in a purchase agreement that requires environmental remediation should consider terminating the agreement and walking away. It is prudent to remember that the first loss is usually the smallest and that remediation is fraught with several issues and problems beyond the purchaser's control. For example, the remediation must be satisfactory to the developer, the seller, the relevant government agencies, the lender, the investors, the tenants, the ultimate users, etc. In addition, the cost of remediation and who pays the cost is always a major problem. The seller typically tries to limit costs while the developer argues that the purchase price assumes an environmentally "clean" property. Beyond the cost issue, environmental firms often disagree on the remediation plan. The issues range from when and how to remove hazardous materials to the efficacy of the removal procedure. Where subterranean contamination is involved, the disagreements can result in cost proposals that are multiples of each other. Remediation contractors seldom give warranties on the results of their work and typically do not command the net worth to back up the warranties they give. Where multiple firms and government agencies are involved, the solution tends to follow the most conservative (and usually most expensive) approach. Only those parties paying the remediation costs are economically motivated. All others respond to different motivations, i.e., safety, quality of life, reputation, limitation of liability, etc.

Where the state government sets the standard for remediation and provides a certificate of completion for the remediation work, a change in political administration can lead to different interpretations of state law. If a proenvironment governor succeeds a probusiness governor, the new political appointee responsible for interpreting the environmental laws can require a multiple of the originally planned and budgeted remediation work by halving the allowable parts per million of the applicable hazardous materials. Often, six months or more elapse before the state administrator certifies completion of remediation.

To complicate matters further, the seller and developer operate under conflicting motivations. If the seller remediates before closing, the developer will want to monitor/control the who, what, and how of remediation to ensure that appropriate corrective action is taken. If the cost of the remediation is placed in escrow at the closing, the developer will want to ensure that more-than-sufficient money is deposited in the escrow account while the seller will want to ensure that the remediation is completed at least cost and that its liability for the hazardous materials has ended. If the purchase price is reduced, the seller will want assurances (indemnities) that its liability will be eliminated and the remediation completed; however, the seller is still liable to third parties and government agencies until the remediation is successfully completed.

Developers who discover a hazardous materials problem but cannot get out of the purchase agreement can minimize the risk of litigation by requesting the seller to remediate under methods and standards approved by the developer. Sometimes, however, going ahead with the intended development is the best or only remediation plan. Nonetheless, negotiating the price and legal protections for each party is extremely difficult. If the seller needs a portion of the purchase price to fund the remediation expenses, the purchaser might consider lending the necessary funds or creating a joint venture whereby he or she does not become an "operator" for environmental liability purposes until remediation is completed. In any case, the developer's basic protection comes from not purchasing the property until assurances are forthcoming that hazardous materials have been remediated.

Satisfaction of Conditions Precedent
In the Purchase Agreement

Typically, the seller and developer must satisfy various conditions precedent (i.e., requirements) in a purchase agreement before the other is obligated to close. For this discussion, we assume that the developer has agreed to satisfy a number of conditions precedent related to his or her ability to develop the proposed project. Setting the time limit(s) for satisfaction of the conditions precedent is always a risk management and litigation avoidance issue for the developer. It is unreasonable to be overly optimistic about how soon the developer can satisfy the conditions precedent. As a result, developers should press for as much time as possible. In these circumstances, there is nothing such as too much time.

Sellers typically want some economic benefit (e.g., more money at risk, increased price, waiver of conditions, etc.) in exchange for each time extension. The developer, however, should look for the seller's leverage points. For example, the seller may have committed funds to either the purchase of something else or a loan repayment. Sometimes, tax considerations motivate the seller. Whatever motivated the seller to offer the property for sale probably still applies and may be leveraged to obtain time extensions.

Other conditions precedent relating to the developer's ability to pay the purchase price, e.g., financing, equity funding, and/or syndication contingencies, are troublesome to sellers because they effectively convert a binding purchase agreement into a purchase option. They also corroborate the developer's lack of financial resources to purchase the property. If the earnest money at risk is low enough or the purchaser is an entity with little net worth, the developer may consider taking the risk of waiving such contingencies.

In the 1980s, the timing of financing was usually the only financing issue. In the 1990s, both the timing and availability of financing (at any price) are issues. Some types of loans are no longer even available from institutional lenders. The seller may require the developer to specify limits on various financing terms (e.g., maximum dollar amount, maximum interest rate, personal liability, minimum term, minimum cash equity, etc.) that the developer must apply for and either accept from any lender or waive the financing contingency.

Given the uncertainties of the 1990s and the possibility that the developer may assign, i.e., "flip," the purchase agreement to another developer, sophisticated sellers now agree to a series of conditions on financing and specify time limits to be satisfied by the developer for each condition. For example, within a specified number of weeks, an institutional lender must confirm to the seller that it has accepted a loan application from the developer on terms not more favorable to the developer than those specified in the purchase agreement. Within a specified number of weeks, such lender must confirm to the seller that it has received certain (or all) due diligence deliveries required in the loan application. Within a specified number of weeks, the lender must confirm to the seller that it has issued and the developer has accepted a binding, conditional commitment for the loan. Finally, within a specified number of weeks, the lender must confirm to the seller that it has received, reviewed, and approved an environmental report and appraisal for the property.

Recognizing that the seller should not (and probably cannot) control the terms on which the developer will seek and accept equity funds, sellers are usually reluctant to accept equity funding or syndication contingencies. However, some sellers grant contingencies because they know the sources of equity funding from institutions such as GE Capital and Wall Street brokerage houses and their practice of rapid decision making.

The key to managing the developer's risk is understanding the financing, leasing, and government approval and entitlement process and negotiating a purchase agreement that allows the developer to complete and confirm the existence of the financing commitments, leases, approvals, and entitlements assumed in the purchase price. Awareness of the following tips and observations can help developers manage risk:

- If the availability of government approvals and entitlements is uncertain, developers should not agree to a purchase price that merely assumes their existence without verification.

- Timing for satisfying conditions precedent is always a problem. Timing pressures become more acute when the developer's financing is contingent on obtaining government approvals and entitlements. It is reasonable to expect delays and roadblocks.

- Developers should not count on a government approval until the appeal period has expired; even then, the approval may be subject to challenges, initiatives, referenda, etc. It is useful to try to lock in government approvals and entitlements with master plan amendments, vesting maps, proffers, development agreements, etc.

- Skipping steps or taking shortcuts with regard to the government review and approval process often becomes the basis of a later challenge.

- When working with the public, developers should take a proactive stance and remain sensitive to issues of concern to the community. Developers should look for allies to broaden their base of support.

Letting the developer initiate physical development before closing the sale of the property is a critical issue for certain projects, such as shopping centers, whose tenants open for business only during specific "time windows" and/or where weather can interfere with outdoor construction for a long period. The problem may be insurmountable because returning the land to its original condition may not be possible and required grading and/or excavation is likely to vary from the seller's plans for the property. In addition, bonding and permitting costs may be prohibitive unless the seller agrees to replace the bond or to complete the work.

Given that delay and change are effective in killing any development project, developers need to bear in mind that the seller will request a large earnest-money deposit to minimize risk, that the seller will want some control during a long contingency period while the developer will not want any such hindrance, and that the seller's property can be "tainted" in the marketplace by the institutional lender's, major tenant's, and/or government agency's refusal to approve the project.

A Special Risk Problem: Seller Carryback Financing
Seller carryback financing usually involves flexible terms that are often based on the seller's cash flow and/or tax needs. Such transactions have a better chance of receiving a nonrecourse designation, i.e., without personal liability to the developer. That is, the developer can argue that the carryback financing is fully secured by the property's value. Where the seller carryback financing is subordinate to institutional first-trust financing, it creates additional risks and potential disputes. More specifically, when the purchase price is known to be high, the seller may decide to risk a portion of the purchase price on the success of the project through subordinated seller carryback financing. In such a case, the developer must carefully plan and negotiate subordinated seller carryback financing. At the same time, the seller seeks to control/minimize risk by placing restrictions on what the first-trust lender and developer can do with the property. Yet, if the first-trust lender does not accept the seller's restrictions, the developer must either abandon the purchase agreement or obtain concessions from the seller (usually at some price and/or increased liability). Unless the debt service coverage is strong, the first-trust lender will always demand to be paid first and prohibit all but regular interest payments on the

subordinated seller carryback financing. The developer must ensure that the seller's terms allow for such a payment scheme and agree to cut off all payments if the first-trust loan goes into default. Many first-trust lenders do not permit subordinated liens under any circumstances. If the developer files for bankruptcy protection, the subordinated lien holder has greater rights against the first-trust lender than do unsecured creditors.

A feasible project can be killed by a release clause in the seller carryback financing that takes all net sales proceeds and does not leave the developer sufficient funds to continue the project. A similar result can occur when the first-trust financing takes all the net sales proceeds. If the seller carryback financing is subordinated, the developer should coordinate the release clauses for all lenders so the developer can sell the lots or units and ensure adequate cash flow to fund the project.

Borrowing by the Nonresidential Developer

If property is the vehicle used by developers, then borrowed money is the most common fuel. No part of the development process works without money. The following is a review of certain issues in the borrowing process that often generate risks and disputes.

Negotiating with Lenders

In the 1980s, developers could dictate loan terms to lenders. In the 1990s, lenders willing to make real estate loans are dictating loan terms to developers. Some banks have recommenced a moderate amount of real estate lending while life insurance companies and other traditional long-term sources of capital are willing to lend but cannot find projects that meet their increased underwriting standards. In the wake of the high-risk loans originated in the 1980s and the real estate acquired through foreclosures in the 1990s, no one can predict if and when institutional lenders will recommence widespread commercial real estate lending. Moreover, lenders have created a whole new arsenal of provisions to protect themselves from enforcement difficulties.

For example, confession-of-judgment clauses are standard for all but the strongest borrowers. In those jurisdictions where the clauses are enforceable, the lender can obtain an immediate judgment against the developer and guarantors if the loan goes into default. Far more common than in the past are guarantees of completion and of the costs of carrying the project until it breaks even or is sold by the lender. Further, where the lender accepts some limitation on recourse, it typically "carves out" liability for misapplication (i.e., wrongful taking) of funds, failure to pay real estate taxes and insurance premiums, damages caused by the borrower's malicious or intentionally wrongful acts, failure to make repairs, etc. In addition, the lender, once again accepting some limits on recourse, typically requires an "exploding" guarantee from the developer's principals. An "exploding" guarantee becomes enforceable only if the developer files for bankruptcy protection. Its purpose is to deter a bankruptcy filing and assure the lender of an uncontested foreclosure sale of the project. Finally, receivership provisions permit the lender to obtain a receiver on an ex parte (that is, done for, on behalf of, or on the application of one party only) basis. The receivership provisions eliminate the developer's control over the project unless the developer is willing to file a Chapter 11 petition in bankruptcy.

Environmental and Toxic Material Concerns

In 1994, the Court of Appeals for the District of Columbia voided the U.S. Environmental Protection Agency's (EPA) 1992 regulations that had expanded the circumstances under which a lender would not be liable for certain hazardous substances found on the property securing a lender's loan. In response, the EPA is drafting replacement regulations to clarify lenders' liability for hazardous substances; however, as of July 1996, no new regulations had been issued.

In today's marketplace, lenders uniformly require perpetual environmental indemnities from all the developer's principals involved in the transaction. Given that any principal who is an "operator" is probably liable under federal and state environmental laws, the indemnity may not as a practical matter increase the principal's liability. Nonetheless, it does permit an additional party to sue to enforce the liability and may give the lender some control over the resolution of the environmental problem. Occasionally, environmental indemnities create disputes whereby the lender seeks to control or expand the scope of remediation of an environmental problem.

The Buildout Process—Draws and Payouts

Lenders seek to hedge their risks by funding last and forcing others to keep money invested in the project. Accordingly, developers need to make sure that their contracts with the general contractor and subcontractors include retainage provisions that match the lender's funding; otherwise, the developer has to fund the difference or placate a disgruntled contractor. In addition, it is important to remember that liens stop funding. Therefore, any plans for escalating a dispute with a party capable of placing a lien on a project demand careful consideration.

Developers who experience problems in performing their loan obligations should communicate with the lending institution, which may assist in solving the problem. Developers should also know and understand the lender's regulatory constraints. Clearly, the institution cannot breach its regulations or accounting policies. At the same time, though, developers should be prepared to contribute something to the solution; otherwise, the lender accepts all the risk and takes the property. It is no longer reasonable to expect the lender to fund the cost of fixing the problem and then leave the developer in control of the project. Finally, developers should keep any partners informed of any material problems. The partners may be displeased, but they probably will be less inclined to sue.

■ Investing with Others in Joint Ventures, Partnerships, Corporations, and Limited-Liability Companies

Few developers have the capital resources to fund all of their projects. Besides using borrowed funds, developers often further leverage their projects by involving investors who provide equity funds in exchange for preferential returns and ownership interests. The following is a discussion of several areas in the developer/investor relationship where disputes often arise.

Setting Up the Parties' Responsibilities

Each of the participants in an owning entity has duties and responsibilities to the other participants. Generally, the law imposes fiduciary duties on the developer in favor of the investors. After adequate disclosure, however, the duties can be modified or reduced by agreement of the parties. Absent a written agreement, state law in the state where the ownership entity was formed controls the fiduciary duties of the parties.

In 1994, the National Conference of Commissioners on Uniform State Laws and the American Bar Association's Business Law Section adopted the Revised Uniform Partnership Act. When adopted by each state, the law will modify the fiduciary duties of general partners in both limited and general partnerships. The act outlines four fiduciary duties: the duty to account for benefits derived from the use of partnership property; the duty to refrain from dealing adversely to the partnership; the duty to refrain from competing with the partnership in the conduct of the partnership's business until the partnership is dissolved; and the duty to refrain from engaging in grossly negligent or reckless conduct, intentional misconduct, or a knowing violation of law.

Generally, while the courts have imposed these four fiduciary duties on general partners for some time, the Revised Uniform Partnership Act codifies them. In addition, the act obligates partners to exercise good faith and fair dealing with each other. The courts exercise broad discretion in defining good faith and fair dealing, thus permitting them to review partners' conduct and grant equitable relief.

The drafter's failure to address fully in the partnership agreement or ownership entity governance documents the responsibilities of each party in the partnership or other ownership entity often causes disputes and litigation. If the governance documents are silent on what the developer is obligated to do for his or her interest in the ownership entity, the developer will want to be paid for work necessary for the project but not explicitly required. The developer's use of related entities and affiliates to perform certain work for the project should be subject to the agreement of the appropriate parties, with a clear arrangement for compensation. Often the work takes much longer than expected, notwithstanding the developer's reasonable efforts. Compensation arrangements should anticipate delays and allocate risk among the participants.

The governance documents should identify and address each party's responsibilities as well as what happens when a party does not fulfill its responsibilities. In other words, developers are advised not to rely on the "money" party's representation that it will obtain financing or some other benefit for the project. If one party is obtaining something for the project (e.g., financing, government approvals, a long-term lease, etc.), the governance documents should specify the terms of the arrangements and what happens if the party fails to perform fully. More specifically, the developer should take note of some circumstances that commonly arise. For example, if the financing requires the developer's spouse to guarantee the loan and ties up all the developer's assets, the financing terms may not be worth the percentage interest the "money" party received in the ownership entity. If the cost of constructing the leased premises under a long-term lease substantially exceeds the developer's budget, the lease may not be worth the percentage interest in the ownership entity given the party that produced the lease. If an institutional and/or publicly held party unilaterally wants to bail out of the ownership entity for reasons unrelated to the developer and/or project, such a party could paralyze the ownership entity. A fair buyout provision can, however, prevent problems with the party's departure. Finally, it should be noted that, with the imposition of the "automatic stay" in bankruptcy, the bankruptcy of a party in the ownership entity protects that party from enforcement actions by the other parties for failure to perform. The ownership entity, however, is not protected by the bankruptcy of one of its parties or of members from outside parties such as lenders, tenants, local governments, etc.

Contribution Issues

Developers need to specify the total obligations for contributions from every party to the owning entity's governance documents. These include when the developer can require the party owning the land to contribute it to the ownership entity and when and to what extent the ownership entity can encumber such land, who funds the development costs first and in what amounts, who funds the last budgeted costs and under what conditions and limits once the project is fully funded, and who has the responsibility to fund unanticipated costs arising from a shortage or halt in lender funding and what right(s) the party receives for doing so. Funding may be stopped when a condition remains unmet or development costs exceed a committed amount. In any event, timing of and conditions for funding underanticipated and unanticipated circumstances are always important and should be clearly specified. Parties can scarcely be expected to agree on these difficult issues at some later date.

The value of contributed property is another common source of disputes. In particular, problems arise with appreciated property in that the contributing party wants to overvalue the contribution. If the contribution is land, developers need to be careful when consenting to a preferred return on its value. Such a return often consumes the developer's equity interest if neither cash flow nor sales proceeds are expected in the near future.

Enforcement mechanisms for missed capital contributions often fail to address adequately the harm exacted on the project. For example, forfeiture of ownership interests can be stopped by bankruptcy and is otherwise difficult to enforce. Converting the missed capital contribution to a loan secured by the defaulting owner's interest creates some protection but must be fully documented and include the filing of Uniform Commercial Code financing statements. Dilution formulas can provide some relief if the ownership entity has equity in its assets; otherwise, the dilution is economically meaningless. Giving the nondefaulting owners the right to sue the defaulting owner for the missed capital contribution works only when a judgment can be collected against the defaulting owner, and such is often not the case.

The Decision-Making Process

Control is a critical issue for the developer; he or she must have control to bring the project to completion. Investors legitimately need some level of control over budget decisions when the project is either over budget or materially off the completion schedule and an even higher degree of control over all decisions when the project is about to create a loan guarantee claim against the investors. The selection of the type of development/ownership entity can affect the decision-making process and the issue of control.

In limited partnerships, the general partner(s) has management control while the limited partners typically control only certain events (e.g., financing, sale, changes in allocations of profits and losses, admission of new general partners, substitution of a general partner, etc.). Limited-liability companies provide investing members with more decision-making control than limited partnerships without requiring the investors to assume personal liability to third parties. Corporations provide the most opportunities for investors to participate in the decision-making process. An investor can be a director and have significant legal and practical control over the corporation without assuming the personal liability of a general partner. Nonvoting stock that becomes voting stock upon the occurrence of specific events is one of the best mechanisms for creating an instantaneous change in control of a corporation. The conversion of stock can be used in a number of situations and is difficult to stop through the bankruptcy process.

Allocation of Profits and Losses

The developer and investors must allocate profits and losses at the formation of the owning entity, usually with little relevant historical financial information. Most disputes occur when the project does significantly better or worse than originally expected. The following observations can help ownership entities specify the allocation of profits and losses:

- Do not oversell the upside of your project to your investors; they may believe you and demand a greater return.

- When the parties want to allocate profits and losses disproportionately among themselves, it is time to seek competent tax advice on how to structure and document your understandings. Significant tax limitations apply to disproportionate allocations.

- Try to match the financial risk with the allocated returns so that the party assuming the risk is compensated accordingly. If not, you create an imbalance between the relative risks and rewards of the parties such that disputes are likely to arise.

- If the parties agree to share their losses on a proportionate basis, the agreement should specify both the contribution arrangement and an appropriate enforcement mechanism. Where subsequent cash contributions are required, due diligence on the parties obligated to fund is in order. Specifically, consider the net worth and liquidity of the various parties. If the loss-sharing obligation is a significant percentage of a party's net worth or liquidity, you may experience difficulty enforcing the obligation. Be sure to include all liabilities of the ownership entity in the loss-sharing arrangement, such as one party's being forced to honor a joint and several guarantee of the ownership entity's loan because other parties are unable or unwilling to do so. In that event, the allocation of profits and losses (and many other factors) should change to compensate the funding party. Finally, keep in mind that between 1990 and 1995, many parties to contribution agreements failed to honor the agreements or were discharged from their contribution obligations in bankruptcies. In many instances, a solvent party in the ownership entity was forced to fund other parties' obligations without adequate protection to recoup its advances.

■ Leasing

When both landlord and tenant are sophisticated parties, they tend to address the issues that cause disputes and litigation. Nonetheless, some common sources of lease-related disputes center around build-outs under leases that require a performance standard as opposed to plans and specifications and operating cost reimbursements. In the first case, the tenant tells the developer/landlord (without including it in the lease) that another developer completed the same building or improvements at a much lower cost. The tenant may also make unreasonable demands in interpreting the performance standard after the lease is signed. The developer/landlord can protect him- or herself by specifying the maximum cost he or she will pay for improvements; of course, the tenant then makes sure that he or she incurs the maximum cost. In the second case, the tenant pays a proportionate share of the total operating costs or a proportionate share of the increases in operating costs over a base year. Setting the stabilized operating costs and real estate taxes can be extremely complex. Where the building has substantial vacancies, adjustments should be made for the vacancy; where the building is recently completed, startup expenses should be deducted; and where the building needs renovation, capital expenses should not be booked as repairs.

Major tenants in shopping centers usually force the developer to "cap" the operating cost pass-throughs and often refuse to pay for certain items. During the base year, the landlord must guard against the tenant that intentionally runs up the operating expenses. The lease should specify what type and how much equipment will be used in the leased premises. If it does not, an unscrupulous tenant can significantly run up base-year operating expenses.

Developers sometimes try to pass above-market fees to affiliates as part of the operating expenses. They may also claim that the leased premises contains more space than it actually does. Considering the current competition for tenants, however, such a strategy makes little sense for the long term.

With the drop in commercial rents in the early 1990s and the unwillingness of lenders to fund tenant improvement money for overleveraged properties, developers often find themselves negotiating creative arrangements that permit the tenant to fund improvement costs. If the tenant contracts to perform the work, the developer/landlord needs to make sure it is completed correctly and paid for. After all, the developer/landlord is still liable for regulatory compliance with federal, state, and local laws. In another arrangement, the tenant may negotiate to perform certain work with an expected cost and then try to "value engineer" a lower cost after the lease is signed. Adding a specific description of the work to be performed may limit the risk of the tenant reducing the scope and quality of the work. Within a certain cost range, however, the work cannot be stopped without communicating a lack of trust to the tenant.

The landlord should try to prohibit assignments and subletting in order to prevent the tenant from making a profit on the lease and using it as a real estate asset. The tenant, on the other hand, wants the right to assign or sublet the leased premises if it no longer satisfies tenant needs. When the tenant replaces itself with another tenant, disputes often arise. One of three scenarios may play out. First, if the landlord accepts the replacement tenant's financial condition, the original tenant will want to be released from the lease in order to eliminate the lease liability from its financial statement. From the landlord's perspective, there is no such thing as too much credit for a tenant; therefore, the landlord will want to retain the liability. Second, if the original tenant pays for any brokerage commissions and/or tenant improvements in connection with the replacement tenant, the original tenant will want those costs repaid from profits on the replacement tenant before the landlord shares in them. Conversely, the landlord may view those costs as the tenant's price for vacating the premises and seek to have the original tenant absorb all the costs. If the original tenant knows that cost sharing will be an issue, he or she can negotiate for the replacement tenant to pay those costs in exchange for a rent reduction, thereby forcing the landlord to share the costs. Third, if the tenant assumes the entire financial risk of finding and moving in a new tenant, he or she will want to keep most of the profit on the new tenant to offset the assumed risk. The landlord, not wanting anyone to profit from his or her property, will try to negotiate a clause in the lease to permit cancellation of the original tenant's lease if a replacement tenant is found, thus capturing the associated profit.

■ Operating/Managing

The property manager is the agent of the developer/owner, who, in turn, is liable for the wrongful acts of its agent. A property management company typically requests the developer/owner to indemnify it from its own negligence in the property management agreement. Any indemnity, however, should specify the responsibilities and liabilities of both the property manager and the developer/owner in various situations. For example, if negligence causes injury to third parties, the developer/owner will probably indemnify the property manager when the negligence was not intentional, grossly negligent, or criminal. If the negligence causes injury to the developer/owner, however, the developer/owner will strongly resist indemnifying the property manager, thereby providing an economic incentive for the property manager to perform his or her duties properly. Further, losses caused by the property manager may not be insured when an agency relationship exists. In any event, the property management agreement should be drafted to maximize the use of existing liability insurance to protect all parties.

Developers/owners and property management companies often disagree over who is responsible for discovering and correcting noncompliance with laws such as the Americans with Disabilities Act, the occupational safety and health acts, environmental laws, various civil rights acts, the Equal Employment Opportunity Act, and other employment discrimination laws. The property management agreement should clearly specify the property manager's obligation to discover and report any noncompliance to the developer/owner as well as the developer's/owner's obligation to fund the cost of remedying any such noncompliance. Many of these laws impose liability on the developer/owner, even though the property manager may cause the liability. Few property management companies have substantial net worth to back up indemnities. Therefore, the developer's/owner's best practical means of reducing risk is to work with a reputable and competent property management company.

The preceding sections identified various circumstances where disputes and litigation risks often occur. The remainder of this chapter focuses on some strategies, methods, and techniques the developer can use to avoid disputes and minimize litigation risk.

■ Dispute and Litigation Avoidance Strategies

Most dispute and litigation avoidance strategies involve the methodical application of common sense. While the strategies are easy to understand, most developers experience difficulty in applying them consistently.

Planning and Goal Setting

No one intentionally plans for a dispute or litigation; however, planning and goal setting are keys to avoiding and minimizing the risk of hostile encounters. Dispute/litigation avoidance and minimization require developer awareness of several characteristics of the legal environment and the project in question. For example, the developer requires knowledge of the legal restrictions applicable to its operation and project and pending changes to such legal restrictions. Planning and research should determine exactly what can be developed on a specific piece of real property and what government consents and approvals are necessary for the planned development. When a developer and/or a member of the development team misjudges the legal restrictions applicable to the property, the parties hurt by the mistake will pursue claims against everyone involved. The natural reaction is for the developer to blame everyone but him- or herself, even if the legal restriction is available for discovery by anyone. Failure to acknowledge legal restrictions may be the worst type of mistake for a developer to make because it is avoidable.

The developer also needs to understand what type of development will succeed on a particular property. Developers must have the vision to see the development possibilities for a property and the judgment to determine if such development is feasible and achievable within acceptable risk parameters. One of the more common mistakes is for a developer to misjudge a market and install the wrong type of improvements on the property. Too many times, the availability of financing and/or investor money drives decisions related to improvements. Instead, the developer should base decisions about improvements on market research, product demand, and other factors relating to the property, the community, and the economy. In a related matter, the developer must develop a sense for the business and legal environment in which he or she is working. The developer can chose the right project for the right property and still fail because the business or legal environment cannot support it. Finally, the developer needs to articulate a set of goals that are both reasonable and achievable. In accordance with those goals, the developer should simulate the planning process both forward and backward. Every step should be tested for its assumptions and feasibility. If it is not possible to complete all the steps, the developer should not initiate the project. Self-discipline is mandatory for survival in the 1990s. Those developers with it will succeed; those developers without it will fail or need luck to bail them out.

Selection of the Development Team

It is imperative that the developer carefully select the development team and those with whom the team conducts business. Too many developers have found the adage "If you lie down with dogs, you will get up with fleas" to be painfully true. The key members of the team and their preferred characteristics follow:

- *Partners/investors.* Selecting good partners/investors is the developer's most important decision. A good partner/investor does not panic if events do not unfold according to plan, consults with the developer on major decisions, and offers perspective and guidance based on a broad view and sound economic principles.

- *Brokers.* The broker is judged and compensated on performance. The developer must determine whether the broker is representing any competing projects or developers and, if so, whether such representation might impair the broker's efforts. Brokers tend to take opportunities where they make the most money. A good track record is essential. It is important to learn whether the broker has been involved in litigation, for everyone can be dragged into a dispute.

- *Sellers.* The developer cannot control the identity of the potential seller but can investigate the seller's business practices and how many times the property has been under contract. Unless you have a reasonable level of trust in the seller and mutual respect, there can be no missteps in the acquisition process. Due diligence must be perfect and the economics of the transaction compelling.

- *Lenders.* Relationship lending no longer exists. In the current market, real estate lenders are hard to find but, once identified, should demonstrate stability and a track record in real estate lending. The current merger mania among banks, thrifts, and life insurance companies makes it difficult to identify lenders who, like the developer's partners/investors, will not panic if events do not go according to plan. Lenders typically have reputations that are easy to discover; if a given lender's reputation is negative, believe it.

- *Architects/engineers.* It is more important for the architects/engineers to meet the project budget than to make an aesthetic statement. If they cannot design a project within budget, then the project has an economic problem no matter how dramatic its appearance.

- *Consultants.* Consultants often are key players in obtaining government consents, approvals, and entitlements. It is important to check their political affiliations before hiring them, particularly in an election year. It is likewise critical to check for any conflicts with competing projects or for opposition to similar projects.

- *Accountants/tax advisers.* Creative and proper accounting and tax planning are essential in real estate development. Project partners/investors and the lender rely on the professionalism of accountants/tax advisers. Any lack of trust or credibility will adversely affect the developer's relationship with key members of the development team.

- *Lawyers.* Project lawyers should be skilled and experienced in each area in which legal services are needed. If the project attorney is responsible for more than documenting negotiated deals, the attorney and the developer should share the same basic approach, philosophy, and level of aggressiveness toward real estate transactions.

- *Contractors/subcontractors.* Again, skill and experience are critical, but size can also be important when fast-track delivery is required. Because a mistake can seriously compromise a project, the developer must engage only reputable contractors, not merely the lowest bidders.

- *Tenants.* Developers should not compromise their credit and quality standards just to fill a building. A bankrupt tenant in built-out space is worse than no tenant in unfinished space. Failure to create good relationships with tenants will result in vacancies.

- *Property managers.* Many developers rely on in-house property management companies that, in general, are poorly managed. Developers planning to manage their own projects should spend the necessary time and resources to ensure a professional performance. The result is dividends in the form of good tenant relations and retention. Experience and economies of scale are important when the property manager is unaffiliated with the developer.

- *Buyers.* For developers able to select a buyer, it is important to make sure the buyer has the capability of closing, even if it means a lower price.

Teamwork among the entire development team is critical. When the team works collaboratively, the likelihood of disputes and litigation is reduced. Good teamwork also reduces overall costs.

Relationships with and Disclosures To Other Parties

Contrary to common wisdom, silence is not always golden—at least not in the real estate industry, which is witnessing an emerging duty to disclose. Partners/investors, lenders, sellers, tenants, and others quickly learn to distrust a developer who fails to disclose relevant and material information—whether the news is good or bad. Building trust and confidence through full disclosures and the sharing of common goals and values is usually the preferred approach.

In structuring agreements with other parties, simplicity and completeness are the hallmark. When all parties understand an agreement that addresses all contingencies, the probability of disputes and litigation is dramatically reduced. In fact, all developer agreements should regularly include alternative dispute resolution clauses. The U.S. Supreme Court has recently upheld the enforceability of these clauses, which are designed to save time and money in resolving disputes.

Changes in circumstances during the development period require flexibility on the part of the developer and the development team. Such changes might include different financial positions and risk tolerance where one party cannot or will not accept a proposed risk. In such a case, any attempt to force the risk on the party will probably result in litigation, signaling the time to look for a replacement party. In another instance, a party's need for cash might override its ability to maximize profit. If possible, the developer should offer to buy out at a discount the party in need of cash all the while recognizing the risks to be assumed and benefits conferred on the other party.

The possible changes in circumstances that can arise over the development period are endless, although some are more likely than others. For example, the developer may have no ability to absorb taxable gain without cash to pay the resulting taxes. In the case of a forced or foreclosure sale of a project, the owners have only a few limited options to defer the gain. In limited circumstances, a tax-free exchange might be used to defer the gain; however, it is difficult to organize and close a tax-free exchange while in default on a loan, and, in a high percentage of cases, bankruptcy only delays the gain. To complicate matters, the IRS is a dangerous creditor with more enforcement options than normal lenders. Another changed circumstance might be the refusal by an elderly or terminally ill party to sell in order to receive a stepped-up tax basis in the property at death. Again, in limited circumstances, a tax-free exchange or a transaction that permits a continuation of ownership can overcome the problem. If, however, the refusing party is incapacitated or does not have access to sound tax and legal advice, the situation may rapidly escalate into litigation. And then there is the case of emotional attachment to a project. The only way to deal with an emotional issue is to convince the party to become rational—and that is easier said than done. Finally, the impact of a divorce among married parties can cause its own problems. Divorces cause ownership divisions that require the cooperation and consent of many different parties. Recourse debt and negative capital accounts are special problems because the parties' individual estates often lack the financial resources of the married estate to pay the liabilities. The only practical answer is to accommodate the divorcing parties without sacrificing any benefits or assuming any risk.

Attitude toward and Mechanisms For Reducing Disputes

The developer's attitude toward dispute resolution, litigation avoidance, and the acceptable level of aggressiveness in business dealings correlates with the developer's sensitivity to other parties' needs. Risk and litigation avoidance depend heavily on attitude and demeanor in dealing with others. Sometimes you win by giving a little. The best advice is to create mechanisms for dispute resolution at the outset of a project. Dispute resolution is a form of insurance and communicates the developer's sensitivity to the other parties. Several different alternative dispute resolution mechanisms are available, and some work better than others in specific situations. The key is always to tailor the dispute resolution mechanism to the circumstances and type of potential dispute.

Many kinds of alternative dispute resolution provisions are designed to avoid costly and protracted litigation. Arbitration provisions are probably the most common type, although many more exist. For example, some jurisdictions permit a judge to hear a dispute informally and then provide an analysis for the parties to use in their settlement negotiations. Mediation is popular but lacks the power to force a resolution on the parties to a dispute.

Developers should review the various types of alternative dispute resolution techniques with their attorney, select those that best suit their needs, and regularly insert them into contracts. The other party will probably not offer much resistance. The provisions are enforceable and should assist in resolving disputes expeditiously.

Selecting an Ownership Entity

The selection of an ownership entity does not just occur; it requires planning. Therefore, developers should choose an ownership entity that protects their assets and discourages affected parties from suing. Aggrieved persons are reluctant to bring legal action when their chances of success are limited.

Subchapter S corporations provide a "corporate veil" against all liabilities except those that are environmentally related and/or result from the failure to conduct the corporation properly. The corporation, however, must command some real net worth before it starts conducting business and must follow the corporate formalities to preserve its corporate protections. In comparison to the other ownership entities discussed below, Subchapter S corporations do not receive as favorable tax treatment. For example, the number and type of shareholders are restricted; severe limitations are placed on multiple classes of stock; allocations and distributions to shareholders generally cannot be disproportionate; and losses cannot be deducted in excess of the shareholder's tax basis.

More than 46 states have passed legislation authorizing limited-liability companies; all states are expected to recognize limited-liability companies in the near future. A limited-liability company is an almost perfect ownership entity. Its tax treatment resembles that of a partnership while its liability protection resembles that of a corporation. Many similar issues apply in forming a limited-liability company and forming a partnership. Specifically, individual members' withdrawal and termination rights must be limited in order for the limited-liability company to qualify for tax treatment as a partnership. Some recent tax rulings and revised state laws have addressed these issues and reduced companies' risk.

Limited partnerships are still a favorite ownership entity when they involve a corporate general partner. They receive the same liability protection as corporations. Investor participation in management decisions is, however, limited by law; otherwise, investors assume the liability of a general partner. In terms of tax planning, limited partnerships offer slightly more flexibility than limited-liability companies.

When using "tiers" of entities for specific needs in a limited number of situations, developers must separate equity from liabilities in order to protect the equity. Tiers of entities can also be used to protect the developer from a disgruntled partner who tries to hold up a transaction for personal reasons. For example, if a person the developer does not trust is a limited partner in the owning partnership, the general partner should also be a limited partner so that other investors may be admitted into the general partnership without such person's consent. The arrangement does not give the developer the right to dilute such person's partnership interest but does permit the developer to raise more capital by diluting his or her partnership interests without such person's consent.

In conclusion, the nonresidential developer can turn to an unlimited number of strategies to reduce his or her dispute and litigation risks. Some are not appropriate in certain circumstances and none of them works in all situations. The best strategy is to deal honestly and fairly with everyone. In that regard, the following is the author's list of Ten Commandments for Avoiding Disputes and Litigation.

Ten Commandments for Avoiding Disputes and Litigation

1. Thou shalt not make a sudden move.
2. Thou shalt not lie (or fudge the truth).
3. Thou shalt honor thy agreements and undertakings.
4. Thou shalt not run another person's business.
5. Thou shalt not bail thyself out with another person's money.
6. Thou shalt keep thine own files clean.
7. Thou shalt seek competent help when the problem exceeds thine own knowledge or resources.
8. Thou shalt work with thy professional advisers, keeping them informed and using their expertise.
9. Thou shalt think carefully before suing anyone.
10. Thou shalt not be arrogant.

CHAPTER 5

Litigation Risk and Avoidance Strategies for Lenders, Contractors, and Professionals Serving the Nonresidential Developer

*Winning is not everything—but making
the effort to win is.*—Vince Lombardi

This chapter addresses litigation risk and avoidance strategies
for lenders, contractors, and professionals serving the nonresidential developer. Most of the chapter deals with identifying high-
risk circumstances and what the lender, contractor, or professional can do to minimize risks in those circumstances.

■ Dispute and Litigation Risks for Lenders

During the 1980s, lenders aggressively competed to make loans to
nonresidential real estate developers. The lending fever reached a
point where several lawsuits brought between lenders challenged
which lender would fund the loan. During this unusual time, the
competition for loans forced many lenders to forget or abandon

many basic principles of real estate lending. Loan underwriting was based on inflationary economic assumptions, which, with 20/20 hindsight, we now know had no basis in reality. In 1986, Congress rewrote the Internal Revenue Code in a manner that drastically eliminated the tax benefits previously enjoyed by real estate. Apartment owners were the first group to feel the impact of the new tax law. Ultimately, it affected all nonresidential real estate adversely and fueled the fire during the real estate recession of the 1990s.

The cost of remedying the mistakes of the 1980s has been staggering: the largest-ever bailout of the savings and loan industry; an enormous number of bank failures; and 1989 federal legislation that straitjacketed real estate lending in order to clean up the ill-advised real estate lending practices of savings and loans and banks. The life insurance industry also suffered significant losses but did not experience the same level of failures and seizures. In September 1996, the National Association of Insurance Commissioners adopted new model legislation to regulate investments, including real estate lending and ownership. The new Investments of Insurers Model Act sets the real estate lending and ownership standards for the life insurance industry for many years to come.

Understandably, the events of the last decade have drastically reduced the number of lenders willing to make nonresidential real estate loans. For those lenders that survived and are willing to continue making real estate loans, the overriding theme is back to basics. Most nonresidential real estate lending principles and guidelines evolved over a number of years and through a number of economic downturns and now need to be refined in view of the volatility in interest rates and the impact of tax law changes. Nonresidential real estate lending will also need to offer a risk premium to lenders as an incentive to make loans.

■ Selection of Borrowers and Loan Commitments

The lender's best protection from disputes and litigation is to select borrowers carefully and to spell out all relevant terms of the loan before either the lender or the developer is committed.

Choosing the Borrower

As trite as it sounds, "People, not property, repay loans." The corollary is also true. "People, not property, sue lenders." Using the real estate recession of the 1990s as a baseline, a lender can easily determine how many times a developer has sued a fellow lender, filed for bankruptcy protection to stop a lender from foreclosing, and/or paid a loan at less than the original terms. While the reasons for these actions may be justifiable, the pattern is a reliable indicator of how the developer views and treats lenders. A loan officer should know the developer's history before proposing the developer as a borrower. If the loan officer is not an enthusiastic advocate for the project's financing, the developer runs the risk of a loan committee rejection.

Negotiating and Documenting the Loan Commitment

The lender's best opportunity for reducing dispute and litigation risks comes while the loan commitment is negotiated and documented. All parties should keep careful written notes of their negotiations and agreements. If the lender intends to include a provision that may be objectionable to the developer and/or guarantors, the lending institution should include such provision in the loan commitment and not rely on the requirement that all documents must be satisfactory to the lender. That just creates a basis for a dispute and will eliminate repeat or referral business. Further, the lender should not use a "short-form" loan commitment unless it is considered nonbinding on the developer. Typically, the terms in such forms are not sufficiently specific to create a binding agreement. The loan officer's report to the loan committee is discoverable. Therefore, any requirement in the report not reflected in the loan commitment may create an inference of failure to disclose all loan conditions. In addition, if either the lender or developer fails to disclose fully all requirements and facts, disputes will arise upon subsequent disclosure.

The lender must create a clear understanding with the developer as to all costs to be paid. The lender should attempt to collect the loan fee or part of it as early as possible to test the developer's commitment to the lender's financing. In addition, the lender should try to budget and control all costs of making and closing the loan. Most developers value certainty over saving the last dollar on costs.

■ Loan Documents and Closing

A checklist should be used when closing real estate loans. Checklists are an excellent means of communicating all of the lender's requirements and identifying who is responsible for satisfying them. They also reduce the risk that the developer will claim the lender provided an oral waiver of a requirement that, in fact, remained in the loan commitment.

Loan documents should be clear, succinct, and understandable by an ordinary person. Enforcement ultimately occurs in a court, and few trial judges and even fewer jurors have experience with nonresidential loan documents. If the lender or its counsel drafts loan documents that are so one-sided that they place the developer in default upon signing them, the lender can scarcely expect to avoid disputes during the closing process or to experience trouble-free enforcement. In fact, the logical assumption is that the lender waives the default at closing. Such an assumption can limit a lender's ability to enforce other provisions in the loan documents.

At least two rules of judicial interpretation must be considered in loan document preparation. First, in the case of multiple interpretations of provisions in loan documents, the court typically interprets the provisions *against* the party that drafted them. Second, if a provision is understandable in a loan document, parole (i.e., oral testimony) evidence cannot be used to interpret it. Therefore, the lender or its counsel must explain unclear or conflicting provisions. A good practice is to provide the developer with "redlines" of revised documents so that it cannot claim that the lender changed a provision without the developer's knowledge.

Personal liability is always an important issue. Those jurisdictions with "one-action" rules (i.e., the lender has the right to foreclose on the property or to sue the developer/guarantor, but not both) cause special problems for lenders. If a lender wishes to make the developer's spouse personally liable, it must follow the requirements of the Equal Credit Opportunity Act or risk that the spouse's signature will be voided. Nonrecourse and partial-recourse loans create drafting challenges. When certain activities and/or conduct are excluded (i.e., "carved out") from the exculpation, they must be carefully drafted to ensure their enforceability. Limited guarantees also pose problems. For example, if a limited guarantee does not specify that foreclosure and casualty proceeds do not reduce the limited guarantee, the lender may find itself without a guarantee if it forecloses before enforcing the limited guarantee. Many traditional nonrecourse lenders (e.g., life insurance companies, pension funds, etc.) have begun using "exploding" or "springing" guarantees to deter developers from filing for bankruptcy protection. Such guarantees become enforceable only upon a voluntary or "friendly" involuntary filing; in many jurisdictions, however, the enforceability of such guarantees has not been judicially determined.

Cognovits or confession-of-judgment clauses that permit the lender unilaterally to obtain a judgment against the developer and/or guarantor after a loan default are important enforcement tools, although they are not enforceable in every jurisdiction. Developers resist the clauses because the judgment lien created by enforcing them effectively stops developers from further advances on other loans or from selling the property without paying off the judgment, which is exactly what the lender wants them to do.

An especially sensitive area for lenders is the obligation to make subsequent advances. Loan committees and regulators are especially unforgiving when a lender is legally obligated to make loan advances when common sense dictates otherwise. Accordingly, lenders should spell out all conditions for subsequent fundings so that anyone reading the loan documents can understand them. In particular, the funding conditions should be made objective rather than subjective to ensure their enforceability. Further, the satisfaction of every condition should not rest on the lender's "sole discretion." For large transactions, it might be prudent to rely on professional opinions for certain evaluations, especially given that experts typically side with lenders. In addition, the funding conditions should specify a mechanism whereby the developer can inject equity funding into the project to bring the budget into balance or to cure a problem. Finally, lenders should not agree to continue to fund over intervening liens in reliance on affirmative title insurance, i.e., title insurance that affirmatively covers a specified type of loss.

The reasons for the last point are many. Anyone who has filed a claim against a title company knows how often coverage is denied or disputed, with the title company refusing to defend or bond off. Even if coverage is accepted, the claim does not have to be paid until the insured suffers an actual loss. Title insurance does not provide the lender with the ability to foreclose or sell the property if its foreclosure sale will not extinguish all intervening liens. Further, title insurance coverage may not include or may be reduced by the title insurer's costs in resolving the claim. If the lender decides to rely on title insurance, the title insurer must promise to provide the same affirmative coverage to the lender's successors, i.e., buyers from the lender after foreclosure, at standard premiums; otherwise, the lender may not be able to sell the property.

If a mechanics' or other lien is filed against the property, any intervening lien must be bonded off if the affected jurisdiction forces the lien holder to exchange its lien for a claim against the bond. Developers are strongly opposed to bonding requirements because, in covering the full claim, the requirements encourage the lien holder to continue to fight and not compromise the lien. Lenders should not rely on affirmative title insurance for these types of liens, which do not permit the developer to lease or refinance the property.

■ Loan Administration and Enforcement

In administering the loan, the lender should avoid surprises and sudden moves and develop an understanding of the legal rights and remedies that attach to the lending function. If a problem is on the horizon, the lender should bring it to the developer's attention and communicate the requirements for solving it. When a problem requires specialized attention (e.g., more experienced loan officers or outside professionals, etc.), the lender should request help early to avoid exacerbating the situation through a poor judgment call. In addition, the loan committee must be advised of major problems, especially if the lender has lost confidence in the developer and/or property.

The lender must set and communicate clear limits to both the developer and the guarantors on what the lending institution is willing to do. The developer needs to know how the lender can help solve any problems. Where appropriate, the developer should be required to satisfy reasonable conditions before the lender is obligated to fund, take, or forebear from taking other action. Well-conceived conditions motivate the developer to solve the problem and, in so doing, protect the lender from later claims that it breached the understanding. The more control the lender exerts over the loan collateral, the more responsibility it assumes. The exculpations and indemnities for the specified lender in loan documents are not always enforced.

Multiple developers and/or guarantors require additional cautions. It is important not to favor one developer/guarantor over others because the lender could be forced to provide the same accommodations to all. In taking an action, the lender must be careful not to discharge any party from liability unintentionally. Unless the loan documents are clear and waivers to future changes enforceable in the affected jurisdiction, the lender should not modify the loan or loan documents without the consent of all parties.

■ Dispute and Litigation Risks for Design Professionals and Contractors

There are numerous situations that create litigation risks for design professionals and contractors. This section identifies some of the more common situations and what design professionals or contractors can do to limit their risks and avoid litigation.

The Architect—Designer and Overseer?

With the recent advent of new liabilities such as the Americans with Disabilities Act (ADA) and environmental laws (which are especially important for lenders who hire architects), the architect's role has become more complex. Owners, lenders, and general contractors expect architects to be both knowledgeable of and, in certain instances, responsible for some degree of compliance with these laws. The growth in the technical information for which architects may be responsible has been exponential. For example, architects are asked to certify that a property has no environmental problems or that a tenant's space plans meet ADA requirements. Such requests may be fair as to some issues but grossly unfair as to others. If an architect designed the entire building and materially participated in its construction, a request for certifications that the building meets the current building code and ADA may be fair. If, however, the architect designed only an addition to the building and/or was limited to monthly inspections of construction progress for loan fundings, the same request would not be fair.

Some years ago, architects' responsibility for performing site visits was changed to responsibility for performing site inspections, thereby preventing architects from becoming guarantors of the contractor's work. The American Institute of Architects Standard Form of Agreement between Owner and Architect No. B141 embodies the change. Notwithstanding this protection, however, traditional protections for architects are eroding. For example, architects are still the object of lawsuits if the owner is out of the area of the project and the architect visits the site for more than just progress payment applications. Typically, though, an owner limits the architect's role and compensation to monthly site inspections for progress payment application. When a problem arises, the owner (or the lender who has taken over the project) may still try to blame the architect for construction problems, claiming the problems should have been discovered during site inspections. The architect's role is further clouded by greater expectations of performance and knowledge on behalf of the other parties to real estate development.

The allocation of responsibilities and risk depends on at least three factors. The first factor is whether the architectural services contract deals with risk allocation. An architect should remain alert to language that specifies a turnkey job or creates responsibilities for reviewing and/or overseeing other persons' work. The architect should be capable of assuming such responsibilities, but only if accorded the needed time and appropriately compensated for discharging such responsibilities. The second factor is each jurisdiction's peculiar slant on the extent of the architect's responsibility. Given that case law varies from state to state, an architect should develop some familiarity with how the laws in question interpret the architect's responsibilities under the architectural services contract with the owner and under the professional services subcontracts the architect may have executed with engineers and other consultants. The third factor is the particular factual situation in each case as it relates to the expectations of the parties and their conduct.

Responsibility for Compliance with the Law

The Americans with Disabilities Act (ADA) is one of the many laws that regulates the design of a new building or the renovation of an existing one. Given the publicity surrounding enactment of the ADA, architects are presumed knowledgeable of the ADA requirements. If they lack the requisite knowledge, they may encounter problems in any of three phases of project development. During the program phase of a project, the architect must understand how the ADA affects the owner's project goals. For example, if ramps are deemed an eyesore but cannot be conveniently and aesthetically located, the architect will have to advise the owner accordingly at program outset rather than after the expenditure of substantial sums of money. During the budget phase of the project, the architect must specify the costs of meeting the ADA requirements. Any contingency established in both intent and amount for unforeseen project costs probably does not cover the ADA. During the design phase, the architect must satisfy the ADA requirements as part of overall code compliance. Courts routinely hold architects liable for code violations regardless of contingencies or the amount of the excess cost to retrofit as compared to overall project cost. Under the general standard-of-care percentage of errors methodology, the architect can remain liable for code violations.

With regard to landlords and tenants, the question arises as to who is responsible for ADA compliance costs. Lease provisions usually allocate responsibility for the ADA as follows: the landlord is responsible for ADA compliance in the building except for tenant premises, for which the tenant is responsible. Building systems or bathrooms are considered gray areas. What if a bathroom is in a tenant's space because the tenant has leased the entire floor? In this case, the tenant is most likely responsible for ADA costs. Government inspectors usually allocate responsibility for premises to tenants and for common areas to landlords, but full-building users and full-floor users may find themselves absorbing more costs. The architect should request the owner to summarize in writing the responsibility for ADA compliance throughout the building so that costs can be properly allocated between landlord and tenant.

An additional layer of exposure for architects comes from lenders' increased liability for environmental problems on projects they financed and then foreclosed on. Previously, the U.S. Environmental Protection Agency had promulgated rules that created a favorable liability standard for lenders. A court decision, however, invalidated the rules. Given that a lender routinely looks to pass on added costs to the borrower, the lender seeks another target when the borrower figuratively dies. So why not the architect who reviewed the property in the loan underwriting or the owner's architect whose architectural services contract was collaterally assigned to the lender in the event of a default? Unfortunately, when a project experiences compliance problems, the architect is always one of the targets for recovery. The two principal means of protecting the architect from these liabilities are to make sure that the architectural services contract and certifications are accurate and within the architect's knowledge and expertise and to comply with professional standards of practice. In creating a standard to measure the architect, the law has developed a doctrine that holds professionals to a higher standard.

The Doctrine of Superior Knowledge and Duty of Care

The doctrine of superior knowledge applies to situations in which a party, by its experience or education, has knowledge of a particular thing or condition that will totally frustrate performance or lead to the failure of consideration; that knowledge is known to be superior to the other party's knowledge; and the party with superior knowledge fails to disclose that knowledge to the other party. The party with superior knowledge will be held responsible for the frustration of performance and/or failure of consideration, even though there was no contractual or other tort liability.

The architect's duty of care can include items about which he or she has superior knowledge but that are not expressly excluded by the architectural services contract. General statements about not being responsible for compliance with laws may not be sufficient protection from the doctrine of superior knowledge if the owner can prove that the architect should have known the consequences of noncompliance.

Working with the Unsophisticated Developer

American Institute of Architects (AIA) documents and practice manuals provide architects with guidelines on how to work with an owner to prepare a program for a project. While concerns about the advisability of a project have not traditionally been the architect's responsibility, the line between feasibility and advisability becomes blurred when the developer is unsophisticated or the project involves an institution that engenders public sympathies (e.g., a church or a university). In terms of feasibility, economic conditions (development dollars are still hard to secure) will continue to require the budget to reflect actual costs rather than mere "guesstimates," especially in the case of the unsophisticated developer who lacks the knowledge or experience to identify missing budget items, lowball estimates, or an inappropriate contingency amount. Accordingly, the developer will rely on the architect.

Who will ensure that the project is properly built according to the program, budget, and design documents? When the developer is unsophisticated, the architect may not be able to assume that the owner can go it alone, with the architect merely approving payment applications. Where there is no one else, responsibility (and risk) may shift to the architect, especially if the architect's role expands beyond payment reviews.

Working with the Contractor Who Makes a Low Bid

In the bidding process, the architect is responsible for assisting the owner in selecting the appropriate contractor and/or subcontractors, not merely the lowest bidder. The sufficiency of the bid must be scrutinized carefully. If the contractor has underbid because of a poor take-off (i.e., missed items), a strong desire to land the job, or an incorrect subcontractor bid, problems will undoubtedly arise. The contractor will then look for changes and claims to remedy the situation as a pressure tactic for extras. The contractor's lack of attention to the project—sometimes a deliberate slowdown—may ensue. Bankruptcy is also a possibility. Certainly, the contractor will blame the architect for poor design documents and the owner for changes. Accordingly, contractors with proven track records and reputations for performing on time and within budget are preferred, even if their cost is higher.

The Budget Process in the 1990s

The architect who assumes that the owner commands more than the contingency may be in for a rude awakening. Many owners raise a limited amount of capital for a project and do not have the resources or willingness to fund beyond the contingency. To avoid liability for an inadequate contingency, the architect should investigate the extent of the owner's financial resources, the overall project budget, and the owner's ability to fund beyond the contingency. Owners/developers will be inclined to pursue litigation/arbitration for major cost overruns, with ample authority to hold architects liable for inadequate budgets.

Professional Liability Insurance

In recent years, smaller architectural firms have deliberately declined professional liability insurance coverage in the belief that insurance invites claims and the lack of it deters claims. This practice may change with increased competition for business and owner requirements for coverage.

Architect's Duty of Care toward the General Contractor

There is a growing trend toward finding architects liable to contractors for design errors that result in harm to the contractor. The absence of a direct contractual relationship, i.e., privity, between the architect and contractor in the AIA documents is not a solid shield.

■ The Contractor—Builder and Designer?

Before the manic 1980s, it was customary for design documents to be carefully prepared, the cost of work to be precisely determined, and profit percentages to be adequate. The handwritten ledgers documenting the cost of construction of the building at 806 Connecticut Avenue, N.W., in Washington, D.C., which housed the Peace Corps, is a prime example of such a project. Each item of work was predetermined and priced, each laborer was accounted for, and his or her wages were predetermined. Projects were funded with more equity than debt such that carrying costs were not a potential disaster if a delay occurred.

All this changed in the 1980s. With higher debt ratios, fast-tracking strategies, higher rents, and greater inflation, appreciation, and demand, project completion became more important than cost control. Budgets included contingency amounts that allowed for less precision in cost determination. Since the recession of the 1990s, however, cost prediction and control have become critical to new projects. Consequently, the early 1990s will be known as an era of renovations, as the cost of out-of-the-ground construction was not justifiable under market rents. For example, a nonbank lender has taken back a Grade B suburban office building and plans to renovate the building and then lease it to recover the loan deficiency. The design is prepared with the contractor's input, the budget and contingency are set, and the lender's board approval is obtained. In accordance with a cost/benefit analysis that caps further funding, no additional funding is available. The contractor submits its bid, which is 25 percent higher than the budget, and is then replaced with a new contractor who can complete the renovation project on budget through value engineering and the use of less costly subcontractors. Some specific situations where the contractor must be watchful and careful are discussed below.

Inadequate Design Documents

The contractor is required to review the design documents and notify the owner of defects. The contractor who observes inadequacies and does not disclose them may be held responsible for later extra costs in accordance with a special (not AIA) "reasonably inferred" provision in the construction contract, the superior knowledge doctrine, or risk allocation by the courts. Claims for extra costs for design oversights also lead sometimes to retaliation in other cost issues.

Inadequate Budgets

The owner whose budget is insufficient may cause serious problems for the contractor. For example, unforeseen conditions often arise in a renovation. The owner then takes the position that the contractor assumed responsibility for these conditions in its bid.

Construction Contracts

The two general types of construction contracts are cost-plus-fee contracts and stipulated-sum contracts. In the first case, the owner pays the contractor for the actual cost of the work, a percentage of such actual costs for the contractor's overhead, and a specified fee for the contractor's services. The fee is the contractor's profit. In the second case, the owner pays a fixed price for the work while the contractor risks the actual costs. The contractor's profit is the difference between the actual cost of the work and the contractor's overhead, on the one hand, and the fixed price, on the other hand. The stipulated-sum contract generates both more risks and the opportunity to make a larger profit.

Missed Items

An inadequate takeoff that results in missed items poses a serious risk to the contractor. To prevent litigation, the general contractor and the subcontractors must pay greater attention to eliminating missed items.

Building on Existing Expertise

Sometimes it is prudent not to bid on a job. Contractors inexperienced in renovations should not bid on projects that are likely to give rise to unforeseen costs. The odds against a contractor making a mistake are lower when the contractor is working in an area of existing expertise.

The Doctrine of Superior Knowledge

The doctrine of superior knowledge, as set forth previously, has its origins in claims against contractors who knew plans were defective, failed to disclose such knowledge, and constructed the design detail anyway. Courts are more likely to find liability under this doctrine where the owner or developer is unsophisticated.

The New Enemy—The Project Manager/Budget Director

Many employees of development companies that went out of business during the recession have emerged as project managers/budget directors, often on rehabilitation projects, for owners (usually financial institutions, vulture fund purchasers, foreign investors, etc.) lacking in-house development or construction expertise. With tight budgets and either guaranteed returns or expected internal rates of return making overruns unacceptable, project managers/budget directors are forced to be more stringent with contractors regarding payment for items that may have gone overlooked in the past.

Contingency

Does the contingency allowance in the developer's budget cover both the contractor's construction items *and* the owner's changes? This issue needs to be determined at the outset to avoid disputes. Nondeveloper owners may view the contingency as applying to their own changes, not to "misses" by the contractor or unforeseen renovation costs. As a practical matter, when the contingency is exhausted, the contractor's ability to obtain approval for additional cost items is adversely affected. Therefore, the contractor needs to know the owner's perception of the contingency, notify the owner if the contingency is insufficient for the project, and monitor the contingency balance to avoid disputes in the later stages of a project.

Warranties

In the past, contractors avoided losses because owners looked to manufacturers' warranties. For example, if a roof failed, the owner would proceed against the manufacturer's warranty if it covered the entire roofing system, not just the product (such as the roof membrane). However, when manufacturers vigorously fight liability, owners look to the contractor to pay for the loss. To guard against this eventuality, contractors may seek to establish their liability as secondary to the manufacturer's warranty, thereby forcing the owner to proceed first against the warranty.

■ Legal Documents

When negotiating and drafting the construction and related legal documents, the contractor can take several steps to avoid future disputes and litigation risks.

- *Know and give effect to the parties' real intentions.* The AIA forms advise the parties to the contract to consult an attorney when drawing up the construction contract. In response, many construction lawyers have developed boilerplate modifications. While these modifications have merit, the challenge in the 1990s is for the parties and their counsel to spend adequate time ensuring that the risk allocations between the parties are determined at the outset and clearly articulated in the construction contract. Conforming the contract to the project is more important than ever before. The attorney must understand the scope of the work and budget constraints, especially in the case of renovations.

- *Simplify the language.* The boilerplate modifications made to the AIA forms have increased over the years to the point that some agreements contain more modifications than form language. Some attorneys have entered the AIA forms and their boilerplate modifications into their computers and added their own modifications, making it difficult for contractors to distinguish readily between the modifications and the AIA form language. This has caused contractors great anguish. Larger contractors have refused to use these modified forms and have insisted on seeing the specific modifications. Many others have simply accepted the revised documents with varying levels of scrutiny. The greater the number of modifications plugged into the documents, the more that risk allocation becomes unclear. Provisions often conflict, or a particular situation may completely lack coverage. More attention needs to be paid to stating the parties' intentions and risk allocation understanding in language the parties can readily understand and to which they can agree.

- *Identify potential disputes.* It is important to determine what the owner and contractor care about both economically and as a matter of principle, particularly when drafting agreements to avoid potential disputes. Such issues should then be addressed clearly and thoroughly.

- *Include "soft" dispute resolution provisions.* Speedy, private resolution with an identified, mutually agreed-upon neutral arbitrator is advisable for certain types of disputes, including those that do not threaten the viability of the project. For example, if the contractor wants to use a specific subcontractor to whom the owner objects, the issue needs to be settled quickly. A delay can be more harmful than the controversy itself. Another example is disputes under a certain dollar amount. At some point, the cost of resolving the dispute exceeds the amount in dispute. In that circumstance, a quick resolution saves money, no matter which side wins. Finally, disputes over other limited issues between owner and contractor provide another example. Contracts often include incentive clauses for the contractor to create cost savings and share them with the owner. To the extent the contractor can value engineer the project, certain types of limited changes may be appropriate to submit to an accelerated dispute resolution mechanism.

While arbitration can resolve disputes over change orders, the process—undertaken in conjunction with the American Arbitration Association (AAA)—is cumbersome and expensive. The AAA's commercial arbitration rules were proposed for large, complex disputes, not simple ones. On the other hand, a specially drafted provision to obtain an inexpensive and quick decision can prevent low-level disputes from escalating and compromising good working relationships. The debate over whether it is better to litigate or arbitrate nonresidential lease disputes continues apace, often focusing on which approach is more effective for a given side. Consideration of the approach that will best avoid disputes may be in the owner's best interest, but distinguishing between types of disputes is also important. For example, failure to pay rent is a life-or-death issue. In that case, litigation, with the probability of a quick judgment that is enforceable, and removal of the tenant from the premises is probably the best approach.

- *Specify the arbitration method.* As a typical issue to be resolved by arbitration, renewal provisions in nonresidential leases have become a contentious matter primarily because the factors to be considered in determining market rent often are unclear. For example, should a vacancy factor be computed on a renewal? Should a full buildout allowance be allowed? Should a broker's commission be deducted even when none is paid? Some drafters are specific on renewal provisions while others are vague—either intentionally or unintentionally. Nonetheless, two common methods of arbitration are used in these situations. The first is the three-broker arbitration method whereby three knowledgeable professionals determine the market rent by majority vote. When two arbitrators agree, the matter is decided. The second is the baseball arbitration method whereby each arbitrator determines a market rent. Then, either the high or low market rent is used, depending on whether the middle arbitrator was closer to the high or low market rent. This method is supposed to encourage the parties to be reasonable.

■ Special Provisions for Risk Allocation and Breach Prevention in Contracts and Nonresidential Leases

Certain typical provisions in contracts and nonresidential leases are important factors in minimizing dispute risks and avoiding litigation. It is not practical to summarize all such provisions here. Therefore, a selection of common dispute protection or resolution provisions in contracts and/or nonresidential leases provides examples of provisions that can be used to reduce risks for all parties to the contract and/or nonresidential lease. The first seven provisions relate to all types of contracts; the last five provisions relate specifically to nonresidential leases.

Indemnifications
Several issues must be considered with regard to indemnifications.

- *Scope.* Indemnification should cover negligence and the intentional acts of the indemnitee and the insured. It usually applies to claims brought by third parties, such as by a business guest who is injured and brings suit against the landlord, tenant, design professionals, and contractor.

- *Enforceability.* Some jurisdictions place limits on enforceability of indemnifications. Research the position of the applicable jurisdiction.

- *Selection of counsel.* The indemnitee may wish to be involved in the selection of counsel; however, such a right must be stated specifically in the indemnification provision. Otherwise, the indemnitor selects counsel.

- *Conflicts.* Conflicts should be considered in determining representation of parties to the indemnification provision. Further, conflicts between the indemnitee and the indemnitor may require separate counsel.

- *Defense cooperation.* In the event the indemnitee has separate counsel, a provision should be included for the indemnitor's counsel to cooperate with the indemnitee's separate counsel.

- *Admissions of wrongdoing or liability.* The indemnitee should request a provision requiring approval before counsel can make any admissions. Injury to reputation and creation of liability not covered by the indemnity are reasons why the indemnitee needs such an approval right.

- *Settlement.* The indemnitee should request a provision requiring notice before settlement is concluded, but the indemnitor probably will not allow interference with or conditions on its ability to settle.

Contractual Indemnification Insurance

Contractual indemnification insurance covers the indemnification provision. The coverage must be specific, and the insurer must be advised of the terms of the contract, particularly the indemnification. The insurance does not cover all conduct but is nonetheless common; however, not everyone is able to obtain coverage. The assets of the insured and the size of the risk are critical factors for the insurer. The insurance generally covers the tenant, contractors, and consultants. It should also cover the negligent acts of the insured as well as the negligent acts of the indemnitee. Some jurisdictions do not enforce these provisions if the indemnitee is intentionally at fault and the insured has no culpability.

Prevailing-Party Attorney Fees

Prevailing-party attorney fees provisions are often included in construction contracts, leases, and many other types of contracts in the belief that they deter a party from taking an unreasonable or indefensible position. While this belief has merit, the provision could become the subject of its own litigation if its language is improper. Three types of such provisions apply. The all-or-nothing provision is viewed as having less ability to deter litigation than the other two types of provisions. If the defendant can show that the plaintiff did not prevail completely, then attorney fees are not recoverable. The allocation provision is more complicated but forces the parties to select the issues over which they will fight. While it can result in more litigation, the allocation is not difficult and less subject to dispute when it is part of an arbitration decision. The reasonableness-of-fees provision uses actual fees to cut down on the potential dispute over what is reasonable; however, many businesspersons believe that they should not pay for the other party's overpriced attorney. Most drafters insert a reasonableness requirement for attorney fees.

The three types of attorney fees provisions cannot be relied on to prevent major disputes or disputes involving principles. Yet, in the case of disputes involving lesser amounts of money, the provisions can be an effective deterrent.

Duty of Mitigation

The duty of mitigation requires each party to take reasonable actions to minimize damages caused by the other party's default. If each party fails to take such actions, the defaulting party can be excused from liability for those damages or for the losses the non-defaulting party could have avoided.

Waiver of Jury Trial

The provision for a waiver of jury trial is intended to achieve a quicker and less emotional decision. It also reflects a belief that complex commercial issues are better decided by a judge than by a jury.

Present Valuation of Damages

Inclusion of the requirement for present valuation of damages avoids further litigation based on whether a damages provision applied to damages incurred over a long period is void for being a penalty because it does not apply a "time value of money" adjustment to such damages.

Liquidated Damages

The provision on liquidated damages is intended to avoid further litigation on the amount of the loss. The challenge, though, is to determine a reasonable amount of liquidated damages. As a result, the provision can act as a deterrent if the amount is sufficiently high.

Critical Nonresidential Lease

The parties may disagree on certain critical issues but not so strongly that either litigation or arbitration is required. Addressing such issues in the nonresidential lease will reduce the risks of disputes. Such issues can include the following:

- Subletting and/or assigning the tenant's interest is an economic issue if rents have increased since the nonresidential lease was originally entered into. Often, the parties negotiate a profit-sharing arrangement. In shopping center leases, the right to assign or sublet affects the shopping center's tenant mix and thus may have an indirect economic effect.

- Alterations to the demised premises are critical if such alterations are structural. The landlord is concerned with making sure the alterations comply with laws and building codes, are completed lien-free, and will be removed at the tenant's expense at the end of the nonresidential lease term if the landlord wishes.

- Changes of use are important in retail leases. The landlord must keep a precise record of any restrictive covenants affecting the shopping center so that any change in use that conflicts with the covenants can be prohibited.

- Operating cost audits is a tenant issue when the tenant seeks to confirm it was properly charged for operating cost pass-throughs. A landlord's resistance to a reasonable request may create credibility problems. A clear and complete description of the operating costs and how they will be allocated is the best means of reducing future disputes.

- Subordination, attornment, and nondisturbance agreements are an important protection for nonresidential tenants. Under such agreements with the landlord's lender, the tenant agrees that its lease is subordinate to the lender's lien and to attorn to, i.e., accept, the lender as its landlord if the lender forecloses on the leased premises. The lender reciprocates by agreeing not to disturb the tenant's rights under its lease or to extinguish the tenant's lease so long as the tenant fully performs its obligations. In most states, a tenant must have a subordination, attornment, and nondisturbance agreement with each lender whose mortgage predates its lease or risk having the lease extinguished by a foreclosure sale.

- Estoppel certificates, i.e., lease status reports from the tenant, are important to landlords. Any sale or refinancing of the project requires the landlord to obtain estoppel certificates from its tenants addressed to the prospective purchaser or lender.

- Buildout design and budget items are important because they both determine whether the tenant receives the premises it expects for its planned use and specify the magnitude of the landlord's and tenant's costs. Again, clarity and specificity are the best protections against disputes and litigation risks.

Covering Nonresidential Lease Risks with Insurance

In the nonresidential leasing area, it is possible to avoid disputes by allocating risks and covering them with insurance. The general concept is that the tenant is responsible for everything that happens in its leased premises, even if the problem is traceable to the building systems or common areas. Therefore, the tenant should consider the following types of insurance coverage:

- liability for physical damage within leased premises, even if caused by the owner (this risk is usually insured under the tenant's policy);

- liability for personal injury within the leased premises, even if the owner has partial liability (this risk is usually insured under the tenant's policy);

- business interruption insurance for tenants to avoid setoffs or nonpayment of rent. This provides a source of replacement income for the landlord who is still obligated to pay the mortgage, even if the leased premises is unusable;

- primary insurance, which identifies whose insurance should cover the first dollars of loss where both landlord and tenant have coverage;

- additional insureds, which allows the other party to make a claim directly under the other party's insurance policy;

- liability for the deductable, which is often either overlooked entirely or covered by a landlord limit-of-liability provision. This issue demands more attention in drafting nonresidential leases, as the deductable can become a major problem if it applies to numerous items or instances of damage; and

- defense issues, such as whether the party wants some control over the selection of counsel and whether settlement should be made.

Right of Redemption

The right of redemption allows a tenant to cure a default after a judgment but any time before actual eviction. It is often used as a delaying tactic and therefore frustrates landlords. The right of redemption is not available in all jurisdictions for nonresidential leases. Insisting on a waiver of the right of redemption, however, or at least limiting its use to one instance during the term of the lease can avoid its application as a delaying tactic.

Tenants' Right to Repair and Set Off

Lenders and landlords vigorously oppose a provision that grants tenants the right to repair where space is uninhabitable and to set off costs against rent due. Experience shows, however, that the lender is better served if the tenant can operate and pay rent. In addition, certain tenants cannot permit interruptions and therefore require such a provision, e.g., all leases to the federal government contain one.

Space Contraction

While expansion rights are a common and complex aspect of non-residential leases, contraction rights are uncommon. Given the prevalence of corporate downsizing in the 1990s, it would be prudent to focus attention on ways to provide limited rights to reduce lease exposure and return space. One possible structure is to tie contraction to the loss of a contract or major client, particularly where government contractors are involved. Similarly, termination rights are tied to gross sales in retail leases.

While market reaction to such downsizing provisions remains unknown, the continuation of corporate downsizing may mean that the provisions will gain widespread acceptance. Landlords in all circumstances will seek to permit downsizing if a new tenant is available at the same or a higher rent. Alternatively, a limit can be placed on the tenant's exposure, with the assumption that the landlord will be able to relet the space. While a loan prepayment methodology may be applicable in computing a space contraction option payment, a downsizing provision will create loan underwriting problems when the landlord seeks to refinance the project. After all, lenders always use the worst-case scenario in underwriting.

■ Dispute and Litigation Risks for Marketing Professionals

Definition of Marketing Professionals

The term "marketing professionals" extends to all brokers, including those handling sales, loans, and leasing; advertising, marketing, and promotional companies; and consultants who serve as "finders" or otherwise seek tenants, lenders, or buyers for real property.

For purposes of this chapter, the term "marketing professionals" applies to nonresidential property only.

Engagement of Marketing Professionals

Marketing professionals need clear authority to act as the agent for the owner, lender, or tenant. Moreover, many jurisdictions require licensed sales and leasing brokers to secure written listing agreements before they show nonresidential property to prospective purchasers or tenants. Such jurisdictions typically prohibit unlicensed persons from selling or leasing nonresidential property they do not own.

Marketing professionals often use legitimate prospects to obtain a listing agreement from an owner. While serious prospects are frequently the necessary catalyst to motivate an owner to make the decision to sell or lease the nonresidential property, the use of serious prospects can backfire if the marketing professional either seeks engagement terms that are too favorable or promises unrealistic results. Each market dictates customs and practice for commission and engagement terms, although such terms vary widely and are highly negotiable. For example, if an owner perceives that the marketing professional is overly aggressive or optimistic, the owner will not trust the marketing professional to market the nonresidential property. In such cases, the owner will limit the listing agreement to specific, identified prospects or severely limit the period for marketing the property. By the same token, if the owner enters into the listing agreement and then perceives that the marketing professional was overly aggressive or optimistic, a dispute may arise, the owner may not cooperate with the marketing professional in marketing the nonresidential property, and/or the owner may not reduce the asking price until the listing agreement expires.

Anyone providing marketing services to a nonresidential property owner, lender, or prospective tenant should be engaged in a written agreement to minimize the risk of later disputes. The written agreement should spell out and protect the rights of all parties, including cobrokerage arrangements, while clearly providing that the marketing professional has neither legal nor apparent authority to bind the owner, lender, and/or tenant; clarify both the owner's duty to provide the marketing professional with accurate and complete information and the marketing professional's duty to use and disseminate such information properly; provide the owner with the means to exculpate the marketing professional and indemnify him or her for permitted dissemination of inaccurate or incomplete information on the nonresidential property received from the owner; clarify how much, when, and under what circumstances the owner must pay the marketing professional; and provide for marketing professionals who are licensed brokers with lien rights in some jurisdictions. Over the past decade, several jurisdictions have enacted broker lien laws that protect marketing professionals from unscrupulous owners.

Disputes over Fees

Most marketing professionals are compensated solely on the basis of results. Given that nonresidential transactions do not occur with the same frequency as residential transactions, the risks and rewards for marketing professionals are much greater. For marketing professionals, fee disputes are the most common type of dispute because they can arise in so many different instances. For example, fee disputes often occur over whether the marketing professional was the "procuring cause" for the transaction. Given that entitlement to a brokerage commission is linked to the marketing professional's services complying with the legal definition of procuring cause, the owner often challenges the role of the marketing professional in the transaction. Disputes also center around fees based on a percentage of the consideration when the owner restructures the contract, loan commitment, or lease to reduce the consideration. Usually, the owner has legitimate reasons for taking any of these actions but might make changes to reduce the marketing professional's commission along with the recording costs and other fees tied to price or rent.

Another common type of dispute relates to when the commission is "earned" and when it is due and payable. In some jurisdictions, the marketing professional earns a commission simply by producing a "ready, willing, and able" buyer who agrees to the purchase in accordance with the terms specified in the listing agreement. The owner takes the risk that the buyer will actually close. In large nonresidential transactions, the same risk is unacceptable to owners such that the commission is often payable only if and when the buyer closes. A parallel issue exists in leases. If the commission is earned at the lease signing, landlords typically are unwilling to pay the full commission until the tenant is in occupancy and paying full rent. Yet another common type of dispute occurs over the division of the commission when cobrokers are involved. Cobrokers often provide different levels of services but typically split the commission evenly. When, however, the listing broker provides little or no services, a dispute usually arises over the divided commission.

Receipt of Incorrect or Incomplete Information

The risk of disputes or litigation over the dissemination of incorrect information about the nonresidential property and/or owner has increased steadily during the past years. Courts have demonstrated a growing willingness to let various parties bring claims against marketing professionals. Accordingly, a marketing professional may not knowingly provide incorrect or incomplete information about a nonresidential property or owner without telling the recipient or accepting some dispute and litigation risk.

The marketing professional must exercise some due diligence in obtaining information on the nonresidential property from the owner or other sources. If the information is patently wrong or incomplete, the marketing professional should obtain correct and complete information or at least avoid using the information that he or she knows is wrong. The marketing professional should not put his or her credibility behind the information obtained from others unless he or she is absolutely certain about its accuracy.

With regard to liability for dissemination of incorrect or incomplete information about the nonresidential property, the best protection is a clause in the purchase agreement or lease that acknowledges the marketing professional's role and confirms that he or she has no liability for inaccurate or incomplete information obtained from the owner and provided to the buyer or tenant. If the parties to the purchase agreement or lease refuse to include such a provision, the marketing professional can obtain some protection by describing in writing from whom and how he or she obtained the information and, before signing the purchase agreement or lease, disclaiming liability for the information's accuracy or completeness.

■ Dispute and Litigation Risks for Property Managers

Duty of Care
With or without a written agreement, the property manager has a duty of care in managing the nonresidential property. If the non-residential property is in financial distress and the owner cannot or will not provide adequate resources to carry out the property manager's duties, the property manager must document the situation and consider resigning if there is danger to persons or property. The property manager should obtain a written list of his or her specific duties as protection against claims by the owner and/or others that he or she was negligent.

Duty to Comply
The property manager has a duty to comply with laws governing the nonresidential property and its operations. Ignorance is usually not a valid excuse. For residential property, fair housing and other civil rights laws have created higher standards of care and the duty both to provide sensitivity and compliance training to employees and to monitor their compliance. Compliance with the Americans with Disabilities Act (ADA) and environmental laws creates additional problems and risks. Such compliance can be evaluated only by a competent professional. Sometimes, however, the owner simply does not want to know about ADA and/or envi-

ronmental problems and chooses noncompliance. For some own-ers, the cost of compliance and/or remediation can be prohibitive. In those cases where the owner cannot or will not evaluate and comply, the property manager may be liable for exposure risks to employees, tenants, and others for providing inadequate protec-tion, even when the owner has refused to pay for such protection.

Indemnification

Indemnification from the owner to the property manager is always a contentious issue. The property manager wants the benefit of the owner's liability insurance if he or she acts negligently, but the owner seeks to limit the indemnification to those circumstances where the property manager was acting within the scope of his or her duties. If the property manager's negligence causes injury to third parties, the owner's insurance can be used to protect both the owner and the property manager. However, if the property man-ager's negligence causes damage to the owner or its property, the owner's insurance does not always provide coverage. If the proper-ty manager violates a local building, operations, or health code, exclusions in the owner's insurance policy may expose both the property manager and the owner to liability.

The indemnification should exclude gross negligence, inten-tional acts, and criminal conduct. If the owner insists, however, on excluding ordinary negligence from the indemnification, then the indemnification is meaningless. Most harm or damage is caused by ordinary negligence. Once an indemnity is obtained, the property manager should make sure it is collectable. If the owner is a "sin-gle-asset" entity with a corporate general partner and no equity in its nonresidential property, the indemnity may be uncollectable except for the insurance coverage.

Incentive Compensation

Many property management agreements include incentive com-pensation provisions for tenant retention, efficient operations, and other performance results. Disputes may arise if the owner or property manager delays or accelerates income in a way that affects incentive compensation. Accordingly, if the compensation formu-la is not clearly defined and preserved, disputes will arise over its interpretation and whether it can be enforced after termination of the property management agreement.

When the property manager relies on incentive compensation as a material part of its income, the property management agreement must have a long initial term or be cancelable only "for cause." The automatic renewal of the property management agreement is necessary to give the property manager sufficient time to earn the incentive compensation and amortize its startup expenses.

Liability for Employees and Service Contracts

For administrative convenience, property managers often place under their name all employees and service contracts associated with the nonresidential property. Although service contracts are usually not a problem if cancelable without penalty on 30 days' notice, the property manager assumes all the employer's liabilities with respect to project employees. To avoid such liabilities, the property management agreement should delineate which liabilities are the property manager's and which are the owner's while the property manager should not employ the owner's staff unless it controls the cash and can make the withholding tax deposits, medical insurance payments, retirement plan contributions, and other benefit payments without owner interference. In addition, the property manager should reserve funds from the owner for the accrued vacation pay of its employees. Finally, if the property manager is concerned that a lender will attach the rental receipts from the nonresidential property because of a loan default, the property management agreement should permit termination of the property manager's obligations unless the lender provides assurances that it will continue to honor the property management agreement through an orderly transition and continued funding of employment expenses.

CHAPTER 6

Alternative Dispute Resolution (ADR) as a Business Strategy: From Setting the Stage to Making It Work

When in doubt tell the truth.—Mark Twain

To lawyers who make their living as litigators in business disputes, what follows may sound like heresy. But the alternative dispute resolution (ADR) strategy discussed in this chapter has helped many clients resolve business disputes cost effectively. It relies on cooperative problem-solving techniques and rejects the adversarial approach to dispute resolution—unless no other option remains.

The strategy is time-tested. Its basic techniques have been used in collective bargaining by labor lawyers as a fundamental approach to dispute resolution for over 60 years. In the 1970s, Roger Fisher broadened ADR's application to general business negotiations as popularized in the best-selling book *Getting to Yes* and in the Harvard Negotiating Project. But ADR's application to business has been slow in coming. Because of the exploding costs of adversarial dispute resolution in business, the time has come to make ADR a part of every business litigator's repertoire.

■ What the ADR Strategy Requires

The ADR strategy demands an upfront understanding of the client's dispute and requires the attorney's active participation with the client in defining and shaping the client's business objectives, legal position, and negotiating leverage before negotiations begin. It also requires the attorney's active evaluation of the opponent's business objectives, legal position, and negotiating leverage before and during the negotiation process.

In addition, while the attorney must assume the customary role of advocating for the client's legitimate business objectives, the ADR strategy requires the lawyer to assume, as necessary, several less familiar roles: investigator, educator, facilitator, and problem solver. Finally, the lawyer must avoid assuming the role of "mad dog" litigator.

■ The Goals of the ADR Strategy and Why It Works

The ADR strategy is effective both before and after the initiation of litigation or some other formal adversarial adjudicatory proceeding. If used before litigation, ADR's goal is to settle the case, if possible, within the client's legitimate business parameters while preserving the client's legal position, should litigation become necessary. If used after litigation has begun, ADR's goal is to settle the case within the client's legitimate business parameters without damaging the client's litigation position.

Typical business disputes embody three features that make use of the ADR strategy a sound business decision. First, business disputes usually involve money: who pays what and when. This, of course, is the stuff of typical deal-making business negotiations, which are normally resolved through a cooperative problem-solving approach. Second, given that business disputes usually involve complicated facts and paper-intensive, multidisciplinary legal and technical issues, they are often a lawyer's dream and a client's nightmare. That is, the parties together (or even singly) might spend more on opportunity costs, attorney and consultant fees, and costs of litigation than the principal amount of the dispute in order to find out who, if anyone, was right. Third, business disputes often involve parties whose overall best interests are to preserve relations with one another, relations that knock-down-drag-out litigation could destroy irreparably.

■ Why the ADR Strategy Is Good for the Client

When compared to adversarial dispute resolution methods, the ADR strategy saves the client money, time, and wear and tear on management resources and preserves important business relationships. The ADR strategy saves money primarily because it encourages the parties to talk openly about the facts that gave rise to the dispute while such facts are fresh in everyone's mind. Facts include the conditions thought to create a claim or defense as well as the size and general dollar amount involved in the dispute. Openness discourages "overkill," "hiding the ball," and other discovery games common to adversarial dispute resolution processes and minimizes excessive attorney time in the fact-gathering and development process.

In addition, the ADR strategy's informality makes it unnecessary to comply with artificial and stylized rules in the presentation of arguments and technical information. The informality simplifies the tasks of technical experts and attorneys in developing the client's position and communicating that position to the other parties to the dispute and, in turn, saves money on fees and expenses.

The ADR strategy saves time because the parties alone control the pace of the dispute resolution process. They do not have to wait their turn for a third party or administrative body to tell them what they may do. The ADR strategy saves wear and tear on management resources because it does not require the time and emotional expenditure required in the adversarial approach, particularly in deposition and witness preparation and appearances. Finally, the ADR strategy preserves relationships by encouraging the parties to focus on their common interests rather than on their differences. By definition, all adversarial dispute resolution processes do just the opposite.

■ Why the ADR Strategy Is Good for the Lawyer

Using the ADR strategy is good for lawyers because they can save clients' time and money and preserve their business relationships while achieving their business goals. A lawyer's association with the ADR strategy identifies the lawyer in clients' minds as a valued professional who, in today's business jargon, "is not part of the problem, but part of the solution." As a result, lawyers should be better able to maintain a long-term relationship with their clients.

■ Setting the Stage

The section that follows is designed to familiarize you with the ADR concept, provide you with an example of an ADR strategy, explain why ADR is a sound strategy for handling disputes related to real estate development projects, and identify the basic types of ADR and their features.

The ADR Concept
ADR is any method of dispute resolution other than litigation.

A Sample ADR Strategy
The following is an example of an ADR strategy statement:

"We seek to prevent disputes involving our company if at all possible. If disputes do arise, we are committed to formulating, negotiating, or mediating sound resolutions to all disputes in which we are involved and to litigating such disputes only if there is no other feasible alternative."

Why Use the ADR Strategy Instead of Litigation?
Litigation should be a *last resort* because it is expensive; diverts management from its main objectives; requires relinquishing control of the dispute to attorneys, courts, and/or juries; is highly unpre-

dictable; is public; is slow; and damages business relationships. ADR should be *used first* because it is less costly, allows management to manage, keeps control in the hands of the parties, is predictable, is confidential, and preserves important business relationships.

■ Basic Types and Features of ADR

There are four basic types of ADR: negotiation, mediation, hybrid, and arbitration.

Negotiation

The word "negotiate" is derived from the Latin word meaning to do business; the definition of negotiation is conferring by parties to try to reach an agreement or bargain. While lawyers have no monopoly on the use of negotiation, many are highly skilled in it. A form of negotiation known as cooperative problem-solving negotiation is discussed below.

Mediation

The word "mediate" comes from the Latin word to be in the middle; the definition of mediation is negotiation with assistance from a neutral third party. Mediation is not a new concept or technique; it has been used in resolving international disputes for centuries. Over 60 years ago, mediation was applied to labor relations disputes; its use in domestic relations and neighborhood disputes began in the 1970s. Since 1990, mediation has been used more and more frequently in all kinds of disputes before and during civil litigation proceedings. Most use of ADR in business disputes today takes the form of negotiation alone or negotiation assisted by mediation.

Hybrid

Hybrid ADR strategies involve four primary variants as follows:

- *Early neutral evaluation.* Early neutral evaluation has been used since 1983, when U.S. District Court Judge Peckham in

San Francisco developed it. A court typically requires early neutral evaluation after a lawsuit has been filed; the affected parties can agree to it, however, without a suit. The parties normally conduct discovery in the suit or have already established a good grasp of the facts of the dispute before they begin the process. The parties choose a neutral party experienced in the subject matter of the dispute and then submit to that party a set of position papers summarizing their positions. The neutral party then guides the disputing parties through a structured (but nonbinding) process to resolve the suit without trial.

- *Conciliation.* Conciliation is also not new but is not used as much as mediation in ordinary business dispute resolution. Like mediation, conciliation involves negotiation with the help of a third party, but it generally implies a more active role by the third party than does mediation. The dictionary definition of conciliation conveys some of the subtle differences between the third party's role in conciliation versus mediation: to overcome distrust or animosity; to placate or to make compatible. The third party thus has a stake in making the sides compatible.

- *Minitrial.* A minitrial is a private, abbreviated trial of a case before a neutral party and the executives of both parties. It is normally conducted after both sides have a firm grasp of the facts, law, and other issues in dispute. The parties agree on a presentation format, which may involve the testimony of key witnesses or presentation of key evidence. The presence of executive decision makers at the proceedings is a requirement.

- *Nonbinding arbitration.* The term nonbinding arbitration is an oxymoron according to the definition of arbitration that follows. The process requires a hearing before an arbitrator, but the resulting decision is advisory only, not final and binding.

Table 1
ADR Procedure for Negotiation and
Mediation before Litigation

Written Notice
Claimant notifies respondent stating the claim, legal basis, pro
posed remedy, and time and place to discuss resolution of the
claim.

Negotiation and Submission to Mediation
If the claim is not settled within 30 days, it is submitted to mediation
by the claimant; if not, the respondent is discharged from liability.

Mediation
If the claim is not settled within 30 days, the mediator issues a
notice of termination. The claimant then has five days to make a
final written settlement demand to the respondent, and the respondent makes a final written settlement offer to the claimant.

Allocation of Costs
Each party bears its own costs and shares the mediator's charges.
However, if the claim is litigated and judgment is equal to or more
favorable to the claimant than its settlement demand, the claimant's
litigation costs and attorney fees are added to the judgment. If the
judgment is equal to or less favorable to the claimant than the
respondent's settlement offer, the respondent's litigation costs and
attorney fees are added to the judgment.

Arbitration

All of the previous types of ADR share a common characteristic:
the parties and only the parties control whether the dispute will be
resolved and how. The final type of ADR—arbitration—does not
share this feature. The word "arbitrate" is from a Latin word
meaning to give judgment. The dictionary definition of arbitration
is to submit a dispute by agreement to . . . one empowered to judge
or ordain at will. Unlike the first three types of ADR, arbitration
yields control to a third party, who then commands all the power
needed to decide the dispute. Generally, arbitration provides for
no right of appeal, except for fraud or corruption of the arbitrator.

Table 2
ADR Procedure for Negotiation, Mediation, and Binding Arbitration

Written Notice
Claimant notifies the respondent stating the claim, legal basis, proposed remedy, and time and place to discuss resolution of the claim.

Negotiation and Submission to Mediation
If the claim is not settled within 30 days, it is submitted to mediation by the claimant; if not, the respondent is discharged from liability.

Mediation
If the claim is not settled within 30 days, the mediator issues a notice of termination. The claimant then has five days to make a final written settlement demand to the respondent, and the respondent makes a final written settlement offer to the claimant.

Final and Binding Arbitration
If the parties do not agree to settle the claim within 15 days of terminating mediation, the claimant has 15 days to submit the claim to arbitration. The arbitration award is final and binding and judgment may be entered upon in a court of competent jurisdiction.

Allocation of Costs
Each party bears its own costs and shares the mediator's and arbitration charges. However, if the claim is litigated and the award is equal to or more favorable to the claimant than its settlement demand, the claimant's postmediation costs and attorney fees are added to the judgment. If the award is equal to or less favorable to the claimant than the respondent's settlement offer, the respondent's postmediation costs and attorney fees are added to the judgment.

■ Making It Work

This section suggests some steps for implementing ADR as a strategy in your business and identifies resources that you and your lawyer might use to institute an ADR program.

Cooperative Problem-Solving Negotiation

Rather than resorting to adversarial or power-based negotiations, your business might first experiment with a form of ADR known as cooperative problem-solving negotiation (CPSN). CPSN is interest-based bargaining focused on the interests of parties rather than on their rights; like ADR, it was popularized in Roger Fisher's *Getting to Yes*.

CPSN involves the following seven-step process:

- Gather information and set forth objectives;

- Plan a strategy and tactics;

- Define your role;

- Initiate dialogue with the other side;

- Reevaluate both sides' positions;

- Continue the bargaining process until reaching a deal or impasse; and

- Agree in principle and memorialize with final documents.

1. *Gather information and set objectives.* As early as possible, the client and the attorney should collect as much information as they can, including the client's objectives and the scope of the dispute.

In the early stages of a dispute, disputants often do not think through their objectives. Yet, everyone benefits if the parties have thought through their objectives as early as possible. It is particularly important to pin down in general terms how much money is at stake in the dispute and how the parties perceive what is at stake. One way to ensure that objectives are both achievable and realistic is for attorney and client to share judgment and experience. A preliminary assessment of liability and damages is a good starting point.

Your objectives and preliminary position should be based on existing information. Armed with that information, you should analyze the known facts regarding both liability and damages, apply them to the relevant law, and construct the most persuasive case you can think of for your side. Roughly calculate the range of recovery under this best-case scenario.

Then, try to get an initial idea of the other side's position by putting yourself in the opposition's position. Anticipate the opposition's best preliminary position based on what you know about the facts and the law on both liability and damages and what you think might be the opposition's likely business objectives. Roughly calculate the likely outcome under the other side's best case.

The first stage may be easy or difficult and time-consuming depending on the dispute's complexity. Under no circumstances should it be shortchanged.

2. *Plan a strategy and tactics.* In this stage, you are establishing a road map for the negotiations, although the map may change as negotiations develop. To do so effectively, you must *establish a principled opening position, anticipate your opponent's moves and countermoves, plan information disclosure, and plan the time and place of meetings.*

- *Establish an opening position.* Your opening position should be "principled." A principled position is one that can be defended objectively with a logical rationale for each element of the position. Your opening position should be high enough that you can achieve realistic objectives but sufficiently thought out and documented so that the other side will take it seriously.

There is nothing wrong with trying to achieve both the upper hand in the dispute and the best possible result for your side. For example, if your side has the facts, the law, and the leverage, you need not fold your tent and compromise if the other side fails to assess the situation accurately. You should, however, afford your opponent the opportunity to see the light and bow gracefully to the inevitable so that both sides are better off than if you peremptorily brought a lawsuit. Nonetheless, experienced litigators know that it is a once-in-a-lifetime case in which one side is in sole possession of the facts, law, and leverage. Therefore, you and your lawyer should develop a realistic opening position that you both believe in before presenting it.

- *Anticipated moves and countermoves.* The goal is to plan a process that will convince the other side of the advisability of settling the dispute in a way that meets your side's objectives. Often, you can best accomplish this goal by putting your side in a position to make a final offer to the other side that, in your opponents' eyes, would be achievable only by spending or risking more than they can or want to. This, of course, is easier said than done but should be your goal.

- *Information disclosure.* Generally, you should put your cards on the table at some time during the negotiation process. You should plan early how and when to disclose your information to maximize its persuasive effect on the other side.

- *Meeting time and place.* You should plan where, when, and how to conduct the negotiations once the bargaining begins. You should also establish a realistic schedule with appropriate benchmarks to ensure that the process does not drag out unnecessarily. Schedule sessions at a time and place convenient to both parties, and don't permit anyone to use the timing or location of the negotiations to inconvenience unreasonably any party or to foster feelings of fear or intimidation on either side.

3. *Define your role.* A variety of roles comes into play in negotiations. Some examples are the mad dog litigator, the nitpicking technician, the bully, the tough guy, and the know-it-all, all examples of aggressive roles. Generally, none of these roles is appropriate in an effective ADR strategy. Usually, they are not particularly effective in negotiation either. Indeed, a recent empirical study concluded that of attorneys considered to be effective negotiators, 78 percent used cooperative strategies and tactics while only 12 percent used aggressive strategies and tactics. The study suggested that it is difficult to be an effective negotiator by assuming an aggressive role, although, at times, the aggressive role impresses certain clients. In fact, entrepreneurs and hard-driving operations managers are often uncomfortable if someone from their side does not play the mad dog litigator. In general, though, better results are achieved by adopting a cooperative approach at this stage of a dispute, with the most effective roles the helpful advocate and clear communicator. Neither role is inconsistent with the role your side might later assume if litigation is indicated or, indeed, if litigation or another adversarial proceeding has already begun. The charac-

teristics of the helpful advocate include courtesy, personableness, tact, sincerity, fair-mindedness, realistic in formulating positions, information sharer, and perceptive and skillful in listening and reading cues.

4. *Start dialogue with the other side.* After you have completed Steps 1 through 3, you and your attorney are ready to start communications with the other side. The two main objectives of the initial communication with the other side are to set the tone of negotiations and to understand the other side's stated position. You should set the tone immediately by playing the role of helpful advocate and clear communicator. Take great pains to create rapport by assuming a friendly and nonadversarial posture. Avoid taking any "bait" from the other side to draw you into a fight.

To understand the other side, listen actively and ask open-ended questions to draw out your opponents' view of the facts and law on both liability and damages regarding their case and yours. Note particularly how their view of the facts and law differs from yours. Avoid the natural instinctive reflex to argue your case at this stage. You are now on a fact-finding mission, and arguing will impede your success. The more information you can gather, the stronger is your position. For example, if the other side has made a claim, what is its theory of liability? What facts do your opponents present for supporting their liability theory? Are their perceptions of their claim consistent with their expressed theory of liability? Do their facts support the range of their claim? Are they willing to send you verification of the facts on which they rely? If you have an obvious defense, how do they say they get around it? What do they say they are trying to achieve?

If the client is making a claim, your attorney's demand letter has probably set out the basics of your claim. In your initial contact with your opponents, find out their defense theories and the facts they use to support those theories. Are they willing to verify the facts on which they rely? Are their defenses partial or complete? If partial, how much do they purport to owe under their theories of defense? Is the range of what they purport to owe consistent with their defense?

To the extent possible at this stage, set out your side's positions in answer to the other side's questions. Except for the basics of your case, it is typically best not to volunteer information to the other side, especially information that might be considered self-serving. Your opponents will attach little credence to such information. If, on the other hand, you convincingly provide information in response to their probing questions and offer to verify it, they will be more likely to credit it.

5. *Reevaluate both sides' positions.* Revisit the issues you considered in Step 2. You now have more and better information because you have the benefit of the information you received in Step 4. You can evaluate who has the edge on the facts and law, whose arguments make more sense, whether the other side shares your assessment of the dispute, and how far apart the parties are from where they say they want to go and from where you think they truly want to go.

Now is also the time to recheck your planned goals, strategy, and tactics. If the other side's case is materially stronger or weaker than you expected, consider whether you should modify your goals and, if so, how. In fact, you should not be afraid to modify your objectives, strategy, or tactics based on information you develop at any time during the negotiation process. You should remain flexible and focus on solving the real problem between the parties. Most often, the law alone will not provide the solution. As you develop more information about the real problem, you can better evaluate whether and how the parties might settle their differences.

6. *Continue the bargaining process until deal or impasse.* The first five steps have prepared you for the essence of the negotiation process. Step 6 is the give-and-take bargaining phase of negotiations; it is a problem-solving game. The "innings" of the game are advocacy, listening, and evaluation until both sides reach a deal or impasse.

As a helpful advocate and clear communicator, you have made your initial principled offer or demand backed up by a reasoned argument. You have listened to your opponents' argument and encouraged the other side to take principled positions backed up with reasoned argument. Now movement from both sides is required to reach a settlement. Clearly, Step 6 is not the time to assume an adversarial role.

Maintain your role as helpful advocate and clear communicator by keeping your moves and countermoves principled. In Step 6, continue to advocate your position constructively by focusing on the needs and interests of both sides and on how your positions reasonably seem to meet those needs. Use all your advocacy skills to persuade the other side that your position fairly meets the opposition's needs. Given the absence of rules of evidence, the materials you use in your discussions is limited only by the bounds of your imagination: charts, graphs, demonstrations, reenactments, site visits, collaborative conferences with both sides' experts, videotapes, photographs, etc.

Use your advocacy skills also to address practical business issues, emotional issues, and external pressures as well as legal and factual issues. Often, business and emotional issues and external pressures are what separate the parties to a dispute. You might find it useful during negotiations to focus on the other side as if it were a jury. Use whatever tools you believe would persuade the other side that your side is "going the last mile" in trying to resolve the dispute.

After you advocate your position, it is your opponents' turn once again to advocate their position. Listen, evaluate, and respond as you did in the earlier steps. The process ends in either a deal or an impasse. "Impasse" means no deal after all reasonable avenues have been explored. You should not consider that you have reached an impasse in a business dispute until the parties invite a mediator into the process to help them determine whether all reasonable avenues indeed have been explored. If the parties do reach an impasse, each side is free to "do what it has to do," which in business disputes probably means move on to arbitration or litigation.

7. *Agree in principle and memorialize with final documents.* If the parties reach a deal, they must first agree in writing to the deal in principle and then memorialize it with final documents. The agreement in principle should outline the essential elements of the deal so that a competent attorney can use it to draft the final documents memorializing the settlement.

The final step in the negotiation process is extremely important. As with any other business deal, many problems may arise between the conclusion of bargaining and the time the parties reach the closing table. The cooperative, problem-solving tone established during the bargaining phase should, however, help minimize the possibility that such problems will preclude a settlement once a deal is reached.

Mediation

If you do not reach agreement using unassisted CPSN techniques, you might consider using a mediator to assist you. Mediation calls for the following four-step process:

1. *Select a dispute.* The dispute should involve a difficult problem, one in which you have nothing to lose. It should be a situation in which you are otherwise unlikely to realize a good solution.

2. *Pick a mediator.* The mediator should be an experienced trial lawyer, but not necessarily a judge. What makes a good judge often does not make a good mediator. It is also important to keep in mind that a mediator decides nothing but rather facilitates and persuades each side. One of a mediator's most effective mediation techniques is acting as a nonthreatening devil's advocate.

3. *Be prepared.* The mediation session may be your only chance to go one-on-one with the other side's business decision makers; do not squander the opportunity.

4. *Use CPSN negotiating techniques in mediation.* Draw on all your creativity during the session. Use illustrations and visual aids and remember that the jury is the other side, not the mediator.

■ Establish an ADR Strategy in Your Organization

The steps in designing and implementing an ADR strategic plan are as follows:

1. *Educate management.* Challenge the litigation culture by exposing its strategy of "wait, litigate, then settle."

2. *Dispel the traditional litigation culture myths* that beating your opponent means that your opponent is weak, winning a jury verdict vindicates your product's quality, and winning at trial means your organization need not change.

3. *Obtain and provide information.* Arrange outside and on-site seminars by ADR providers; usually, only a nominal fee is involved, although sometimes the service is complimentary. Sources of ADR information and services include consultants; the National Institute for Dispute Resolution (NIDR), which produces studies and reports; the Center for Public Resources (CPR), which makes available model procedures and documents; the Society for Professionals in Dispute Resolution (SPDR), a professional association of neutrals actively participating in all forms of ADR that provides information on ethics and other issues related to ADR services; the American Arbitration Association, which produces training programs and provides information; and the American Bar Association Section on Dispute Resolution, which is the newest ABA section.

4. *Solicit support.* Enlist the support of every part of your business, from the top to the trenches.

Establish the Need for an ADR Strategy In Your Business

To analyze the need for an effective ADR program, your business should perform the following steps:

1. *Determine the scope and extent of problems by area.* Perform a break-even analysis by project over the past three to five years to determine the volume of product you must sell to pay your direct litigation expenses (all payments to opponents plus your total attorney fees and costs). The formula for a break-even analysis is the direct litigation expenses divided by the pretax return on sales. For example, assume that you paid your attorneys $250,000 and costs of $50,000 to defend successfully a construction defect case and that your pretax return on sales was 20 percent: $300,000 / 20% = $1,500,000. Therefore, you need to sell $1.5 million more product to break even.

2. *Determine the scope of the program needed to fit problem areas.* A broad range of programs is available, from a full-scale ADR program to a simple corporate ADR awareness program.

3. *Identify risk areas.* Examples of risk areas include development disputes, construction disputes, construction defect disputes, lender disputes, labor and employment disputes, Americans with Disabilities Act disputes, vendor/supplier disputes, commercial contract disputes, and landlord/tenant disputes.

4. *Set goals for each risk area.* You need to ask what specific goals are realistic and achievable in each risk area.

Design an Effective ADR Program for Your Business

To design an effective ADR program, your business must follow a multistep approach.

1. *Employ early settlement strategies in existing cases.* Work with your litigation counsel to establish sound business objectives for each case and encourage your litigation counsel to develop a settlement strategy consistent with those objectives. Early settlement consistent with your objectives normally results in overall savings.

2. *Match ADR techniques to each risk area.* To the extent you need to maintain control over the process, choose negotiation and mediation; to the extent you need finality, choose arbitration.

3. *Consider key decision points.* The following questions should be considered:

- Who will decide whether and when to use ADR within a department or in a particular case?

- Will the use of ADR be encouraged or required? Will targets or quotas be imposed?

- Will form contract provisions be developed? Will your business encourage mandatory negotiation and mediation before adjudication, other procedures such as nonbinding arbitration, or an administered (using a service that provides arbitration administration) or nonadministered process?

- Will the neutral service provider be named in a preset agreement or identified on an ad hoc basis by agreement of parties?

- Will neutral parties be national, local, or regional?

- What type of facilities will be used?

- What type of ADR services will be used, e.g., neutral party, scheduling, training, forms?

4. *Start with a pilot program.* Start small and consider using ADR in one project or with one type of matter (for example, warranty claims) or to resolve disputes with controlled entities such as divisions within the same corporation. Incorporate ADR provisions into all agreements with subcontractors and suppliers in the given project or area and then monitor the results.

5. *Appoint an ADR point person.* Select a point person who understands the importance of saving litigation costs and who has an incentive for doing so. The person should have a budget that enables him or her to become involved in selected ADR organizations in order to keep abreast of developments in the field.

6. *Institute ADR training.* Recognize the need to institute training. Lack of information and lack of skill are the primary reasons for resistance to ADR. The strategy has been receiving a great deal of attention since 1989, but many lawyers and risk managers still are not up to speed. Formal training is available from the ADR providers and professional associations previously listed.

7. *Apply ADR to other areas.* Extend the ADR process used in the pilot program to other projects in the company; monitor results and modify as necessary.

8. *Sign the "ADR Pledge."* The Center for Public Resources (CPR) developed the ADR Pledge, which is a formal agreement with other signatories (over 500 companies and the law firms that represent them) to consider ADR in any dispute between or

among signatories. Signing this pledge is a tangible sign that your company has a sound ADR strategy.

9. *Develop an ADR manual.* After your business establishes an experience base, it should record successful systems in a manual for distribution to management and claims-handling personnel.

10. *Tell your lawyers and law firms.* Your lawyers should be fully informed about your company's dedication to its ADR strategy and told that they will be expected to comply with that strategy.

11. *Publicize your commitment to ADR.* Many companies have found that their ADR strategy is good for business. Consult your public relations professional on how best to publicize your commitment.

12. *Monitor and modify as necessary.* Develop feedback and case tracking systems and perform "dispute autopsies."

Like any strategy, an ADR strategy needs persistent leadership to ensure its success. ADR is not a "quick fix," and it cannot be implemented overnight. Disputes will always be a part of the real estate development process, but resisting the temptation to use litigation as a first resort will surely pay dividends in the long run.

CHAPTER 7

When the Ox Is in the Ditch: Managing the Claim, Managing the Legal Team, Controlling the Costs

It is not enough to fight. It is the spirit which we bring to the fight that decides the issue.—George C. Marshall

This chapter deals with litigation management as the risk of litigation turns into reality. Something has gone wrong in the business relationship, whatever that relationship might be. There is a dispute; one or more claims can mature into litigation. Several questions arise.

- How should you implement damage control?

- When do you use "the best defense is a good offense" strategy, and what separate risks does this defense create?

- How should you manage the crisis?

- Who should be in charge? Who makes the ultimate decisions?

No matter how effective the litigation avoidance strategy, litigation often results. Therefore, it is important not to lose the psychological edge, not to become defeated mentally and emotionally when a suit is filed. This point cannot be stressed enough. Managers still must manage. With the battle lines drawn, your skill, attention, and balanced judgment are necessary now more than ever.

At this stage, a number of additional issues arise, including the selection and role of litigation counsel, the formulation and approval of a litigation strategy, discussion of and agreement on a process for periodically determining litigation tactics for implementing the strategy, and agreed-upon benchmarks for what and under which circumstances settlement will be acceptable. (Remember: total victory is rarely achieved and then often at intolerable cost.)

These issues and many others deal with your control over the litigation. For example, there is the issue of the relationship between the insurance company and the insured and which party controls the litigation. The policy terms and nature of the working relationship between those parties are both important on this point. In any event, you should not delegate to your attorney important managerial responsibility for litigation control.

Another related but separate topic is your control over the litigator. At this point, it is worth mentioning that not all lawyers are litigators and that few litigators are trial lawyers. Most litigators deal in motions, discovery, and the preparation for the actual trial. True trial lawyers are a special breed with particular skill and experience. At different stages in the handling of your matter, you may need and want a transactional lawyer with substantive knowledge of your matter and your business. Later, you may need the skills of a trial lawyer. The roles and relationships become important not only to the ultimate outcome but also to cost control.

Although the two aspects of control—over the litigation and over the lawyer—essentially represent two prongs of the same fork, they differ in detail. The loss of one will at the least degrade the other. Therefore, litigation and attorney control give rise to several issues.

The first involves the mutual understanding of goals between client and attorney and is premised on the notion that the client is ultimately responsible for all decisions. For the process to work, however, the attorney must have the ability to make tactical decisions along the way and must be in a position to make meaningful recommendations for strategic decisions. Accordingly, attorney and client must achieve a mutual understanding of basic goals that are established early and reviewed regularly. The second issue relates to the client's need to acknowledge its right to ultimate decision making. Such authority, however, does not mean that the client can or should exercise its responsibility lightly or foolishly.

Other issues center around identifying and obtaining the best advice possible, agreeing on systems for efficiency with regard to time and cost, agreeing on and honoring budgets, establishing a periodic reporting mechanism so that the attorney keeps the client informed, and modifying goals and objectives as necessary.

Still other issues pertain to agreeing on who will work on the matter (i.e., addressing the problem of "associate of the week"). You need to know that the attorney with whom you feel comfortable and in whom you have developed confidence will be assigned and committed to your case. The attorney may be a partner or an associate; the keys are comfort and confidence. In a similar vein, it is essential to determine who is responsible for the litigation track and who is responsible for the settlement track, although that individual may be the same person. Above all, the success of your effort turns on clarifying ultimate accountability.

■ Effective Damage Control

Effective damage control requires a sensitive balance of emotions and reactions. On the one hand, it is necessary to be aggressive in asserting the strengths of your position and the weaknesses of the potential plaintiff. On the other hand, it is necessary to maintain a productive line of communication if settlement rather than litigation is to remain an option.

Temper and ego are major contributors to excess legal fees. Therefore, effective damage control initially requires a damage control plan that is a genuinely well-considered written plan; the assignment of responsibility to someone preferably not involved in the dispute to oversee execution of the plan; established limits as part of the plan; and an acknowledged and continuing statement of the dangers of temper and ego.

All too often, cases settle after years of negotiation and litigation at or about the price they could have been settled for before those years of cost and disruption. It is important, therefore, to know how to evaluate the strength of a claim, i.e., the question of liability; assess the degree of monetary exposure for that liability, i.e., the question of damages; assess realistically the potential direct and indirect cost of litigation other than potential liability; construct the most cost-effective yet mutually acceptable alternative for satisfying damages; acknowledge that you may not be able to settle the case for the value you assign to it however realistic that value may be (to you); force self-acknowledgment that you may be in the wrong (at least in part); and prepare the manager who has the authority to settle the case, although that individual probably has his or her own preconceived notion as to the value of the case.

Damage control also presupposes a knowledge of essential legal principles: not only the substantive law of the potential claims but also the principles that encourage the filing of the suit. You need to understand these thoroughly. Further, you must be in a position to communicate them convincingly to the other side. In a construction defect claim situation, for example, even though there is no duty to sue, the argument could arise that the association must sue or the board will breach its duty. In addition, while you must do your best, you are no guarantor. Be fully informed on each situation so that you know if there is a defect and can act accordingly. Do not act out of a sense of perfection or guilt, but learn the facts and acknowledge that problems are not necessarily your fault. Finally, business judgment allows you to exercise judgment.

The earlier chapters, particularly Chapter 3 dealing with the construction defect claim, as well as articles and case citations contained in the appendices thoroughly discuss and explain these principles.

Some tactical tips may help you in formulating a damage control plan.

- Be a tiger not an ostrich. Prepare to defend your position and not to put your head in the sand. Gather the relevant facts and know the law that applies to those facts. It is also important to know the politics of the particular situation. In most cases, it is the "people" factors that are most important. If you and/or your lawyer are not "people-sensitive," you will experience greater difficulties than necessary.

- Evaluate who is behind the dispute. What do the opponents really want, what is really the problem, what makes the case so important from their perspective?

- Know the politics involved. Develop an understanding not only of people but also of the dynamics of the opposition. Do not leave this to litigators who argue that they can beat opponents in court. Too often their argument prevails, and a case goes to court where it may or may not be won, even though the political realities of a dispute could help resolve it. The goal is to avoid court, but the natural litigation tendency is to try to "win the fight."

- Determine what the potential plaintiffs really want. Disputes are often about something other than the apparent subject. A dispute cannot be resolved if its real subject is hidden. This may be a simple principle, but it is too often ignored in the rush to court and the "litigation solution."

- Build a file on the potential plaintiffs. Your file should include the letters, newsletters, memoranda, etc., that allow counsel to know the other side and to look for defensive positions as well for possible offensive positions.

- Do not create martyrs, but do determine how to make the role of plaintiff a difficult job.

- Evaluate the relationship between potential plaintiffs and their attorney to determine strengths and weaknesses.

- Be firm but fair; do not alienate undecided parties.

- Do not make fundraising easy for the other side by being unreasonably tough and contrary.

- Neither expect much from nor fear press coverage.

- Do not fear the opposition's tactic of "going over your head" to upper management. If you have the confidence of management, senior managers will support you.

- Be responsive; *do* not stonewall!

To control damage, it is also important to know the nature of that damage. The acquisition of such knowledge and a plan for dealing with it require a prelitigation discovery program, a record retention and management plan, and a well-considered, disciplined discovery plan. In a prelitigation discovery program, you and your team perform a discovery review of your own documents so that you are fully informed as to what the other side will find, thereby allowing you to do a better job of evaluation. As for a record retention and management plan (already discussed), it is important to note that once the litigation process begins, you may not destroy documents. Finally, a well-considered, disciplined discovery plan is vital to both sides, but it is also an attorney's annuity unless properly managed and budgeted.

At the same time, successful damage control requires you to remember that what you say, especially in writing, can and will be used against you. Moreover, a case will never cost less to settle than before it is filed in court. As discovery goes forward, not only can the positions harden and become stronger, but the emotions and pain will start to run up the legal bills. Therefore, you should "cash it out" early if possible. Throughout the damage control process, keep your confidence and believe in yourself. You are not the only person ever to be sued, nor will you be the last; you are not alone.

Once litigation begins—and technically that could be before a suit is actually filed—the attorney for one side may not contact the other party except through that party's attorney. You can. Do not waste that opportunity.

■ Some Strategic Suggestions

With regard to litigation, some specific tips about crisis management, many of which are dealt with in more detail in the appendices, follow:

- Know what you are willing to give up.

- Appear to be in a life-or-death struggle but make decisions on the basis of sound business principles.

- Show—but do not act on—emotion.

- Do not make unnecessary enemies.

- Be reasonable in tone and manner.

- Do not bully . . . or be bullied.

- Do not shoot the messenger, especially if that messenger is your attorney.

- If your lawyer cannot convince you that you are right, you are probably wrong.

- Righteous anger, skillfully applied, can be a highly productive tool.

- Attack the cost and pointlessness of litigation.

- Remember the concept of "divide and conquer."

- Believe in yourself, your product, and your team.

- Never ever underestimate the plaintiff group, especially property owners and their attorney.

- Be willing to toll the statute of limitations by agreement so that talking may continue; running the statute can frighten people into filing suit.

A strategic decision for the defendant in any litigation is whether "a good defense is a good offense." There are often legitimate arguments to support countersuits against the plaintiffs or suits against third parties. Certainly, when a party is sued for actions committed by a third party—for example, a defective roof installed by a roofing subcontractor—the case is relatively clear for a third-party complaint. A countersuit against the homeowners' association or group of tenants are two additional considerations. Asserting such claims can mean that the emotional cost of being sued is paid by both parties; the cost to prosecute increases; the effectiveness of the contingency fee system is reduced, as plaintiffs must incur their own cost of defense; the potential for conflicts of interest for the plaintiffs' attorney increases; the plaintiff group is potentially fragmented; plaintiffs face added confusion, especially when they are homeowners who must communicate the status of the suit to other owners; the plaintiff group's illusion of achieving a quick victory is shattered; and the plaintiff group must start evaluating your case, responding to your questions, and playing on your turf. Strategically speaking, it is better to be characterized as a plaintiff (the aggrieved party). So, if you know a suit is coming and you have a legitimate claim against the other side, file yours first. It sends a message. If the other side is bluffing, it calls your opponent's bluff, although you are still in court.

It is important to note that disadvantages attach to the "good defense is a good offense" strategy. For example, you should never bring an action for which you do not, at least arguably, have a reasonable and good faith legal and factual foundation. In addition, your costs could go up, and the action may distract you/your counsel from defending against the main claim. The completion of a settlement becomes exponentially more complicated by the number of parties and the number of claims. Your counterclaim may be better used as a negotiating point, or it may be more effective in another, nonlitigation forum. Should there be consideration of counterlitigation, potential causes of action might include libel/slander, failure to anticipate damages, failure to maintain and repair, bad faith litigation, and failure to pay/perform an obligation.

Finally, it is appropriate to repeat that strategic planning, both for avoiding litigation and for the litigation itself, is a complex process. The final plan must be tailored to fit the many variables in the particular case (see the appendices for further guidance).

■ A Word about Litigation Counsel

The selection of legal counsel is as much art as science. Perhaps the most important factor is trust and the personal quality of the relationship. You must be able to work together and trust one another. A second consideration is knowledge. Many skilled litigators lack knowledge of the disputed subject. A personal injury insurance defense attorney, for example, may not be the best choice for construction litigation involving a homeowners' association. Some questions to consider when seeking counsel include the following:

- Does the candidate specialize in the particular field in dispute?

- To what extent does the candidate appear knowledgeable of the field generally and of your situation specifically?

- Does the candidate specialize in representing one side or another or both?

- Does the candidate understand the people involved as well as the legal aspects of the situation?

- Does the candidate want the job? Of course, he or she would like to earn a fee, but does he or she really want to be your attorney?

- What is the candidate's fee, billing, and cost recovery proposal?

- How does the candidate react to your concerns and proposals regarding cost control, reporting, and the fact that you are ultimately in charge?

- Does counsel have a "go to court at all costs" mentality? If so, he or she is probably not the attorney for you.

- Will the attorney with whom you are dealing/talking at the beginning be the one involved on a day-to-day basis? What is the quality of the team?

A third factor in selecting litigation counsel is the personality (style) of the plaintiff's attorney. Large corporations usually hire attorneys on the basis of reputation and seniority. These attorneys sometimes come across as "stuffy" to a jury while the plaintiff's counsel may seem more populist and appealing. A fourth factor is corporate attitude/strategy. If you want to settle, you may need a "negotiator" as opposed to a "litigator."

These and other special concerns apply when the attorney is supplied by your insurance carrier. Special steps are needed to ensure that the proper relationship exists from day one. As mentioned, the client and attorney work together as the first members of the team to create and implement a linked negotiation and potential trial strategy. Vital factors in this strategy are ultimate goals, settlement limits, a cost containment plan, a reporting plan and schedule, and agreement on who is in charge. It goes without saying that the outside counsel's plan must be consistent with yours.

Controlling legal costs requires two different but related actions: control over the litigation and control over your lawyer. To ensure the latter, it is helpful to consider the following hints:

- Stay a month or so ahead of the attorney in monitoring the plan by knowing the facts and the schedule. Expect to give a lot of time and attention to the case.

- Stick to the budget.

- Request a detached, knowledgeable professional to review bills; be fair but businesslike.

- Require lower-rate professionals to perform any task within their skill/experience level.

- Do not tolerate excessive "group lawyering" or research by "attorney conference."

- Control discovery by requiring explanations of who, what, when, why, etc., before discovery.

- Be organized, focused, and efficient.

- Make decisions in a timely manner and stick to them.

- Consider value billing, which uses agreed-upon fees for particular tasks based on the nature of the service and its value.

- Execute a thorough engagement agreement.

- Require periodic status reports.

CHAPTER 8

Conclusion

The only limit to our realization of tomorrow will be our doubts of today.—Franklin Delano Roosevelt

In conclusion, it is appropriate to reflect on the one central theme that runs throughout the text: preventive law and the necessity for the client to function as an active participant in the process of risk avoidance and management. Just as most other business activities involve process so does the avoidance of liability. That process demands involvement, participation, and interaction. It requires understanding, indeed more understanding than is traditionally seen, of legal and practical concepts, of the real world, and of political challenges.

One last demand falls on those who would change the system and find new and better ways to deal with risk and business disputes. That demand is to "think outside the box" and to look to and for new models and approaches. The greatest obstacle to finding and following successful new approaches is that we are all attached to our old ones. We know that the old ways are flawed, yet we continue to rely on them. If it is true that the perpetual obstacle to human advancement is custom, then our opportunity and responsibility is to learn from what has been customary and use that knowledge as a point from which to advance rather than as a point at which custom becomes another word for regression.

Failing to find new solutions and new approaches will be a regression—one that we cannot afford. It is hoped that this book will help advance the process of moving from what is customary to what is innovative in and responsive to a rapidly changing world.

Appendices

Checklist of Documents And Materials to Be Retained by Developer

■ I. Building and Development Process

- Copies of all promotional material and sales literature (including any public reports, offering statements, sales training materials, or other disclosure documents that were required to be provided by the developer to purchasers pursuant to any state or federal law or regulatory requirement).

- The names, addresses, and telephone numbers of the development entities and the officers, directors, and key personnel of those development entities.

- The names of any real estate sales or brokerage organizations that were granted, either jointly or severally, rights to market any of the property.

- The names, addresses, telephone numbers, and Social Security numbers of all persons who have served as sales or marketing agents or employees for the development.

- Photographs taken by the developer during the development and construction process or that depict the completed buildings or amenities at the property.

- Any document specifying any warranty work to be completed by the developer or work that the developer has agreed to perform or to undertake on the common elements during and subsequent to the transition period. (Follow-up may be necessary.)

- Copies of the original master development plan and all revisions thereof and all other plans, specifications, proposed or actual, used or prepared by the developer in the construction of the property.

- All punchlist records.

- All construction files, daily logs, draw requests, models, maps, shop drawings, and any other on-site renderings and inspection reports of lenders.

- All architectural/engineering reports, proposals, drawings, conceptual drawings, and promotional drawings that have been rendered in regard to any portion of the property or common area. (Should be kept by the developer's attorney.)

- All building permits, licenses, and filings.

- All deeds, all purchase contracts, all settlement statements, all HUD 1 forms, and all certificates of occupancy.

- The names, addresses, and telephone numbers of all building inspectors, fire inspectors, and environmental inspectors (if applicable) who inspected the property and copies of all approvals or other documents received from such inspectors.

- All bids received by the developer and all current and past contracts and agreements of any kind executed by the developer in connection with the development, including builder contracts.

- The names of key personnel for all companies with which the developer has a contract or agreement of any kind in connection with the development.

- A complete set of all builder and construction guidelines and all as-built drawings and plans of all buildings, facilities, water and sewer systems, major subsystems, utilities, and drainage and irrigation systems.

- All tract maps.

- Copies of all surveys.

- Copies of all grading plans.

- Copies of all landscape drawings and specifications.

- The names of all builders, construction companies, and contractors who performed work on the property, including all principal subcontractors and the key contact person at those companies, and the name, address, and Social Security number of the on-site foreman or supervisor for each company. (Explanatory memorandum of builder qualifications and hiring policies may be necessary.)

- The names of any product representatives and all promotional materials at any company whose products were used in the development.

- A detailed written report at the end of development of a walk-through and on-site audit of the physical condition of the buildings and facilities, the common property, and any and all other items within the association's maintenance responsibility conducted by or with the assistance of an independent licensed or registered architect or engineer. (Should be kept by the developer's attorney.)

- A list of manufacturers of all construction materials, all building components, all structural material, all subsystems, all paints on the surface buildings, and all major equipment or fixtures on the common property or within the association's maintenance responsibility. (Explanatory memorandum may be necessary regarding choices of materials.)

- All interoffice memoranda of the developer and all correspondence between the developer and builders, contractors, subcontractors, product manufacturers, and any other parties with whom the developer entered into agreements relating to the development.

■ II. Maintenance and Future Improvements

- All plans or proposals for capital improvements or major repairs in progress or to be undertaken in the future.

- Estimates of useful life and analysis and evaluation of all planned repair and maintenance programs for all major components, structures, and improvements, including buildings, roofs, streets, paint, major mechanical equipment, or amenities such as swimming pools, tennis courts, etc. (Association and developer need a copy.)

- Copies of all warranties, maintenance agreements, or service contracts on equipment or facilities owned or maintained by the association.

- Copies of all assignments necessary to transfer any property to the association, if in the name of the developer.

■ III. Government Relationships

- All zoning requests, approvals, variances, waivers, and zoning letters of intent granted or pending for the property or that may affect the property. (Follow-up may be necessary.) (A copy should be kept by the developer's attorney.)

- A delineation of the limits and divisions of responsibility for road maintenance, fire and water mains, cable television, electric and telephone service, and other utilities showing which matters fall under the association's responsibility and which matters fall within the public utility's or local government's responsibility.

- Verification that all periodic government inspections or reviews have been conducted and that all certificates of compliances or licenses are valid and are in effect (including, for example, those for club operation, swimming pools, restaurant or grills, lakes, or golf courses).

■ IV. Legal

- A complete and compiled set of all legal documents for the association, including, but not limited to, copies of the recorded declaration, the recorded bylaws, any adopted rules and regulations, and any amendments thereto. (A copy should be kept by the developer's attorney.)

- All corporate documents for the association, including, without limitation, copies of the articles of incorporation, the certificate of incorporation, and the name reservation certificate; the bylaws of the corporation and all amendments thereto; copies of all annual reports to the secretary of state; copies of all tax returns filed by the association; and the names and addresses of every person who has served as the corporation's designated registered agent for service of process and the written resignation of any such agent and the written appointment of a new agent, if appropriate. (A copy should be kept by the developer's attorney.)

- Copies of all recorded rights-of-way and recorded easements, including utility easements, and any licenses that have been granted by the association or the developer in, under, or over the buildings or the common property. (A copy should be kept by the developer's attorney.)

- A list of any liens that may have been filed, even if filed erroneously, against the association or the common property, including tax liens, liens for unpaid water charges, or mechanic's, materialmen's, or laborers' liens.

- Current reports from the developer's and the association's legal counsel on all pending or threatened claims or litigation involving the association.

- The names and addresses of the association's present and all previous attorneys and the key contacts within those law firms.

- Copies of all recorded plats and plans for the property.

- Copies of all documents or agreements settling or resolving disputes or claims against the association.

- An evaluation of the legal status and relationship of any clubs or other organizations to the association, if such a relationship exists, and any documents related to or concerning this relationship, including any contracts, agreements, covenants to share cost, and the articles of incorporation, bylaws, rules and regulations, membership applications, summary, membership list, and other relevant documents of such clubs or organizations. (Developer needs to retain copy.)

- Copies of any other documents recorded in the local land records relating to the development.

■ V. Association Operations

Copies of the following should be obtained from the association:

- all minutes of the association meetings and board meetings;

- all resolutions adopted by the association (including any resolution authorizing checking accounts in the association's name);

- all reports of committees, special investigations, or projects that have been made to the board of directors of the association;

- all correspondence regarding the association;

- all records regarding the enforcement of any provision of the documents against any unit owner, including records relating to the levying of fines or other enforcement action taken in the past or presently being considered against any owner disputes over architectural changes or assessments;

- reports on pending assignments or projects being undertaken by management, committees of the association, or present officers and directors;

- complete records of all matters voted on or approved by the membership of the association;

- any written approvals and disapprovals of sales or rentals made by the board of directors (explanatory memorandum may be necessary.);

- copies of all newsletters or items that were forwarded to all members of the community, such as rules and regulations, policy changes, or other items of general interest;

- the written resignations of all directors and officers appointed by the developer whose terms have not otherwise expired under the terms of the association's bylaws;

- copies of all current and past contracts and agreements of any kind executed by the association; and

- the names of key personnel for all companies with which the association has a contract or agreement of any kind.

■ VI. Association Organization

- A list of the names and addresses of all owners and the principal mortgagees of the units, including mortgage account numbers.

- A list, by unit, of all original purchasers of units from the developer, organized by unit.

- A list of the names and addresses of all prior officers and directors of the association.

- A list of all association committees and their functions, including the names and addresses of all current committee members and the names and addresses of past committee chairs.

- The name and address of the association's current management company and the principal individuals to contact.

- A copy of the current management contract and all previous management contracts entered into by the association.

- The names and addresses of the current association manager and all previous managers, including all on-site management.

- The names, addresses, and Social Security numbers of all employees of the association, if any, and all payroll records, employment contracts, and employment records and filings relating thereto.

- A copy of the records of all approved and disapproved architectural changes undertaken by individual unit owners and any and all maintenance agreements, easements, or other documents executed by the association and the owners in connection therewith.

■ VII. Developer and Association Financial Books and Records

- All checkbooks, check registers, and cancelled checks of the developer. (Should be kept by the developer's attorney.)

- Copies of all checkbooks, check registers, and cancelled checks of the association.

- A list identifying all of the developer's bank accounts, investments, intangibles, and negotiable instruments, including the names and addresses of the relevant institutions and the relevant account number(s). (Should be kept by the developer's attorney.)

- A list identifying all of the association's bank accounts, investments, intangibles, and negotiable instruments, including the names and addresses of the relevant institutions and the relevant account number(s).

- All financial books and records and ledgers of the developer. (Should be kept by the developer's attorney.)

- Copies of all financial books and records and ledgers of the association from the date of its organization to the present.

- The names, addresses, and telephone numbers of bank, brokerage, or professional personnel having regularly serviced the developer's and/or the association's accounts.

- Copies of all signature cards, authorizing resolutions, and other documentation necessary to transfer control of and the right to withdraw funds from the association's accounts.

- Audit and verification of all accounts receivable of the developer. (Should be kept by the developer's attorney.)

- Audit and verification of all accounts payable of the developer. (Should be kept by the developer's attorney.)

- Copies of audit and verification of all accounts receivable of the association.

- Copies of audit and verification of all accounts payable of the association.

- Copies of all audits and financial statements from the inception of the association until the present.

- The names and addresses of all of the developer's and the association's present and former accounting firms and key contact personnel at those firms.

- All receipts, invoices, documents, and other evidence supporting payments made to the association by the developer.

- Copies of all receipts, invoices, documents, and other evidence supporting payments made by the association to third parties or the developer.

- All loan documents, agreements, or other records regarding loans made or accepted by the developer.

- Copies of all loan documents, agreements, or other records regarding loans made or accepted by the association.

- Copies of all budgets, budget worksheets, and draft budgets for the association from its inception to the present.

- A complete audit of all of the developer's books and records by independent certified public accountants.

■ VIII. Insurance

- All policies of insurance currently in force held by the developer.

- Copies of all policies of insurance currently in force held by the association.

- A written review of the insurance requirements of the association documents and the applicable state statute and a thorough audit by an independent agent of the association's insurance needs and the adequacy of current insurance coverage.

- All prior insurance policies held by the developer and copies of all prior insurance policies held by the association that may provide continuing coverage to the developer or its employees, even though the policy period has expired (for example, certain types of liability, fidelity, and directors' and officers' insurance).

- Names and addresses of all insurance agencies that have acted on behalf of the developer or the association and key contact personnel.

- Identification and verification of all pending insurance claims.

- The history of all insurance claims made from the formation of the association to the present.

- An accounting of any and all insurance payments or settlements received.

- Copies of any and all compromise settlements or releases between the association and any insurance carrier.

Builder Program Conceptual Plan

The following summary provides a general overview of the benefits of a builder program for a master-planned community.

■ 1. Builder Program Overview

A builder program provides organization, coordination, and a clear system of management for the construction and sale of homes within a development. A good builder program anticipates problems that may arise and provides an efficient means for addressing them. A builder program allows a developer strict architectural control over the style and quality of homes constructed within a master-planned community. Typically, the program includes the following steps:

- application and approval process for builder to be admitted to the builder program;

- presentation and summary of design guidelines and procedures and negotiation and execution of the master builder agreement;

- negotiation and execution of parcel and lot purchase contracts and preparation of a standardized home sale contract for use by builders; and

- design review process.

■ 2. Participating Builder Application/ Financial Statements

To protect the interests of other builders and the community as a whole, each candidate shall submit a participating builder application and current financial statement dating back over the last two years prior to contract. The developer's goal is to choose companies that meet certain criteria, such as financial ability and a proven record of superior workmanship and customer satisfaction.

■ 3. Builder Criteria

The success of development rests in participating builders with the ability, integrity, and understanding to deliver the promise of an exceptional lifestyle and environment.

The selection of firms to participate in the program may be limited to a small group of qualified builders. The selection process begins with the participating builder application, which must be approved and reviewed by the developer. The developer is committed to involving builders who will support the concept and architectural standards that will be established for the development. The evaluation of potential candidates will be based on the following:

- professional background and experience;

- product design /impact/acceptance;

- quality construction;

- value (price in relation to quality);

- satisfied buyers;

- customer service program;

- financial/credit rating; and

- enrollment in a ten-year limited warranty program.

■ 4. Presentation and Summary of Design Guidelines

After a builder has been accepted for the program, the developer may require the submission of preliminary design documents for a model home to be built. Review of these designs and meetings with the builder will provide the developer with control over architectural matters. The program will also dictate the timetable for construction, taking into account the possibility of delays that are beyond the builder's control. During construction, the program will set forth site maintenance requirements, requiring the builder to keep the lot free of debris. These requirements will be flexible but sufficiently strict to ensure that the interior and exterior of homes built are presentable and attractive. Obviously, these requirements benefit both the participating builder and the developer.

■ 5. Construction Deposit

Each participating builder will be required to submit a construction deposit in the amount of $_____ per lot/parcel at the time of the schematic design conference until a maximum of $_____ is received per participating builder. The construction deposit will be held by the developer until the home/parcel is completed and the design review committee receives a final survey. If necessary, the construction deposit will be used to cover the cost of repairing damage to the property and site improvements caused by the participating builder or his subcontractors and for trash removal and routine maintenance of completed homes, if not properly provided by the participating builder. This deposit may also, at the sole discretion of the design review committee, be used to bring the site or the residence up to a level of compliance as set forth by the design review committee.

■ 6. Insurance

The participating builder must provide the developer with proof of a public liability policy with limits of no less than $1 million. The developer must be named as an additional insured to protect him or her from any claims that might arise from the builder's activities on the construction site.

■ 7. Warranties

Before closing of the first home, the builder will be required to submit for approval by the developer a limited ten-year warranty that will apply to all homes constructed by the builder in the development. Enrollment in an approved homeowners' warranty program will substitute for submitting a limited warranty.

■ 8. Construction Commencement

Repurchase provisions may be included in the builder's contract to ensure that construction is completed in a timely manner. The developer may retain a right of first refusal for the repurchase of any property. This right may be exercised if the property is not developed within a specified time frame or if the builder wishes to convey an undeveloped lot to another builder who does not meet the quality control standards established for the project. Such provisions would set forth the repurchase price, notice requirements, and other details.

■ 9. Marketing

The developer will reserve an approval right on all sales documents to be used by the participating builder in order to ensure uniformity and the veracity of any statements made. This is necessary because representations in marketing materials or in statements by sales staff can be held to be implied covenants that may bind the developer to unintended and undesired requirements with respect to the property and/or the project.

■ 10. Master Builder Agreement

Each participating builder will execute a master builder agreement that will address many of these matters upfront and will control all further purchases of property by the builder in the project. A master builder agreement will be entered into by the developer and builder before the consummation of an agreement between the parties for the purchase and sale of property. The master builder agreement will set forth all the general controls the developer wishes to assert over the participating builder as well as the developer's enforcement remedies. This will simplify the individual lot or parcel purchase contracts by avoiding the need to repeat these controls and remedies at length in each purchase contract yet will give the developer the needed control over construction within the community and a practical means of enforcing compliance by each participating builder.

APPENDIX 3

Disposition of Amenities— The Legal Issues

©1988 by Hyatt & Rhoads, P.C., all rights reserved

■ Part 1. The Practical Concerns

Holding that "in today's complex, social, economic, business and legal communities reasonableness must be the standard, rather than the extreme," the District Court of Appeal of Florida, in *Old Port Cove Property Owners* v. *Ecclestone*,[1] ruled that the developer of a large-scale homeowners' association did not breach his fiduciary duty to the association when he "sold the entire road system of the project to the POA"[2] but retained for himself a rent-free easement in the road system to allow access to the commercial areas. Relying on the complexity of the development itself and the fact that the "values of the condominium units had actually been enhanced by the recreational and commercial area development to a greater degree than comparable condominium units," the court held that the "profit motive alone, however, does not constitute a breach of the fiduciary duty."[3] In this case, the court, in effect, relied on the old adage "Pay me now or pay me later" to uphold the conveyance of the roads subject to long-term lease payments as an appropriate alternative to increasing the price of condominium units to recover the costs of road construction.

The *Ecclestone* case is a fitting point to begin a discussion of the disposition of amenities in large-scale planned developments. This topic is a major issue in real estate development in the late 1980s and is not limited to traditional "resort" developments. The legal, operational, and economic problems relating to amenity transfer can occur in any large-scale project with substantial amenities, whether a resort or primary home community. The regrettable fact is that many business transactions centering around amenity disposition ultimately become litigation matters when, in reality, that last unpleasant step should never be necessary.

The primary sources of amenity disposition problems rest with poor planning, poor project documentation, inadequate disclosure, and overly aggressive marketing. Developers can and must have the flexibility to deal with a major asset in various ways—to sell it to a club, to sell it to a third-party operator, to sell it as part of the common area, to retain and operate it, etc. The homebuyer has a right to rely on the development plan as originally represented and on the certainty that flows from this reliance. The development plan must therefore include flexibility, specific options for the developer, and some protections for the home purchaser. When these provisions are absent, lawsuits too often result.

In keeping with the author's philosophy of preventive law, this article is oriented toward identifying problems, suggesting solutions to those problems, and seeking ways to achieve a desired business objective without the cost in dollars, hours, and physical wear and tear that results from litigation. The first part of the article is therefore designed to identify the major business factors and their legal consequences so often seen in amenity disposition transactions. The second part of the article is more legally oriented and is designed to identify in a case study approach the major areas of substantive law that are involved in amenity disposition transactions. It discusses the half-dozen major causes of action that are generally alleged in amenity transfer litigation and identifies for the businessperson those actions, often taken (or not taken) at the earliest planning stages, that can trigger causes of action.

Finally, attached to the article is a planning checklist recommended by the author as a basic planning tool to guide each individual transaction, thereby ensuring that the major questions are asked, the major disclosures made, and the essential options preserved.

Much of the literature and most of the workshops on this subject generally deal with the mechanics of an equity conversion. From the perspective of this paper, those discussions "put the rabbit in the hat" by assuming that the mistakes made and lessons learned have all come out the right way and that a successful sale of country club equity is concluded to dispose of the amenities. Accordingly, this paper leaves to others an in-depth discussion of equity conversions. The focus here is on ensuring that whichever option for conversions is selected, it is not thwarted by earlier mistakes.

What Are You Selling?

When discussing mistakes made and lessons learned, it is important to acknowledge that one recurring, threshold mistake is the failure to perceive that the large-scale residential project with substantial amenities contains two major asset bases, both of that are independently subject to disposition. A basic assumption in the amenity disposition discussion generally and in this article specifically is that the businessperson considering amenity transfer is not in the business primarily of developing and operating the amenity package. Rather, assumption is that the amenities are constructed as an adjunct to the primary business of the development and sale of land either in parcels or individual housing units.

Anyone in the business for more than a few days understands the tremendous increase in value to the housing unit that results from either the golf course or waterscape components of the development. It is therefore obvious that the price of the parcel or of the housing unit increases with the increase in value of the amenities. The developer/builder readily perceives the importance of maintaining access to these amenities and sustaining a high level of maintenance and community peace. Just as readily, he or she perceives a decline in value of the amenities as the housing units or parcels are sold. The thinking goes that the "loss leader" has done its job and has no residual value.

Too often, however, the developer/builder does not appreciate that the amenity itself carries significant intrinsic value. Further, the assumed decline in value of the amenity as land is sold leads to a decision to leave money on the table. When the development plan does not properly include a method to realize the value of the amenity through the disposition process, the developer/builder loses money.

To realize the amenities' intrinsic value, the developer/builder must understand that the amenities as a separate part of the development have great value to the homeowners both individually and collectively. In all probability, the amenities have been paid for substantially or completely through the sales prices of the parcels and housing units and therefore can continue to be operated by fees and assessments generated from property owners and nonresident users. In other words, an asset with significant intrinsic value is available for disposition on a debt-free basis if planning is properly carried out.

The Lesson Learned: Planning

In the creation of any homeowners' association, the developer/ builder is always well advised to use a development team approach. This approach is not intended to increase the paperwork and complexity of development planning but rather is a device by which all professionals whose services are required in the creation of a project have an opportunity to work together rather than as independent operators. The goal should be coordination of activity, timing, and the decision-making process so that the lawyer, for example, can draft what the planner has conceived and what the manager can deliver, all in a manner consistent with what the developer/ builder intends and can afford. The product of the team effort should be an operational plan that allows everyone to know how his or her actions affect others and how the entire process is expected to come together in an integrated whole that ultimately produces a profitable development.

In a large-scale planned community that includes substantial amenities, it is extremely important that the development team and the development plan carefully and thoroughly address an amenity strategy. The strategy must obviously include a number of nonlegal creation issues that go beyond the scope of this article and are treated fully elsewhere.[4] In addition to creation issues, four key areas must be included on any thorough planning checklist.

The first area concerns the care, custody, and control of the amenity package itself. Planning should address these issues not only for the period of development and sale but equally for the posttransition period. It is possible that the developer/builder or a successor will need easements of access, rights of use by third parties or by subsequent, noncontiguous developments, assurances of levels of maintenance and hours of operation, and other varied rights. As shall be seen subsequently, the panoply of subissues involved under the general topic of "care, custody, and control" includes those most volatile in property owner/developer relations;

however, experience has taught that when these issues are carefully planned at the outset with rights specifically reserved in the project documentation, the level of expectations is properly established with a concomitant reduction in future hostility. Perhaps more important, however, is the establishment of procedures to ensure that development interests are protected over both the short and long terms without regard to the ultimate question of disposition. In other words, the objective is to plan and to prepare the project documentation in such a way as to permit development needs to be met properly without concern for issues of ownership and management authority.

The second key area on the planning checklist deals with the method for rational transfer, which, of course, is the subject of this article. The decision on how the amenities ultimately will be held or conveyed is not important at this stage but is vital to ensuring disposition options for the developer/builder. It is entirely appropriate, for example, for the documents creating the planned community to specify that the developer/builder may convey the amenities to a third party, hold and operate them as a for-profit component of his or her own business, convey them as an equity club, convey them to the homeowners' association as common area, or some combination or other approach. Such document provisions, if carefully drafted, do not create significant buyer resistance within the marketplace and have even gained the acceptance of the secondary mortgage market and various state regulators. The goal is to satisfy the third key planning objective, which is flexibility.

If truth be told, none of us can forecast how a large-scale project will build out and sell over a period of years. Most businesspersons would generally consider a business plan longer than three to five years as more speculation than sound planning, yet building plans for large-scale projects with pro formas and sales predictions running out eight, ten, 15, 20, or more years are not uncommon. Such planning and projection is necessary, but it must be accompanied by marketing and legal planning and sufficiently flexible language to meet changing conditions that will exist over the course of the business plan. Maximum flexibility in these matters is generally legally permissible and obtainable so long as it is clearly disclosed in the sales message as well as in the appropriate documentation creating the project. The documentation should include the covenants, conditions, and restrictions; sales contracts; information packages and advertisements; filings with the appropriate regulators; and other such materials. Flexibility is as important as location in a large-scale, amenity-intensive project. Flexibility must be created, however, for it will not exist on its own.

Flexibility can and often is lost when the developer/builder's actions are inconsistent with the planning effort or the documentation and representations. A developer/builder is wise to institute a program to monitor the sales process to ensure against inconsistent representations that could ultimately result in an abrogation of the flexibility thought to have been built into the development plan and amenity strategy.

The fourth key planning area concerns the timing of ultimate transfer of the amenities. As with most business decisions, there is no absolute and little certainty on this topic. It is a given that planning should be performed early, yet a question still relates to the best time for the execution of the plan—early in the project's life, at mid-life, or late in the buildout stage. Clearly, a mid-project conveyance would attract the smallest number of adherents, but, as always, timing issues are affected by the realities of the particular project, thus making generalizations difficult. It is therefore appropriate to identify some of the considerations inherent in the decision for early and late dispositions of amenities.

Perhaps the most often heard suggestion calls for an early transfer of the large-scale amenity package, particularly when the transfer is to an equity club composed of property owners. The reasons in support of this suggestion are compelling and include certainty regarding the transfer of responsibility, a reduction in potential hostilities, transfer of repair and maintenance responsibilities, and the immediate generation of another source of income through the sale of memberships. The reasons to delay, however, are equally compelling. The author can point to first-hand experience with a large-scale resort and primary home community in New England whose substantial club facilities were transferred at an early stage to the property owners. From the developer's perspective, that decision resulted in nothing but trouble. The property owners used the leverage resulting from ownership and control in each and every subsequent dispute. Therefore, one of the considerations in disposition must be that of care, custody, and control. Who is going to pay at what level for what period and permit what variations on use by which groups of owners and nonowners, members and nonmembers? For example, what problems result when the facility is conveyed early and the marketing plan changes and focuses on a convention business in a project conceived and marketed as primary and secondary homes with little or no rental or "national" business expected?

A secondary but significant issue inherent in early conveyance concerns the fiduciary duty of those in control of the entity to which the amenities have been conveyed, e.g., a homeowners' association or private club. In another words, problems arise when the developer/ builder controls the entity but is subject to the fiduciary duty to exercise control in a manner consistent with the best interests of the entity and its members, even though control on behalf of the entity may conflict with the developer/builder's own control. If, on the other hand, the developer/builder owns the facilities and is not subject to a specific fiduciary duty outside his or her own business in operating them, he or she enjoys greater flexibility in making business decisions.

Financing and secondary mortgage market considerations must be addressed as well. In projects that wish to take advantage of VA/FHA programs, project planners must take account of regulations dealing with amenities. The VA/FHA, for example, requires the transfer of encumbrance-free amenities to the homeowners' association before the first closing. Obviously, this requirement is not consistent with reality in a large-scale, amenity-intensive planned community. Fortunately, through drafting and negotiation with agencies, the developer/builder can usually modify such black letter rules. It is important, however, that all parties work from the same list of assumptions and understandings. If not, as is often the case, the marketing director, who is particularly concerned about taking advantage of all available financing options, will experience conflict with the planner, who sees the need for long-term control over the amenities. Both will encounter difficulties with the attorney looking to them for guidance in drafting the necessary documents.

Finally, in the case of an early transfer of amenities, the basic documentation must protect the rights of the developer/builder and nonmembers for access to and use of the facilities. Once protected in the documentation, this right must be carefully preserved by controlling the representations made, particularly in answer to purchaser questions.

The late disposition of amenities also evokes significant pluses and minuses; again, the decision is project-intensive and must be made on a case-by-case basis to reflect what actually applies under a particular set of circumstances. Among the several factors to be considered in any project is the flip side of those just discussed regarding early disposition. The longer the disposition is delayed, the greater is the buildup in expectations, rumors, and representations, with the result that flexibility may erode to the point of nonexistence. In addition, the likely need for the repair and replacement of amenities upon conveyance increases while substantial expenditures may be required to bring the facilities to a condition that the new owner, whatever its form, finds acceptable. Delay and repair issues can be the basis for organized homeowner opposition and, potentially, litigation.

While delaying disposition defers the recapture of the value inherent in the amenity package, it does permit longer-term control and heightens the flexibility that comes with that control. It allows the developer/builder to consider and select the appropriate market and the appropriate entity to which disposition should be made. Obviously, the best candidate at one stage may, as time and circumstances change, prove not to be the best both from a financial and operational point of view.

One interesting aside concerns the developer's retention of the amenities to allow the project to qualify as a de minimus PUD under applicable secondary market regulations. The author recently worked with a client who thought that this approach offered a way to minimize the time and expense involved in Fannie Mae processing; however, for this approach to work, project documentation must specifically prohibit the amenities from ever being conveyed to the association. In other words, this approach lops off a major branch of the flexibility tree. While the greatest area of profitability in disposition may appear to come from conveying the amenities to an entity other than the association, the *Ecclestone* case makes it clear that assuming that disposition is limited to one or two approaches is shortsighted. The goal remains maximum flexibility, the maximum number of options, and maximum disclosure.

A Significant Lesson Learned: The Effect of Representations

Salespeople usually do not lie; therefore, buyers usually do not win misrepresentation lawsuits. But misrepresentation lawsuits do not go away easily, and they do not go away early. They generally involve factual disputes that make summary disposition at the motions level inappropriate, with the result that cases are often concluded at or just before the trial. Such cases are therefore expensive in terms of time, money, and lost opportunities. Accordingly, it is extremely important to monitor representations. This importance is heightened by the fact that while misrepresentation cases are often resolved in the developer/builder's favor, representation cases (that is, those in which the salesperson made affirmative statements inconsistent with an ultimate development plan) are often won by the property owner/plaintiff. It is here that the innocent answers of the salesperson that run counter to the perceived or intended flexibility take over and become the controlling factor in what a developer/builder may ultimately do. Employing a sales staff that has been trained in the legal and development issues addressed in the development plan and amenity strategy and whose work is regulated and periodically tested becomes vital to the preservation of disposition flexibility and the reduction of potential liability.

A survey of mistakes made and lessons learned points to several key areas of concern relating to representations. The first pertains to the type of facilities to be constructed both at the outset of the development and in the future. This representation could include what is believed to be the development plan or could simply be the result of "gilding the lily" by applying adjectives that are not thought to have legal significance. For example, the author is aware of litigation concerning, among other items, representations that a community would include a "championship" golf course. The PGA has developed specific guidelines on what constitutes a "championship" course. As a result, developer/builders using such a term of art must realize that legal significance attaches to their descriptions.

The second area of representation concerns levels of maintenance and is closely connected to the third category, which concerns the cost of facilities maintenance and operation to be borne by the unit owners. Suffice it to say that these two areas of representation are important to the consumer who may have developed enough unreasonable expectations without any encouragement from a marketing person.

The fourth category relates to the date the facilities will be available for use. Here, the developer/builder/seller should exercise considerable caution and realize that the buying public will more readily accept a promise of a lengthy delay when that delay is explained upfront than it will unfulfilled expectations, particularly when those expectations are premised on representations made at the point of sale. When dealing with both the type of facilities to be constructed and the date the facilities will be available for use, the developer/builder should qualify his or her representations by using such words as "proposed" rather than "planned." Additional protections can take the form of tastefully executed legends on plats and other sales depictions that make clear that depictions are not ultimately binding but rather are subject to change as required by circumstances and conditions. Such disclaimers will not cost a significant number of sales. To the extent that sales are lost as a result, the type of lost potential purchaser is probably one with a low tolerance and high potential for adversarial conduct. While the potential for lost sales is low, the potential to reduce future litigation is high and thus worth the risk.

The nature and extent of nonowner/nonresident involvement in facilities development and management is an extremely significant item in the minds of the owner group, particularly the resident owner group, and is the fifth area of concern. Careful planning should be devoted to the nonowner/nonresident issue, with maximum flexibility built into the development plan and any representations made. Experience has shown that the natural divisiveness that results from the different interests of the different classes of users within a large-scale resort community can be one of the most troublesome ingredients in such a community and can be exacerbated by poorly conceived and executed development plans. The careful drafting of basic homeowners' association and club documentation in conjunction with carefully structured sales and disclosure materials can help avert problems.

The sixth and final major category of concern in dealing with representations presents the ultimate question: the extent to which owners acquire some legally enforceable interest in the amenities. This interest could range from some right of use all the way to an ownership right. The second part of this article addresses the associated legal issues in detail as well as the potential causes of action that arise in cases dealing with implied vested interests. It is appropriate at this juncture, however, to note that the developer/builder should exercise great care in reviewing advertising materials. Such advertising lines as "Your home comes with a $5 million recreational facility" or "Mr. Smith just bought his wife an Olympic pool and four tennis courts" may seem innocent enough to the marketing personnel and the advertising agency. These slogans play well in the Sunday real estate sections and on television, but the developer/builder needs to ensure that they play equally well from the plaintiff's point of view in the courtroom.

What Concerns the Property Owners?

As noted at the outset, legal planning and development planning should be preventive. In that regard, it is surprising that most of the "texts" dealing with amenity disposition focus on what developers want and need and how developers can obtain a substantial profit through amenity transfer or "equity conversion"—all without regard for property owners and their concerns and how to bring developers and owners together.

The successful amenity disposition plan gives considerable thought to homeowner concerns and specifies what will be done in the areas of greatest concern to homeowners to maximize the attractiveness and acceptability of the plan while minimizing the potential for disputes and litigation. The developer/builder usually can satisfy homeowner concerns easily if he or she simply takes the initiative and follows a reasonable approach. Regrettably, though, the developer/builder too often underestimates the significance of homeowner concerns from both marketing and legal points of view.

Each of the "lawyer's dozen" concerns listed below demand considerable planning and discussion and involve business decisions of an economic, practical, legal, and operational nature. It goes beyond the scope of this article to discuss these issues in detail; at this juncture, it is sufficient to identify them and to recommend that the developer/builder and his or her development team give these questions appropriate time and attention after reflecting on the lessons learned from mistakes in amenity disposition cases.

Some of the significant concerns of property owners are as follows:

- The maximum number of units.

- The maximum number of members available to use the facilities. The developer/builder needs experienced consultant assistance in determining, for example, how many people can use the golf course, when more than one golf course is required, and how to accommodate the conflict between owners' expectations and reasonable profitability.

- The transferability of the membership. Representations that a membership will be transferable at the sale of the purchaser's home or lot can present a variety of subsequent problems, including the creation of claims that may bar a subsequent equity conversion if a "membership" granted at the original time of home or lot purchase purports to be perpetual and transferable. Transferability of membership is one of the most sensitive concerns from everyone's point of view and needs a great deal of informed thought.

- Whether the amount of permitted cost increases that can be passed on to owner/members is capped.

- Use of facilities for some other purpose in the future, e.g., rental, commercial, convention, or simply a change from a recreational amenity to residential or commercial use. The case law and factual settings in which the issue arises are so plentiful and varied that an entire article can and perhaps should be written on this subject alone.

- Membership, initiation, and user fees now and in the future. Guarantees of any economic charges in light of present economic realities, if such guarantees extend for more than a relatively brief period, are somewhat foolhardy. The buying public will look for such guarantees, but the developer/builder must resist giving them and ensure that any such guarantees are carefully considered and researched.

- The rights of nonresidents or nonowners in the facilities. If nonowners have acquired membership rights, prospective purchasers will be concerned to know if nonowner or nonresident membership rights phase out so as to permit future purchasers of housing units to be able to acquire memberships. This question obviously must be asked and answered in conjunction with the total number of memberships permitted and in light of how the numbers of residents, nonresidents, and future residents relate to that total. The overall question of rights of nonresidents and nonowners is an extremely emotional one that also carries significant economic impact.

- Whether the membership offering is a security and, if so, how it is to be handled.

- "Haven't we already bought this?" Invariably, any disposition of amenities other than one given to the homeowners without charge gives rise to the assertion that the amenities were "bought and paid for" in the price of the housing unit sold. The developer/builder and his or her development team must realize that this assertion will be made and must stand prepared to deal with it forthrightly, correctly, and with sufficient factual foundation to support the legal argument when the response to the assertion is "no."

- The nature, number, and extent of amenities. No matter what the developer/builder does, it will not be enough to satisfy some people. As a result, upfront disclosure is important to keep expectations within the realm of reality.

- Issues of "national" members, timeshare, and rental-convention business. These highly charged, emotional-economic issues are, on the one hand, often vital for the economic success of a particular project but, on the other hand, anathema to the full-time or part-time "permanent" resident. The only way to deal with such issues is forthrightly and at the outset. They require a considerable amount of planning. Carefully drafted documentation can significantly ameliorate problems by disclosing and preserving at the outset rights that are less likely to be objectionable to an individual in the excited blush of enthusiasm over buying into a given project.

In connection with this last point, it is probably appropriate to conclude this part of the article with the admonition that the developer/builder and particularly the consultants who work with and for the developer/builder should never underestimate the ability of the owners within a community to enhance the success of the project. The author has spent almost his entire practice representing hundreds of homeowners' associations and working with developers. From that experience, it is easy to develop a keen sensitivity to what the owners can do and indeed have done under all types of circumstances in making large-scale planned community projects successful either as a part of a "partnership" with the developer or after the developer has completed the transition of control and disposition of facilities. Included in that experience is an awareness of the litigation that often results as well as an overwhelming appreciation that litigation is not an issue in most communities if the process is carefully planned, structured, and executed.

This last comment about working with the association is not intended to imply that great care and a posture of self-defense are not needed. The disposition plan should build in a release and a covenant not to sue so that the developer/builder is ultimately protected and so that contingent liabilities can be put to rest. The suggestions for working with the various components of a homeowners' association are not to be construed as a statement that those components cannot spin apart and result in fractious, expensive litigation. Too often that is exactly what happens, especially when the planning and preventive structuring of the transaction were inadequate from the outset. It is appropriate therefore to turn to a discussion of the fundamental legal issues involved when mistakes lead to charges of "Haven't I already paid for this?" that cannot be resolved short of litigation. In each and every case, the developer/builder and his or her consultants must work through these issues and see how they do apply or may apply in the future to a particular project. Only by doing so can the development team take some comfort in the knowledge that the ultimate goal of a profitable, harmonious disposition of assets is achievable.

■ Part 2. The Substantive Law Issues

Several distinct and significant areas of substantive law can be involved in the disposition of amenities. In one form or another, each leads to the potential creation of certain property interests or other rights in property owners to use and enjoy the amenities that the developer must inevitably address.

Many developers initially reject vested rights arguments as theoretical, "make weight" arguments. Such a belief is a misperception. The various legal theories that can be used to establish rights of use, access, and ownership of amenities in homeowners are plainly established. Nothing magical occurs. Only the actions of the developer and those who work for him or her can create vested rights out of thin air. If the developer does not do so, he or she may obligate him or herself at the very least to make amenities reasonably available to residents at reasonable fees. At most, the developer may create ownership rights in homeowners and may obligate him- or herself to convey the amenities and facilities to the homeowners—essentially giving away the golf course and country club.

The various legal theories that may be used to establish vested rights are as follows:

- express or implied easements,

- implied covenants,

- estoppel,

- breach of fiduciary duty,

- breach of contract, and

- fraud.

Express or Implied Easements

Theories of express or implied easements, including negative easements, may be used to assert that purchasers of lots obtained an express or implied easement for access and use of the amenities under certain terms and conditions. These property rights run with the lot and cannot be subsequently modified or taken away. The theory of negative restrictions simply asserts that certain property may not be used for any purpose other than that specifically represented at the time of sale and conveyance of the unit or lot. For example, an area on a recorded plat that includes parcels marked "open space" or "golf course" and that are referenced or incorporated into a deed of conveyance of an individual lot creates a negative easement restricting the use of that land to open space or a golf course. Future use of that parcel for any other purpose is precluded.

In *Walker* v. *Duncan*, 236 Ga. 331 (1976), the court stated that where a developer sells lots according to a recorded plat, the buyers acquire an easement in any areas set apart for their use. An easement acquired in this manner is considered an express grant and is an irrevocable property right. In *Hendley* v. *Overstreet*, 253 Ga. 136 (1984), the court held that where a declaration of restrictive covenants describes a park or lake area for the use of lot owners, the sale of lots by deeds referencing the declaration creates an irrevocable easement in such an area for the lot owners. The rationale in both cases is that lot owners have paid a higher price for lots because of the presence of the area reserved for their use. Thus, either a designation on a plat or a statement in written covenants may create the right for surrounding lot owners to use and enjoy the described area permanently.

Implied Covenants

The theory of implied covenants is similar to the theory of implied easements; indeed, the two are often used interchangeably. The difference, however, is that implied covenants may include affirmative obligations to perform certain acts or duties while implied easements generally are permissive or restrictive. Implied easements generally do not require any affirmative action by the owner of the property burdened with the easement. An implied covenant, however, may include the affirmative obligation on the part of the developer to perform certain maintenance duties on amenities and facilities.

The best-known case applying the theory of implied covenants is *Shalimar Association* v. *D.O.C. Enterprises, Ltd.*, 688 P.2d 682 (Ariz. 1984). The case provides a virtual checklist of developer actions that may conspire to create an implied covenant in favor of the lot purchasers. The developer showed potential lot buyers a plat of the proposed development, which included a golf course. The plat was recorded in the county land records along with use restrictions that referenced the tract of land on which the Shalimar Estates golf course would be constructed. The recorded plat showed an easement for a golf cart path. The developer placed brochures and sales materials depicting the golf course on file with the state department of real estate. Throughout the sales period, purchasers were told that the golf course and the recorded use restrictions on the residential lots would be maintained until the year 2000 with provision for an extension of 25 years.

The court applied the theory of implied covenants, holding that the developer's actions had created a covenant restricting the use of the land to a golf course. That covenant now binds the current owner of the golf course and all subsequent owners until the year 2025.

Estoppel

Estoppel is a claim based on equitable arguments rather than on express legal obligations. Homeowners may assert estoppel if the developer made certain promises or representations that home-owners relied on to their detriment. In such event, the developer might be precluded from later denying those representations or acting in a manner inconsistent with them to the detriment of homeowners who had relied on them. If a developer represents that certain property will be maintained as a golf course or other recreational facilities and homeowners rely on those representations in improving their property or purchasing houses, the developer may be estopped from either making other arrangements for the use of that property or denying maintenance responsibility.

Estoppel, however, generally applies only where the affected land is well defined and its restrictions clear. A representation that a 1,000-acre tract of land is reserved for pleasure and recreational purposes may not preclude a different activity on the land while a promise to maintain a certain 100-acre tract as a golf course would probably estop the developer from later changing its use.

A good example of the application of estoppel principles is *Oceanside Community Association* v. *Oceanside Land Company*, 195

Cal. Rptr. 320, 522 P.2d 427 (1983). A developer recorded a declaration of covenants, conditions, and restrictions restricting certain property adjacent to the Oceana community to use as a golf course for 99 years. The declaration stated that the covenant was to run with the land. The developer built the golf course and operated it for several years. A reference to the declaration was included in the deeds of all purchasers who bought at Oceana.

The court held that a successor developer could not deny the existence of the covenant to maintain the property as a golf course or the fact that the covenant ran with the land and bound successor purchasers of the golf course. The court imposed an equitable lien against the golf course land that could be foreclosed by the lot owners whenever the developer was not in the process of renovating and maintaining the golf course. In this case, the developer clearly defined both the tract of land and the restriction to be imposed.

Breach of Fiduciary Duty

Breach of fiduciary duty may be applicable if the developer places him- or herself in a position of trust and confidence of the homeowners. The position of trust and confidence gives rise to certain duties on the part of the developer. Fiduciaries who handle property or operate a business on behalf of others must do so as if the property or business were their own. Breach of these duties by a developer may be the subject of a lawsuit by homeowners.

Fiduciary duties arise in at least two situations: the developer is in a position of total control of an existing recreational club on behalf of the homeowners, or the developer has undertaken to perform services for a recreational club on behalf of the homeowners. In such situations, the developer is in a "no-win" position since he or she must evaluate any amenities disposition plan from the viewpoint of the homeowners rather than from his or her perspective. Self-dealing in the form of a "sweetheart" deal for the sale of the amenities or simply a disposition contrary to the interests of the homeowners may lead to substantial liability against the developer and sometimes personal liability against those persons in the decision-making role.

Again, it should be emphasized that fiduciary responsibilities are not created out of thin air. The developer creates such responsibilities by placing him- or herself in a position of control over activities conducted for the benefit of the homeowners. Sometimes the developer creates the responsibilities to portray him- or herself as a "good guy." In any event, the developer can avoid the pitfalls of a fiduciary by paying careful attention to issues of ownership, control, and expectations regarding the amenity package. It has been the author's experience that homeowners will accept virtually any reasonable plan for the operation and eventual disposition of amenities so long as they are aware of the situation and possibilities from the outset.

Breach of Contract

A contract between the lot owner and club may exist if the developer, as the owner of the amenities, established a club that lot purchasers can join and represents that certain rights will be granted in exchange for payment of initiation fees and periodic dues. If so, changing the terms of the "contract" in an amenities disposition deal after payment of initiation fees and dues may constitute a breach of contract.

The key is the extent to which the developer has protected him- or herself by retaining the right to modify unilaterally the terms, fees, and rules of the club. If, in the process of accepting lot owners as members in a club, the developer makes oral or written representations that the club will be transferred to a homeowners' association, the representation becomes part of the basis of the bargain of membership in the club. Without the express right to modify the plan for disposition, the developer can be held liable for breach of contractual obligation. Homeowners may recover damages for the breach or force the developer to perform the obligation to convey the facilities.

Fraud

The final theory is that of fraud. Fraud is extremely difficult to prove since the state of mind and intentions of the persons making representations are at issue. The key elements of fraud are an intentional misstatement or misrepresentation, knowledge on the part of the developer that the statement is false, and justifiable reliance by the buyer.

Statements of opinion, hopes or expectations, or normal sales puffery as distinguished from intentional misstatements of fact do not suffice. Developers often represent which specified amenities will be transferred to a homeowners' association after a certain period of time. If the developer, at the time he or she makes such a representation, does not have any such intention, homeowners may be able to force a transfer of the amenities free of charge based on a successful allegation of fraud.

It is implicit in each theory that the developer must "do something" in order to create rights in homeowners. Determining whether the developer has created rights in homeowners is fact-intensive and can cover virtually every aspect of a project's development from initial planning to marketing. The contents of any one of the following items can be critical in determining whether the developer has created irrevocable rights in homeowners to use or own the facilities and amenities:

- state and federal (HUD) property reports;

- the covenants of the project;

- the master plan of the project, including all revisions;

- recorded plats for the project;

- written advertising materials, sales brochures, and sales handouts;

- representations of sales agents, both written and verbal, regarding the amenities;

- documentation for the country club or other amenity, including application forms and related materials; and

- sales contracts for the lots in the project to determine the nature and extent of any representations regarding the amenities.

The developer spends considerable time and money to create high-quality amenities and must take care not to lay the foundation for later claims that he or she gave away those amenities.

■ Checklist of Documents to Review and Issues to Address

Documents

- Zoning letters of intent;

- Written (and oral) representations of sales agents regarding access to and availability of amenities;

- Original project master plan and all revisions through current master plan;

- Recorded plats referencing or showing amenities;

- Restrictive covenants or declaration of covenants, conditions, and restrictions;

- Federal (U.S. Department of Housing and Urban Development) and state property reports from the original to the most recent filing;

- Minutes of developer-controlled homeowners' association meetings regarding amenities;

- Country club documents and related materials, including articles of incorporation, bylaws, minutes, rules, and application form;

- Sales contract regarding written representations and references to the amenities; and

- Written advertising materials, sales brochures, maps, and drawings involving the amenities.

Issues

- Restrictions on the transferability of the amenities or country club property;

- Representation that homeowner members will not pay an additional lump-sum charge upon sale of amenities to a third party;

- Transfer of amenities at the option of the developer or the members;

- Transferability to a homeowners' association as relates to compensation of existing members, accommodation of nonowner members, option or right of first refusal of members to purchase amenities from developer, and obligation of homeowners' association to accept the facilities;

- Restrictions on future use of amenity property;

- Transferability of memberships as relates to ability to transfer to grantee of lot and potential for profit to member upon transfer;

- Disclaimers informing the association and its members that they acquire no proprietary or other interest in the amenities;

- Maximum number of members;

- Membership qualifications such as residency in development or membership in association or membership requirement if resident or association member;

- Priority of certain persons, especially residents in development or association members, to obtain memberships in club;

- Nature, type, and extent of voting and/or management rights and obligations of homeowner members;

- Representation that purchase of lot or membership in association entitles owner to membership in club or right to use the amenities;

- Existence of special-privilege memberships or special categories of membership;

- Advertising regarding extent of availability of amenities or use rights in amenities; and

- Applicability of restrictive covenants to amenity property.

■ Notes

1. 500 So. 2d 331 (Fla. Dist. Ct. App. 1986).
2. Id. at 332.
3. Id. at 335.
4. See for example, the ULI–Urban Land Institute publication *Developing with Recreational Amenities* for a discussion of these issues.

■ Bibliography

Hyatt, Wayne S. *Condominium and Home Owner Associations: A Guide to the Development Process*. Colorado Springs: Shepard's/McGraw-Hill, 1985.

Hyatt, Wayne S., and Philip S. Downer, eds. *Condominium and Homeowner Association Litigation*. New York: John Wiley & Sons, 1987.

Phillips, Patrick L. *Developing with Recreational Amenities: Golf, Tennis, Skiing, and Marinas*. Washington, DC: ULI–the Urban Land Institute, 1986

Urban Land. ULI–the Urban Land Institute. Various issues.

■ Applicable Cases

Atlanta Association of Baptist Churches v. *Cowan*, 183 Ga. 187, 188 S.E. 21 (1936), on remand, 186 Ga. 10, S.E. 780 (1938)

Case v. *Morrisette*, 475 F.2d 1300 (D.C. Cir. 1973)

Cree Meadows, Inc. (NSL) v. *Palmer,* 68 N.M. 479, 362 P.2d 1007 (1961)

Drye v. *Eagle Rock Ranch, Inc.* 364 S.W.2d 196 (Tex. 1963)

Hendley v. *Overstreet*, 253 Ga. 136, 318 S.E.2d 54 (1984)

Horseshoe Bend Properties, Inc. v. *Duquemin*, No. C85-2895A (N.D. Ga. Sept. 20, 1985)

Oceanside Community Association v. *Oceanside Land Company*, 195 Cal. Rptr. 14, 522 P.2d 427 (1983)

Piechowski v. *Case*, 255 N.W.2d 72 (S.D. 1977)

Shalimar Association v. *D.O.C. Enterprises, Ltd.*, 142 Az. 36, 688 P.2d 682 (1984)

Ute Park Summer Homes Association v. *Maxwell Land Grant Company*, 77 N.M. 730, 427 P.2d 249 (1967)

Walker v. *Duncan*, 236 Ga. 331 (1976)

Protecting Your Assets While Dancing with a Gorilla: The Lender and the Master-Planned Community

©1991 by Hyatt & Rhoads, P.C., all rights reserved

■ Introduction . . . What Should Be the Goal?

The primary goals of those involved in the creation of any master-planned community should be to maximize development flexibility, minimize development liability, and maximize project marketability. In creating the legal documentation and reviewing the collateral marketing materials, the attorney should ensure that nothing is said or done to interfere with the accomplishment of these three primary goals. In the case of a distressed master-planned community in which construction and development loans are in default and the project is in difficulty, these goals remain paramount and deserve special planning and response. Inherent in this effort is the need to address many diverse issues; ultimately, however, for a project to be successful and for its developer and lender to achieve a satisfactory business result, marketability and flexibility must be maximized while the liability of all parties must be minimized. This article addresses these issues and suggests proven approaches for both creating new developments and dealing with existing but troubled projects.

Certainly, each master-planned community is unique, with differences magnified and multiplied when a project is in distress or owner/developer/lender litigation is rife. In dealing with a distressed master-planned community, the affected parties face peculiar characteristics that exacerbate the process and significantly differentiate the workout from any other real estate transaction. The most significant of these characteristics is that people have direct and indirect ownership interests in the collateral and that an independent legal entity exists in the form of the homeowners' association, whose interest in the collateral is independent of that of the lender, the developer, or the individual property owners. For its part, the lender obviously desires to protect its collateral and to find alternatives that allow the development and marketing of the project to go forward as an earning asset.

Definitions of Essential Terms

Most terms are equally applicable to any type of real estate workout. In the context of a distressed master-planned community, however, two terms merit special analysis: declarant and community association. The declarant is the owner of the land who has the authority to impose on that land, through the recordation of covenants, certain affirmative and negative restrictions that create the general plan of development and the attendant rights and responsibilities that are a part of the plan. In most instances, the developer and the declarant are the same person or entity. Inherent in the discussion of the lender and the master-planned community are such questions as who may be a successor-declarant, whether a given person or entity wishes to be a successor-declarant, and what are the rights and liabilities of a successor or of the lender short of becoming a successor. The rights and responsibilities of the declarant are integral to the overall implementation of a development plan and thus to anyone seeking to effectuate the original or some workable plan of development.

Obviously, a lender can become a developer and thus a successor-declarant either voluntarily or involuntarily, but however it is done, it is vital that the successor-declarant understand the consequences of assuming this role. Developers and indeed lenders with some community association experience are mostly likely to be successful. The individual or entity that finds itself in a position of assuming the declarant's responsibilities without the benefit of hands-on experience with community associations must quickly avail itself of various resources necessary to appreciate the legal and practical consequences of being the "declarant" and develop and implement a workable plan of development for the community association.

What, then, is a community association and why does it require specialized approaches? In answering this question, it is helpful to think of the duality of purpose involved in creating and selling a master-planned community. First, there is a product, which is some item in the shelter industry—whether a condominium unit, single-family house, undeveloped lot, or other form of shelter. Second, there is a process, which is the mandatory-membership community association of which each purchaser of that unit, home, lot, or other product automatically becomes a member. The association is vested with significant powers and responsibilities, such as the power to control the use and enjoyment of property—not only its own but also that owned by its members and, in some cases, by third parties. In addition, it has the power to tax or impose assessments and to enforce those assessments through encumbrances on title and through other judicial and nonjudicial remedies.

The unique qualities of a community association give rise to particular powers and roles, all of which have significance in the declarant's, successor-declarant's, and lender's relationship to the association and their efforts to structure or restructure a project. These roles and functions have best been described as both business- and governmentlike and are discussed in detail later. Initially, it is important to note certain attributes and to understand the declarant's relationship to the association.

A critical point to remember is that the association has a separate existence from the declarant in that it exists from the time its documents are recorded. While the declarant, in accordance with the basic documents, has the ability in most cases to exercise significant control over the association, the declarant, any successor, or any intervening lender must govern itself in accordance with the principle that the association is a separate legal entity constituted under local law. Therefore, the association has its own responsibility, interests, and powers; and anyone who acts in a position of authority in relation to that association is governed by applicable principles of law, including those pertaining to fiduciaries and others in a position to control the interests of third parties. The declarant and any successor have limited ability to control the interests of the association and, in so doing, must act in the association's interest even when that action may run counter to their own interests. This simple statement can prove to be a significant barrier to the lender's resolution of issues in a distressed project.

Some Basic Principles

Experience in working with the creation and re-creation of master-planned communities indicates that several basic principles apply. The first principle is that community building is a "team sport" requiring a variety of disciplines and professionals. The ultimate objective is to structure and market the project successfully whether through individual or bulk sales. Accordingly, the development team should develop an operational plan to permit the achievement of this objective. The team's purpose is coordination, communication, and control throughout the process. As with a "mission impossible" team, the team composition varies but usually includes some of the following disciplines and professions: architect; engineer; land planner; insurer; attorney; economic consultant; marketing consultant; club consultants in organization, management, and marketing; and a community association consultant as well as representatives from marketing, management, and development interests. In the case of a distressed community, the lender's representative plays a major role and may substitute for the developer as the party in charge. The team's initial objective should be to perform a legal and operational audit of the community to determine exactly where it is, how it arrived there, and what is necessary to the greatest extent possible to correct those issues that led to the project's distress.

The general economy and market forces in the community's geographic area certainly play significant roles in the circumstances surrounding the project, although the team can do little to affect those circumstances. The legal and operational audit, however, has as a primary objective the determination of those conditions that can be altered and an evaluation of what course will best allow the distressed master-planned community to exist successfully within the overall circumstances. The team therefore has as an operational priority the legal and operational audit, operational and marketing analyses, and the development of a proposed solution. Nonetheless, the audit, analysis, and solution battle plan must reflect the legal and operational realities inherent in the fact that the master-planned community has owners in place whose interests potentially diverge from those of the developer and lender.

The existence of individual property owners and a community association introduces the second basic principle: the team must be flexible in seeking solutions. Any solution to any community association problem should draw on all available legal principles and authorities. Too often, the team seeks an answer only in real estate law while the solution lies elsewhere among corporate, municipal, administrative, or many other areas of legal scholarship generally bundled into "community association law."

Perhaps the most important maxim is that the team should not start with an answer and seek its justification. Whether from a legal or practical viewpoint, the realities of the project, the project's life cycle, and the internal legal-political issues of the community association must be addressed candidly rather than under the assumption that one party is always right, another party is always wrong, and "might makes right." In dealing with community associations, those with that attitude often find that "might makes wrong."

One recurring mistake made by lenders, successor-declarants, and their counsel is the assumption that the existing owners of units, lots, homes, or other product are, at worst, a necessary evil to be tolerated and, at best, totally ignored as an insignificant irritant. Those who plot such a course do so at their considerable peril and, more seriously, do so at the loss of a potentially valuable alternative to liquidation or other distressed sale. At all stages of a project's development and sale, existing owners are a potential resource that should be properly nurtured and harvested.

The third basic principle is objectivity, which requires the avoidance of scapegoating, placing blame, or developing structural solutions solely for self-justification or protection. Objectivity is an essential ingredient in any problem-solving effort, but experience has shown that the tendency is to inquire how one found oneself in a predicament in the first place. Under such circumstances, it is easier to look for a safe harbor than for a course through the storm.

Fundamental Considerations in Analysis

Finding that course requires a clear understanding of the concepts involved in community associations. If you do not know how to create an association in a market where buyers want to buy and lenders want to lend, then there is no hope of fashioning a solution to a partially developed, partially sold project in an era of rampant litigation. A great failure in the community association industry is that too many have ample appreciation for what is necessary to produce the product but far less appreciation for what is involved in the creation and operation of the process.

In addition to understanding the "normal" factors pertaining to a given project, the team must understand the particular project from the community association's point of view. Factors include geography; amenities proposed and in place; demographics; the delineation of responsibility among and between such players as the declarant, the association, and individual owners; the amenity strategy (both in the creation and disposition phases); and the delineation of maintenance responsibility. In looking at the delineation of responsibility, the team must ask what the association is responsible for, what it will do, and what it will own. The same questions must be asked of individual owners, the declarant, and any other member of the community.

Analysis of the project must reflect the marketing and development plan initially in place and how that plan has been followed or modified during the course of development. The analysis should examine the level and degree of participation in the operation of the community association as originally intended for the declarant and the owners and the actual extent of such participation.

Finally, to understand the particular project, it is necessary to understand the financing concerns applicable to the unit, houses, lot, or other real estate product. These concerns are manifested in a wide variety of ways ranging from the simple availability of financing to support the sale of the product through title issues, secondary market issues, association and operation issues, and many more issues discussed in greater depth throughout this article.

Failure to understand the product as a unique combination of real estate product and community association process has probably doomed more developments to distress, failure, and litigation than any other single cause. The combination of any other adverse causation with the failure to understand and appreciate the workings of a master-planned community will, at best, ensure a difficult situation.

Assessing the Situation—Due Diligence

General Real Estate Analysis Tailored to Master-Planned Community

Much has been written about the requirements for due diligence in real estate projects. As with any real estate project, participants must perform a thorough examination of a variety of factors ranging from the state of the title to hazardous waste to local political conditions and requirements. When confronted with a troubled master-planned community, however, participants need to consider additional factors, with the due diligence examination appropriately tailored.

Participants may but should not operate on the simplistic assumption that a valid master-planned community exists. Instead, it is important to ask the following questions:

- Is the association validly formed?

- Is the association valid as to all of the units, lots, houses, or other real estate product that might be contained within the community?

- Is the assessment valid as to these products?

- Will the title policy insure or affirmatively state the validity of the association?

Tailoring for the Master-Planned Community

Analysis of Project Documentation

In answering the above questions and tailoring the due diligence examination, the team must initially perform an analysis of the project's documentation. That task requires a review of the recorded copy of the declaration of covenants, conditions, and restrictions or the declaration of condominium. Too often the available documentation is not a recorded copy and therefore may or may not be accurate. Additional documents to be reviewed include the bylaws; articles or charter of incorporation; the rules and regulations applicable to the community; any leases, contracts, easements, rights-of-way, or other such instruments applicable to the property; and, perhaps most often forgotten, any amendments to these documents.

The conduct of an analysis of project documentation means something more than a perfunctory read-through. Frankly, even experienced professionals in the field may look at a stack of community association documents and dismiss them as nonessential boilerplate with no more relevance than problems relating to pets, parking, children, and trash. Such an unenlightened approach can result in adverse consequences. Accordingly, the analysis must be firm, informed, focused, and open-minded.

It may well be that one or more important provisions are missing from the documentation. In addition, the team needs to examine carefully the possibility of amending one or more of the essential documents in order to add, delete, or modify them to effectuate the redevelopment plan. In essence, the nature of the analysis is to ascertain what is or is not contained within the documentation as well as the consequences of the presence or absence of certain provisions—all with an eye to developing and ultimately implementing a strategy based on the analysis itself. Therefore, one area of analysis must be a determination of the ability to amend the documents before or after foreclosure or other transfer.

Other areas requiring particularly close analysis are the basic rights and responsibilities of the declarant and any successor, including the necessity to determine what constitutes a successor-declarant. Often the covenants, conditions, and restrictions or declaration of condominium contain a specific section or article entitled "declarant's rights" or some similar nomenclature. That article should contain the most specific statement of rights, which is reserved for the declarant; however, such declarant's rights as assessments, leasing, control of the association, matters relating to marketing, and a wide variety of other substantive issues are often scattered throughout the document. It is therefore incumbent on the examiner to ensure that he or she does not focus merely on the obvious but also combs the documents in such a way to ascertain as thoroughly as possible what rights and indeed what responsibilities and obligations exist. As part of that examination, it is important to determine which, if any, of these rights and obligations pass from the original declarant to some successor-in-interest or merely to some third party, when the passing would take place, and how it would take place.

An essential declarant right normally set forth in a substantive article deals with the ability to affect the property physically by adding, withdrawing, or converting real estate to or from the regime created within the governing documents. The ability to grant easements, the ability to terminate easements, the rights to build or use facilities already built are powers that demand the understanding of those seeking to structure a revised general plan of development and actually serve as the bedrock of development flexibility. Considerable flexibility exists within these provisions if the team appreciates the process.

The examination should explore association operational issues, including the declarant's right to participate in operations and indeed to affect operations through such powers as the appointment of the board of directors, the exercise of a declarant veto, the fixing of the annual budget, etc. The goal is to ensure that the association runs smoothly and that the association's smooth operation supports the objectives of maximizing flexibility, maximizing marketability, and, particularly, minimizing liability. How the association operates and the nature of the declarant's or its successor's relationship to the association can greatly influence these objectives for good or ill.

A vital area of examination deals with subordination and estoppel issues. To perform a thorough job, look beyond the covenants applicable to the property from the community association's point of view and examine those documents in conjunction with the loan documents themselves. The documents must present a complementary package of the rights of the lender, the declarant, and the association and its members and set forth the priority of those rights. Acts taken in one context may have unintended consequences; for example, a lender who grants releases on unit sales may be estopped to deny the validity of a community association regime even though loan documents have not been subordinated to the community association documents. Accordingly, the analysis must be broadly based and must, as discussed in the next subsection, be designed to uncover the snakes.

Uncovering the Snakes

One uncovers snakes by getting out in the field, turning over the stones and the brush, and poking around with a sharp stick. It is better to find the snakes during project conception and governance structure planning than when spreading the picnic blanket for the luncheon celebrating completion of development or redevelopment plan. An excellent place to begin this particular search is by taking a site tour of the project to observe construction and maintenance, ask questions about sales patterns, review collateral materials, and take notes of positive or negative actions dealing with such matters as document compliance, design review, rule enforcement, and other matters that directly impinge on the nature and quality of the development and its marketing. Perhaps most important, a site visit provides an opportunity to assess the degree of satisfaction among those who reside within the community.

The steps and areas of examination in the following discussion relate to an existing project in which "trouble" is present, although the same type of examination in the context of initial project creation is appropriate, with some modification. During the site tour, ask questions of the marketing staff while reviewing marketing materials to ascertain the earlier representations that have been made and the reliances purchasers have placed on the representations. All areas of examination are crucial in analyzing the existing owners' expectations and level of hostility toward the developer and, vicariously through the developer, toward the lender and any successor. Strategically, it may seem desirable to position the successor as a white knight, and doing so is possible only if the problems are understood initially. Moreover, existing owners can be a valuable ally in the restructuring process, but failing to understand and appreciate their present positions obviates any opportunity to use these allies as resources.

Uncovering the snakes is a challenge associated with any thoroughly planned and executed legal and operational audit of a community association. The checklist of documents and materials necessary for such an audit includes the following:

- Building and development process;

- Maintenance of existing improvements and plans for future improvements;

- Government relationships;

- Legal documentation, including existing or pending litigation;

- Association organization;

- Association operations;

- Financial records, including budgets, statements of reserves, list of delinquents, tax returns, and audits; and

- Insurance policies and procedures.

As with much of the analysis, the legal and operational audit occurs on two levels: general association operation and the declarant's relationship to that operation. Accordingly, it is necessary to look at the nature of management and the declarant's subsidies, guarantees, and representations made in relation to that management. Also bear in mind the legal implications of principles such as the business judgment rule and the declarant's fiduciary duty to the association. Always ask, "Who is minding the store, and how so?" To do otherwise may well result in seeing the colors but missing the snake.

One often overlooked serpent lying in the weeds is an invalid scheme of development. Others pertain to common area and construction questions. The examiner must also inquire as to the nature and extent of any encumbrances on the common property and how and when such encumbrances, if any, may be released and at what cost. Are there encumbrances on any privately owned property, and, if so, are they valid? Has access been reserved in the roadways? Do easements and other necessary licenses exist? Finally, who holds title to the common property? Is title held validly? For example, title to the common property may remain in the declarant but, because of plats, deeds, or other express or even implied representations, may have passed either as a matter of law or equity to the association, its members, or third parties.

Most distressed communities can point to a pending or potential claim relating to construction defects. It is therefore advisable as part of the common property analysis to perform at least a basic engineering study of construction so that the revised plan of development can avoid repeating earlier mistakes and, at the same time, account for the potential costs in time, money, and effort required to deal with and resolve construction problems. Certainly, the successful reliance on existing property owners as a part of the revised plan means that disputes over earlier conduct must not be permitted to fester. In other words, the ways of the real world necessitate curing one problem before advancing to the next.

The final area requiring close attention when uncovering serpents is the amenity development and disposition plan. With an amenity strategy vital to the overall success of a master-planned community, the due diligence examination should include questions relating to the existence and nature of that strategy. Once again, the strategy should have as a fundamental principle the maximization of flexibility and marketability and minimization of liability. Therefore, the plan must match the mix, quantity, and quality of the amenity to the market and ensure that it reflects the overall project. The amenity should be consistent with the site, balance the population and demographics of the ultimate consumers, and reflect a realistic analysis of experience with the amenity within the overall area. The strategy should determine the amenity's priority within the community by asking questions such as who will own it and who will operate it for how long, on what schedule, and at what price.

The strategy should reflect the fact that while the amenity is an integral part of the real estate it also carries an independent value and role of its own. At each stage of the analysis, the team should carefully consider the adequacy of control over the amenity to ensure that the developer or successor commands the necessary control while minimizing the exposure that so often comes with that control. Finally, the strategy must provide for a rational transfer and address a variety of issues relating to disposition, representations, and reliance. A later section considers these and other questions in greater detail.

At this point, it is worth noting that amenity issues should be high on the list of questions asked of existing owners and marketing people about what representations have been made. It is from these representations that obligations and potential liability may well arise. In structuring the analysis of club or amenity planning, one should realize that timing can be crucial. Maximum flexibility is generally legally permissible so long as it is clearly disclosed orally and in such appropriate documentation as contracts, sales materials, advertising, covenants, registrations with appropriate government agencies, etc.

Questions of timing also apply to the construction of amenities, the availability of amenities for use and enjoyment, and whether options are retained to vary schedules not only of the delivery of amenities but of when, under what circumstances, and at what cost to whom. Once again, the checklist of relevant questions dealing with amenities in club issues is lengthy; however, the time and effort required to review that checklist is a wise investment given that so much potential liability and so many infringements on flexibility often flow from these very issues.

Analysis of Developer and Designated Successor
The final area of analysis is that of the developer and any designated successor. Their ability, experience, and knowledge not only of the product but also of the process involved in master-planned community development are crucial to ultimate success. Accordingly, the due diligence review should include all data concerning these issues and a review of any and all pending litigation. This is not to say that there is a touchstone or numeric listing of qualifications that permits a developer to go forward with a master-planned community. Moreover, those charged with performing the due diligence are perhaps no more qualified to select the ultimate champion developer than anyone else; however, analysis is in order to quantify the risks and opportunities associated with the existing level of ability, experience, and knowledge.

Duality of Due Diligence
Due diligence's dual nature requires a look forward and a look backward. For due diligence to be meaningful, it must extend to a host of facts from past activities as the basis for evaluating the ability of people and things to be successful in the future. It is therefore most helpful to have some appreciation for what the future plan entails in order to unearth and evaluate the bits of evidence from earlier actions. It is not enough to engage in a due diligence review simply to find out the state of the project at a given moment; this is the functional equivalent of an archeologist who simply wishes to recreate the village as it was at the time the volcano erupted. Because of the challenges inherent in attempting to restructure distressed projects, the due diligence review must take the "archeological find" and extrapolate forward to what can be done not only to reposition the village but also to avoid damage by

a future eruption of the volcano. The goal should not be to identify things to avoid but to create an affirmative plan of action.

Declarant and Successor-Declarant

In restructuring any distressed master-planned community, one issue that quickly comes to the fore is who will act in the role of the declarant with all the attendant powers and rights as the implementation of the redevelopment plan unfolds. The role of successor-declarant is a two-edged sword. On one edge rest those rights and powers vital to the implementation of an overall development plan. These are the "declarant's rights" reserved in the original documentation and created by amendments or agreements. They allow for the orderly, structured unfolding of the general plan of development. However, these rights come at a price, for upon the other edge rest the liabilities and responsibilities that evolved on the original declarant and that, in many cases, pass to the successor. The question then becomes whether as a part of the redevelopment plan the lender or its designee wishes to become a successor-declarant, and, if so, how to accomplish the transfer at minimum cost and, if not, how to complete the necessary development.

The project documentation may provide for successor status by its express terms but may also again be a trap. Frequently, as documents say that one who expressly takes the powers and responsibilities of the declarant shall be deemed a successor-declarant, thereby potentially imposing liability for earlier acts. Other modifiers and provisos may either limit the ability of the successor to acquire the declarant's powers or impose the powers on someone not desiring them. In other words, the document drafting or initial analysis of the roles to be played in the redevelopment process demand a careful review of the project documentation, loan documentation, and applicable state law as well as of the course of conduct that has governed the various parties to determine whether successor-declarant status is available, desirable, or obligatory.

In some cases, the lender is exposed to liability not because of documentation but because of an earlier course of conduct. The courts appear to be uniform in the opinion that active participation in the development of the project beyond the role of "mere lender" combined with active participation in construction and marketing increases the likelihood of liability, especially when participation is either direct or through the exercise of control over the activities of another. What the test of participation requires, however, remains unclear. The cold hard fact is that when the lender becomes an active participant in the project and starts making development decisions, marketing the product to ultimate consumers, and otherwise conducting itself as if it were the developer, it assumes tremendous risks. The key is involvement, direct or indirect. The problem is that in many cases there is no way to end the distress affecting the project without this involvement.

As part of each redevelopment plan, the team should carefully and specifically address the issue of whether successor-declarant status is necessary. It may well be that the lender should merely pass the property in bulk to a genuine successor to insulate the lender from liability. In each case, ask why it is desirable to be a successor-declarant and whether the desired benefits can be achieved with a minimum of burdens.

Categorically taking the position that one can have the powers of the declarant without the attendant responsibilities is naive. Regrettably, however, lenders and others frequently adapt such a position. In these circumstances, the redevelopment plan asserts that the lender or its designee has the power to market, add phases, control boards of directors, fix budgets, and address other such matters in relation to the community association that are specifically reserved to the declarant but absolutely denies any responsibilities. Legally speaking, this approach does not work. The sword has two edges and is an area requiring careful thought and creative problem solving, for the liability potential is great.

"Dancing with the Gorilla—I": Areas of Liability

As noted earlier, developer and successor-developer liability fall into three categories: construction, association operation, and marketing representations. Much has been written about this substantive area of community association law; however, for the purposes of this article, it is appropriate to identify once again the basic areas of concern and to highlight the need for a preventive approach in the preparation of any development plan. First, it is important to seek to minimize the exposure for earlier actions; second, it is essential to seek to develop a program that presents minimal exposure for future action.

Construction

In the construction area, the courts and legislatures have evolved areas of exposure for the builder/seller of real estate products. Depending on the jurisdiction and its law, the individual who constructs a unit, house, or other product in the shelter industry can face a variety of potential challenges. Perhaps the most common challenge is the imposition of liability for an implied warranty of habitability. Such a warranty is imposed as a matter of state law predicated on a perception of inequality of bargaining power between the builder/seller and the purchaser. Such a warranty is normally construed to state that the product has been constructed in a reasonably workmanlike manner and is fit for habitation. The implied warranty is not a function of a specific contractual promise made from the seller to the buyer; rather, it is imposed by operation of law on the parties and may not be abrogated by action of the parties. In many cases, however, the best mitigation of implied warranty liability is an affirmative statement as between the parties setting forth an express warranty.

An express warranty is obviously a creature of contractual agreement between the purchaser and seller and spells out in specific terms what has been warranted for how long and under what conditions. While the express warranty cannot take away that which state law provides, it can institutionalize the warranty obligation, thus increasing the understanding of the consuming public regarding what to expect and in large measure circumscribing the exposure of the builder/seller. Express warranties are particularly important in matters such as the length of time the warranty runs and the time within which the aggrieved purchaser must notify the responsible seller of any alleged defect. In these areas, certainty becomes a critical factor that has both tangible and intangible benefits.

In some states, the builder/seller's construction liability goes beyond the express or implied warranty and is a matter of strict liability or of statutory warranty under state law and is best summed up by the idea that if the builder/seller built it and sold it and it has a defect, the builder is strictly liable for that defect. Such exposure is perhaps unrealistic, but it is the law in several jurisdictions. The primary area of dispute thus becomes a matter of damages rather than of liability, and the attempt to quantify the exposure and risk is a major challenge requiring careful consideration.

Perhaps the most common cause of action throughout the country is predicated on negligence in the design or construction of the project. Of the three major areas of liability in the construction category, negligence is the most difficult for the plaintiff but is fraught with considerable exposure for the seller because of the presumption that certain things speak for themselves as to negligence when the lender may not have the willing witnesses and appropriate evidence readily available to rebut such a presumption.

The construction exposure is a basic consideration. If the product is built defectively, the builder/seller—and, in many cases, the successor to the builder/seller—has tremendous potential for that defect. The redevelopment or workout strategy must address these issues from both preventive and defensive perspectives.

Operation of the Association

The second major area of potential liability concerns association operation. The person or entity in control of the association has a fiduciary obligation to that association and its members to act free of self-interest or self-dealing. A problem can arise because the declarant or successor is often placed in a position in which the issues once again have multiple edges, with decisions most difficult to make without benefiting one interest at the expense of another. The duty has best been summed up as one of "undivided loyalty" that applies when the board of directors of the association considers maintenance and repair contracts, operating budgets, creation of reserves, etc., such that the directors may not make decisions for the association that benefit their own interests at the expense of the association or its members. The fiduciary responsibility exists because of the special confidence placed the board to control the interests of others. When board members are developer appointees, the risk of conflict of interest is great.

The fiduciary responsibility embodies two levels of this obligation. One is best summarized as the requirement for members of a board of directors to exercise their decision-making responsibility in accordance with sound business judgment. It can be met with ordinary and reasonable care and supervision over those to whom some authority has been delegated. The director, as with any good businessperson, must exercise good faith, diligence, care, and skill in making the association's business decisions. The second level of obligation, sometimes referred to as the "higher" duty, requires the board member to disclose any real or potential conflicts of interest to avoid self-dealing and to ensure that decisions reflect the best interest of the association. Regrettably, sometimes the association's best interest is in direct contravention of the developer's or the successor's best interest. In those circumstances, the decision-making process is troublesome indeed.

As noted earlier, the association is charged with two basic roles: that of a business and that of a "minigovernment." Therefore, the board of directors of an association functions as the board of a small business and as the governing body of a private government delivering public services. In each instance, rules and procedures govern the operation. As with any rules, sanctions are imposed when the rules are violated. The areas of potential liability involved in the operation of the association are fraught with a greater-than-normal likelihood of liability because, by their nature, they present inherent conflicts. In the analysis of what has taken place and in the preparation of a plan for what is to take place, the team should pay particular attention to these matters, although the examination should certainly not be limited to them. The potential areas of conflict follow:

- *Contracts and Leases.* These are agreements between the association and the declarant, the lender, or some entity related to either the declarant or the lender.

- *Assessments, Budgets, and Reserves.* These items embrace the entire topic of the adequacy of assessments; the necessity and adequacy of reserves; whether assessments have been collected in a timely fashion from owners unrelated to the developer; whether they have been collected from units, homes, or lots owned by the declarant; and how the funds have been handled, invested, and reported. The required stewardship is great, yet the sophistication afforded these aspects of association operation is often well below the necessary threshold.

- *"Acceptance" of the Common Property.* It is common for a representative of the developer to conduct a punchlist walk-through of the common property with a representative of the association to develop a list of outstanding defects and a timeline for curing those defects before the association's assumption of maintenance responsibility. This approach has worked well in a number of projects. It does not work well, however, when the association's representative is a developer appointee and the "punchlist agreement" is obviously not entered into as an arm's length transaction reflecting the equality of bargaining power on both sides of the agreement.

- *Maintenance Decisions.* Decisions made by the board of directors as to whether a defect is a maintenance or construction problem sometimes call for fine shades of judgment. When resulting from improper maintenance, the defect is the responsibility of the association and its members rather than of the developer/builder/seller. The troublesome issue is who is making the decision, under what circumstances, and how. A developer-controlled board of directors may make the right decision, but the decision will appear to have been made for an improper reason. These matters can be resolved properly but require considerable integrity, skill, documentation as to the rationale, and communication to educate those concerned as to why something was done.

- *Enforcing Obligations.* Too often, representatives of the developer on a board of directors forebear from taking judicial or nonjudicial action to enforce the development documents or rules. Such forbearance frequently results from a desire to maintain tranquility within the project and to avoid the appearance of dissension, litigation, and intra-association divisiveness. All of these are laudable objectives unless the underlying purpose of the forebearance is to enhance sales; thus, the decision is made for a reason beneficial to the developer rather than to the association to which the board members owe their duty. The companion to this problem is the board's unwillingness to enforce obligations against the developer itself. Interesting cases have revealed the liability of individual board members who have failed to take actions for such reasons.

- *Architectural Issues.* The same basic principles apply in the overall issue of enforcing the architectural and design review process. Here, however, the potential divergence of interest is starkly drawn. The declarant sees the need for unbridled freedom to permit builders to construct housing that reflects a marketplace willing to purchase that housing. At the same time, existing owners have a genuine aesthetic and economic interest in seeing that the requirements and guidelines in place at the time they purchased and constructed their homes are followed so as not to denigrate their housing, thus depreciating the value of both house and investment. The twin horns of the dilemma—certainty on the one hand and flexibility on the other—best summarize the problem and challenges for those attempting to adjust a project's plan to reflect a dramatic alteration in the maket while maintaining a collegial community free of dispute and litigation.

- *Claims against the Developer.* How can members of a developer-controlled board deal with potential claims against the development entity that is their employer without a genuine potential for conflict of interest and widely divergent opinion as to how claims should be resolved? Stating the problem frames it sufficiently. It is important to note that the courts have indicated that not every problem requires a litigious response and that those charged with making decisions in accordance with sound business judgment are afforded the freedom to do just that. Sound business judgment does not always require unanimous approval by the plaintiffs' bar but rather requires an objective analysis of the facts and a decision made in good faith, with diligence, care, and skill.

The due diligence examination, which looks backward and forward at the same time, must give these matters considerable thought. Well-drafted documentation; disclosure; homeowner involvement at an early, phased transition of control; a highly refined sensitivity to the nature of the community association and to potential problems can all militate against costly errors. Institutionalizing procedures and practices for association operation can not only reduce exposure for earlier actions but can also help innocent mistakes that might create future exposure. As part of this procedure, board decisions should be carefully considered, documented, and communicated. Finally, assurance that the association's structure is adequate, accurate, in place, and operational will in large measure significantly reduce risks.

Representations and Reliance

The third area of potential exposure rests on representations made as a part of the marketing process and the degree of reasonable reliance purchasers placed on those representations when making their purchase decisions. It has been said that salespersons (usually) do not lie; therefore, buyers do not often win misrepresentation cases. Nonetheless, such cases do not go away easily because they involve one side saying "yes" and another side saying "no" and require resolution by the trier of fact, which is normally a jury. A judge is typically not in a position to grant summary disposition, thus necessitating costs in time, money, energy, reputation, and lost opportunity to resolve the issue. Once again, the twin horns of certainty and flexibility come into play. What will be done within a project, what amenities will be provided, how the club will be structured, or when the amenities will be constructed or conveyed all become issues about which buyers so often hear one thing, program another, and subconsciously act on a third.

The legal theories of liability are varied and range from express and implied covenants, express and implied easements, implied negative reciprocal easements, basic contractual provisions, fraud and misrepresentation, and estoppel to principles of fiduciary duty and on to the Racketeer Influenced and Corrupt Organizations Act, which so many in the plaintiffs' bar like to trot out as the ultimate "boogey man." In each of these instances, the essential ingredient revolves around some oral or written expression of a present intention regarding a future fact; yet, a well-structured preventive plan can mitigate the risks almost into insignificance. Too often, however, that plan is not prepared and implemented.

Representations and expectations can arise from oral and written sales representations, master plans, recorded plats, deeds, sales contracts, zoning letters of intent, initial documentation, land sales registrations, the basic community association documents, minutes of the board, and a wide variety of other sources. The redevelopment team must analyze this mass of material to evaluate the exposure that may exist and to determine the feasibility of the existing amenity plan and the flexibility to change that plan. Implicit in a workable amenity plan is a disposition component, which is an exit strategy that allows, indeed preserves, maximum flexibility in disposing of amenities or other bits and pieces of property within the community in a light most favorable to the overall general plan of development and its economic feasibility. The strategy, which must be written and understood but must not be public, specifies the amenities; the time of disposition; the permissible owners; responsibilities for care, custody, and control; method of transfer; and the retained flexibility to meet changed market conditions.

Developing the disposition plan requires disclosure, control over implementation, and constant testing of those who interact with the public to ensure that nothing is said, done, written, or spoken that can be construed as amending the plan or speaking in contradiction of the plan. All of this—analysis, plan creation, and plan supervision and implementation—must be a critical responsibility of the redevelopment team. A successful plan is flexible, unique, and realistic. Most important, there must be a plan.

Land Sales Regulation

Two other areas of potential exposure permeate the entire process and require a brief discussion: land sales registration and securities registration. Local, state, and federal law may impose an obligation to register the sale of the real property product and to provide certain disclosures and other information. If properly conducted, the due diligence examination, of course, includes a review of registration issues. It is important, however, to reflect on these issues as more than just another item on a due diligence checklist.

It is important to ask such questions as, Is registration required and, if so, is a valid registration in place? Such questions go beyond pro forma compliance with a bureaucratic annoyance. Failure to register may create rescission rights in existing purchasers and obligate the successor-declarant to time-consuming and potentially expensive registration processes before engaging in future marketing. Adverse consequences may also arise if the failure to register unfavorably affects existing remedies specified by the lender in the loan documentation.

Registration is not just a matter of the federal Interstate Land Sales Full Disclosure Act but also an issue of state law in many jurisdictions. Each project must analyze not only the nature of the product but also the scope and extent of the marketing plan in order to ascertain the relevant requirements and the best means of meeting them. A concomitant part of that marketing analysis demands knowledge of the requirements of provinces, countries, and other governments throughout the world to the extent that marketing will extend to those areas.

Securities Laws Issues

Although the prevailing maxim is that the sale of real estate does not create a "security" necessitating compliance with state and federal securities laws, the nature of complex real estate developments represents an ever-grayer area. When memberships are sold in a golf course or initial deposits are taken and used as the equivalent of venture capital for the construction of the project, the likelihood increases that securities regulations apply under either federal law or, in some cases, more restrictive state law. Currently, the sale of a "traditional" primary residence community does not give rise to this issue. However, there are fewer and fewer such communities. As mixed-use, highly amenitized, resort-residential communities and other such permutations and modifications of the development art enter the market, financing, marketing, or development issues suggest the possibility of securities involvement.

A major problem in securities analysis is not whether a state or the federal government takes action but rather whether failure to comply gives purchasers and prospective purchasers rescission rights or private causes of action. The rise and fall of markets and the resultant change in an individual's perspective on his or her investment can be the cause of a securities claim with rescission as the ultimate goal. Securities claims thus become one of many arrows in the quiver of the aggressive plaintiff's attorney who seeks to achieve some economic return through applied leverage.

"Dancing with the Gorilla—II": Developing a Risk-Averse Strategy

It has been said that dealing with a master-planned community is like dancing with a gorilla: one goes round and round until the gorilla tires. The idea that a 1,000-pound gorilla can sit anywhere has taken hold of American humor and politics, but the fact is that the gorilla is trainable. Developing a strategy in a master-planned community requires a willingness to take the time and expend the bananas necessary to make that dance mutually beneficial if not necessarily enjoyable. That process must begin with a focused strategy for dealing with the owners. The following comments pertain to existing owners, for that is the context in which the lender most frequently becomes involved. Ensuring that the initial documents and project planning anticipate owner issues and situations should be on the lender's list during project formation.

Dealing with Existing Owners

The first and perhaps most important consideration is to avoid the reflex response of negativism so often seen by developers, lenders, and their successors in dealing with owners—and vice versa. Experience has taught the value of using owners as an available resource. This resource will not be available, however, if the team's attitude is that the owners will be used but not informed or involved in the development of a proposed strategy. The team must take care in selecting the people with whom to deal in order to avoid any appearance of impinging on owners' independence. At the same time, though, the team wishes to deal with reasonable, capable people.

The selection of leaders and the activation of the community behind a plan are both served by communication and education as to the problem, potential solutions, and ultimate solution. The team must not seek to use bribes, direct or indirect, but rather must make the problem and the owners' involvement in the solution of the problem part of an ongoing process. Someone sold those individuals on the project in the first place, and that person should be in a position to sell them again. Most significantly, the redevelopment team should not be rigid, and the lender in particular should not reject the owners as noncreditworthy, nonbusinesslike individuals. In case after case, the individuals who directly or indirectly represent the control group for the community association have considerable business experience; in many cases, far greater experience than the loan officer making the decisions on behalf of the lender. Yet, these people are dismissed as "mere homeowners" or retirees looking for something to fill their time. Such an approach is ineffective.

Examples of owner involvement in project restructurings abound, and those involved in developing the workout plan should avoid costly misconceptions and review the available examples. Owner involvement represents an effective alternative because, first, owners are there. Second, they have a genuine interest in seeing the project work because the asset subject to consideration represents, in all probability, the single largest investment in their portfolio: their home. Third, they very often have available the necessary financing or access to financing to make a restructuring process work in whole or in part. Fourth, in many cases, they have the business experience that allows them to understand and appreciate what is being done and what needs to be done.

It should not go unmentioned that, because of their fear of some other alternative and their perception that they can benefit from a restructuring in which they are involved, owners may well represent the best buyer for some or all of the property involved. Once again, examples of such solutions abound, and the redevelopment team should examine these histories as part of their backward- and forward-looking due diligence/strategy development. This is not to say, however, that the redevelopment team should take the approach of the lamb any more than it should always assume the role of the lion. The existing owner group often has highly inflated expectations of what should be provided and an attitude that economic depreciation resulting from circumstances beyond any individual's control should be compensated for by the successor developer or lender. Accordingly, the approach to the existing owner group should reflect a balance between competing interests.

Lenders and declarants would be amazed at the documentation that resides in buyers' attics, basements, and memories. Much of that documentation surfaces in the years subsequent to the purchase. Accordingly, the best advice is to involve owners at the beginning; in the case of a redevelopment, the beginning is a moving time frame that starts not only when the original development team began conceptualizing the project but also when the redevelopment team goes through that process again. It is never too late to let buyers know the reason for changes. It is too late only when the teams make changes without informing the existing constituent group and expect to ignore the howls of protest.

An informed, trained sales staff that knows what to say and what not to say is most important. It is easy to ensure that people know what they are marketing if they are properly trained. While we allow our sales staff to tell the story of the product, too often salespersons do not understand the process. The redevelopment team wastes one of the best potential advocates for the totality of the redevelopment plan by not providing training sessions on documentation, title issues, and other subjects so that the sales force can sell the process at the same time it sells the product.

Experience has clearly shown the importance of a posture of responsiveness and information sharing. The redevelopment process should designate a person to act in accordance with an established procedure to deal with construction problems, warranty problems, alterations to the documentation, and other matters in which the declarant, successor-declarant, or lender directly or indirectly interacts with existing homeowners. Once the procedure is established, it should be followed.

It is also important to fix little things. In many cases, successor-declarants take the position of stonewalling the existing community on the assumption that they are the lender and can get away with it. The author was once on a panel with another attorney who said that, in representing a large bank, his approach to the community association was "to grind it down" by turning off the water, stopping services, and otherwise exerting pressure. The author is reminded of the story of Goliath. The lender was undoubtedly a giant, as was Goliath, but Goliath was brought low by little David. Lenders who take the position that they are the 1,000-pound gorilla usually find themselves bogged down in a morass; and the more they attempt to badger and bully, the more tightly they are stuck. If at all possible, the goal should be to develop a working partnership to produce an "era of good feelings." If that is not possible, crisis management and damage control issues come into play.

Communicating what is being done and why can go a long way toward ameliorating dissension and dissuading owners from litigation. However, the development team should be prepared and aware. For example, legal counsel should not only be knowledgeable of title or lender issues but should also reflect specialized training and understanding in community association issues from both transactional and litigation perspectives. A team and a team leader should be in place to ensure that the negotiation strategy, redevelopment strategy, and potential litigation strategy are complementary rather than divergent. The team leader and ultimately the client need to know what they are willing to give up. While they need to appear to be in a life-or-death struggle, they need to base decisions on sound business principles.

Dealing with restructuring a master-planned community is in many ways more of a political process than a real estate law process. The goal should be to put everyone on the same side pulling in the same direction. Doing that requires more finesse than power, yet most players understand only power. Regrettably, they do not even always know how to use what power they may command.

The problem in redevelopment activity, both in re-creation and potential litigation, is that the lines of communication are too often closed off rather than opened up, building in hostilities rather than minimizing and diluting them. Trust is a fragile commodity; however, it existed at some point in the relationship and, if it can be reestablished and built upon, it will make the process work.

Problem Projects May Reflect Problem Documents
In an earlier article, the author commented that "the declaration and bylaws therefore, must be flexible and realistic in anticipation of changes in time, personalities, and residents' needs, desires and abilities. They should be sufficiently unique in order to ensure that they fit the particular project." Stated in support of a discussion on how to draft "documents that work," that maxim is certainly relevant today and applies equally to the creation of new documents and the re-creation of documents as part of a redevelopment plan.

Often, problem projects reflect problem documents. Although many distressed projects result from economic circumstances and market forces beyond anyone's control, the documents become "problems" because they lack sufficient flexibility to respond to the difficulties created by extraneous forces. Thus, it is incumbent on the redevelopment team to explore ways of altering loan documents, title documents, and master community association documents to reflect "new realities."

No matter how creative the team in dealing with issues of finance and lender/borrower relations, if the title and community association documents affecting the property itself are not workable, the redevelopment process will not succeed. For this reason, the due diligence examination must be coupled with a plan for how to modify the documents. An earlier section of this article dealing with due diligence and the analysis of project documentation includes a list of several substantive areas covered by the documents that require particular examination during the due diligence phase. Obviously, each of these substantive areas becomes critical during the reworking phase when the redevelopment team explores the possibility of making additions or deletions to the documents to bring them in line with present marketing and operational realities. For the sake of brevity, we will simply refer to that section to incorporate those substantive areas. Yet, experience has shown that the following specific problem areas fall out from those general substantive categories:

- the definition of declarant and the definition of successor-declarant;

- specific delineations of the declarant's rights and obligations;

- a reservation of retained rights, as, for example, the right to grant or modify or terminate easements;

- the right to add or withdraw property to or from the community association;

- use, access, and maintenance provisions;

- the ability to amend the documents before or after a foreclosure or transfer of title;

- boundary definitions of total property, units, homes, lots, or other product;

- percentages of ownership, percentages of interest;

- ownership of particular amenities and how those amenities are to be operated;

- governance issues;

- the power of assessment;

- the freedom of the declarant from paying assessments;

- issues relating to subordination of the community association documentation and the loan documentation;

- the ability to use some or all of the facilities for marketing;

- the right to control the design review process and how that design review process is to function;

- title issues relating to validity of submission of units, lots, or homes to the declaration;

- applicable provisions allowing the documents to satisfy the secondary mortgage market, including the Veterans Administration and the Federal Housing Administration as well as the Federal National Mortgage Association;

- issues of the validity of the association's organization under state law and its basic documentation; and

- the validity of plats and plans recorded with the governing documents.

Several alternative approaches are available for curing many of these problems. Drafting is an art that allows the implementation of most development or redevelopment plans if sufficient experience and creativity are brought to the task. Those who see a set of forms and only one way to go lack the creativity needed for problem solving. Not only does restructuring offer a clean slate for creativity, but several proven approaches make the process work. For example, if one association has too many problems to make restructuring feasible, the remaining unsubmitted property may be submitted to a revised, second association with contractual agreements between the two to provide joint benefits in operation. Associations can merge, contract, dissolve and be reconstituted, and do a variety of other things permitted not only by real estate law but also by corporate and other areas of law.

The regular membership may be unwieldy and cumbersome, but use of the voting member or representative approach can eliminate the cumbersomeness and unwieldiness from the process, allowing the association to function much more smoothly and efficiently. Establishing neighborhoods, villages, or parcel structures may build in cohesiveness, establish the "mood" needed for marketing, and divide a large project into discrete service delivery areas, thus providing for a much more tailored and cost-effective method of operation.

Distinguishing between and among types of owners, particularly in resort property, may well permit levels of service to meet levels of need. It may also allow a newly tailored redevelopment plan to gain the acceptance of different groups whose needs and thus willingness to pay for services vary widely. The key is to analyze the project and to analyze it carefully. In that analysis, the development team must ask, "What did I want to create? What do I want to create now?" Then it must determine what will work best. By identifying a project's problems and peculiarities, the team is able to decide how to restructure the documents to overcome problems, maximize benefits, and satisfy peculiarities. The team needs to remember to use all of the available tools, including, of course, real estate law, corporate law, municipal law, political "give and take," and, in extreme cases, resorting to the courts to seek a traditional reformation of documentation that satisfies no one's expectations at the time of the creation.

These are but a few illustrations of approaches to restructuring community association and club documentation in order to cure problems. There are as many approaches as there are distressed properties if one only understands the process.

Some practical tips for getting the job done are worthy of mention. First, it is important to understand the overall concept of the "power source." The governing documents are the power source of the community association and, to the extent that the power source is modified, most things are possible. Courts have held that documents may be amended for "any lawful purpose," thus providing an opportunity for the curative process to take place. Obviously, the requisite votes must be obtained in order to approve the amendments. In some cases, the first step is simply to amend the documents to provide greater flexibility in amendment. Coupling that effort with emotionally and politically charged issues may quickly result in a negative vote, whereas simply amending the documents to make them more fully amendable may be a "motherhood and apple pie" issue that will receive the necessary vote. Which issues are voted on in which order by which group and at what time all become vital in achieving the desired and necessary result.

The redevelopment team should check the statutory basis of the association and borrow from available statutes such as the Uniform Condominium Act and the Uniform Common Interest

Ownership Act. There may very well be statutory ways of making the necessary changes; it may be possible to amend one document and achieve the desired result, whereas it may not be possible to amend another. For example, bylaws may more easily lend themselves to amendment than the declaration of covenants, conditions, and restrictions. In the event that the problem is one of ambiguity in documentation and impossibility of performance, judicial action to make the changes may necessitated. Simply attempting to amend the document through the existing association may be less efficacious than re-creation, termination, or reconstitution of the property into different associations.

Dealing with the dynamics of people, of course, is always a challenge, but educating existing owners to the need and purpose of the amendment, framing the questions in a way most likely to achieve the desired results, and structuring the methods of voting and approval can all enhance the process. For example, if all approvals must be achieved "at a meeting," the likelihood of obtaining the necessary turnout and thus approval is reduced. However, combining a meeting with a written ballot or powers of attorney enhances the likelihood of achieving necessary approvals. Keeping the time for approval open works wonders. A California court has held that the time for approval may be open-ended as long as it is not so long as to show that fraud took place in obtaining approvals.

The point is that there are as many approaches to developing a solution as there are problems. Certainly, not all of them work, but the one-shot, dogmatic, do-it-my-way approach is guaranteed to fail in most cases. Creative drafting combined with creative association marketing has a much higher rate of success. Moreover, it vests the community with a spirit of interaction and interdependence and is thus much more likely to guarantee the long-term success of the redevelopment plan. That, after all, should be everyone's goal.

Conclusion

Working out problems in distressed master-planned communities is expensive and frustrating and involves significant potential liability. The lender is increasingly aware that the greater its involvement in restructuring and operating a project, the greater is its potential exposure to liability for a variety of causes of action arising from the conduct of the original declarant-developer. As with so much in business today, working out the problems of a distressed master-planned community is not a spectator sport but rather is one that requires active and informed participation by persons with ultimate decision-making authority. So often, that authority rests solely with the lender.

Accordingly, the lender must become involved, and with a talented supporting team able to perform a comprehensive job of creating a redevelopment plan. The team must be forward-looking and must appreciate all the risks and duties inherent in the creation, re-creation, and operation of the project. The team must be prepared to use all available resources, including the existing owners, to achieve the desired objective.

The team must be imbued with the determination to avoid a reflexive, responsive negativism that rejects the use of all resources because of the perception that some group or individual does not bring to the table the same attitude and experience shared by the rest of the team members. Reflexive, responsive negativism also includes a failure to acknowledge the obligation to act on behalf of those in charge of the community association and a failure to acknowledge the realities of who may act and how they may act in accordance with business judgment, reasonableness, and fiduciary responsibilities. In other words, the realities, the "realpolitic" of community associations, must of necessity be acknowledged and worked with to salvage the distressed master-planned community. It is the failure to acknowledge, accept, and work with these realities that causes the project to be distressed in the first place.

The team needs to achieve and maintain a level of confidence in itself, its ability, and the process. One of the initial critical mistakes made in the master-planned community arena is the lack of confidence in what the master-planned community can do. Too many experienced developers say that the community association is a necessary evil. To the contrary, understanding community associations and using them wisely and well will allow the project to work.

The team needs to guard against overreacting and must bear in mind that threats and intimidation rarely achieve a positive result. In the short term, threats produce the desired result by pushing people into silence and acceptance; however, the long-term result is the creation of a body of opposition destined to ensure that the long-range prognosis is negative. The team needs to be creative, and it needs to anticipate what is about to happen. Working through a distressed master-planned community should be a process that begins before the master-planned community is in default.

The team should adopt a preventive approach and take steps to anticipate and plan for the operation of the association and any potential problems. For example, the team should perform legal and operational audits at different stages of the project's life. Seminars for marketing people and the operational staff can ensure that that marketing representations are exactly as intended and that those operating the association on behalf of the developer know their duties and responsibilities as well as the limits on their power.

A periodic document review should ensure that changes may be made, structures altered, and actions taken before the problem reaches its worst. A disclosure certificate, a warranty certificate, and other disclosure methods should be a standard part of the sales documentation. Early on, a title review should ensure that terms are consistent among the project documentation, the loan documentation, and the title documents. The title review should take place after the land acquisition closing when all the dust has settled and all the heat, tension, and pressures of the moment have evaporated. At this early stage, curative actions can be taken that do not then become bargaining chips in a negotiating strategy. Before problems reach an acute stage, everyone will want to cure a title defect. Later, it may be necessary to pay some extortionate request to a group whose consent is a prerequisite to effecting a cure that truly benefits everyone.

In the early stages, all concerned need to understand the risks and theory involved in community association development. They need to be active and not just reactive, and, most important, they need to be willing to learn. Perhaps the final note should be that all those involved should be as professional and innovative on the process side as they are on the product side in the creation, operation, and, if necessary, restructuring of the master-planned community. If so, both the product and process will be successes.

Creating the Community: Senior Housing and the Fair Housing Act

■ I. Introduction

A developer of a senior housing community must thoroughly understand the Fair Housing Act's prohibition against discrimination on the basis of familial status. Penalties for violating the Fair Housing Act include compensatory and punitive damages (including damages for emotional distress), injunctive relief, and imprisonment. A senior housing community is not subject to this prohibition if it falls within one of several narrowly defined exemptions from the Fair Housing Act. A developer of senior housing must be certain about which exemption he or she intends to use and have a plan for satisfying all of the requirements of the exemption.

■ II. Scope of the Fair Housing Act

The Fair Housing Act, 42 U.S.C. §3604 et seq. (the Act) prohibits discrimination in the provision of housing on account of race, color, religion, sex, or national origin. The Act is monitored and enforced by the U.S. Department of Housing and Urban Development (HUD). In 1988, the Act was amended to include familial status and handicap as protected classes under the Act. This amendment prevents discrimination against families with children in the provision of housing and related services. Familial status is defined as one or more individuals who have not attained the age of 18 being domiciled with a parent or legal guardian or the designee of such person. Familial status also includes any person who is pregnant and anyone in the process of acquiring legal custody of a child.

Providing separate housing for senior citizens violates the Act's prohibition against discrimination on the basis of familial status unless the senior housing fits into one of the three exemptions from the Act. The first exemption is for housing that is provided under any state or federal program and that is designed and operated to assist older persons and approved by the secretary of HUD.

The second exemption is for housing intended for, *and solely occupied by*, persons age 62 or older. A developer who intends to use this exemption must ensure that only people age 62 and older occupy the housing. If any occupant is under 62, the housing provider will be considered to discriminate on the basis of familial status and will be in violation of the Act.

The first two exemptions are straightforward and infrequently relied on by developers of senior housing because of their inflexibility. Thus, this article focuses on the exemption that is most likely to be used by developers of senior housing. This third and most significant exemption is the one provided for housing for older persons. Older persons are defined in the Act as being 55 years old or older. Housing intended and operated for occupancy by older persons is exempt from the Act if the "housing provider" satisfies three criteria: the 80 percent requirement, the provision of significant facilities and services, and the publication of and adherence to policies and procedures.

A housing provider under the Act is the owner or manager of a housing facility or the owner or manager of any common property included in the senior housing community. Initially, this is likely to be the developer and eventually may be a community or condominium association. See *Massaro v. Mainlands Section 1 & 2 Civic Association*, 3 F.3d 1472 (11th Cir. 1993).

1. The 80 Percent Requirement

At least 80 percent of all occupied units must be occupied by persons age 55 or older in order to qualify for the exemption for housing for older persons. For new communities, the 80 percent requirement goes into effect once 25 percent of the planned units are occupied.

The minimum number of units that must be occupied by persons who meet the age requirement is set at 80 percent rather than 100 percent to allow younger spouses continued occupancy of a unit if the person who is 55 or older dies or otherwise ceases to reside in the unit. In addition, the 80 percent requirement allows heirs or other successors in title to a unit to occupy it even if they do not meet the age requirement.

The developer of a senior housing community should take a regular census of all residents to ensure that the 80 percent requirement is met. It is important that the developer always have proof that the senior housing community satisfies the 80 percent requirement. If a charge of discrimination is ever brought against a developer, the developer must be able to document that the housing satisfied the exemption requirements at the time indicated in the complaint (that may be several years earlier).

The 80 percent requirement applies to occupants, not owners. Therefore, merely keeping track of the age of title holders will not be sufficient to ensure that the community meets the 80 percent requirement. The developer of a senior housing community should require all owners to provide notice of the date of birth of the occupants of the unit whether they are tenants, family members, or others.

The developer of a senior housing community should not use the 80 percent requirement as an opportunity to allow adults who are not 55 or older to occupy 20 percent of the units. While this practice technically may be correct, it does not allow for the strong likelihood that older residents will die while younger residents will continue to live in the units, and consequently the number of occupants over the age of 55 will fall below the 80 percent requirement. In addition, in the event that an enforcement action is brought against the community, HUD will not look favorably on a developer who takes advantage of the 80 percent requirement and will most likely use it as evidence that the community was not intended to provide housing to people over age 55 as a good faith exemption from the Act.

2. Significant Facilities and Services

The second requirement of the exemption for housing for people age 55 and older is that the housing include significant facilities and services that are specifically designed to meet the physical or social needs of older persons. The term "significant facilities and services" is not defined in the Act, and this omission has caused much confusion. HUD has proposed regulations to define the term, but the regulations have not been formally adopted.

The key to satisfying the significant facilities and services requirement is offering facilities and services that set the community apart as a senior housing community. The regulations that were published in 1988 at the time familial status was included in the Fair Housing Act provide several examples of facilities and services that meet the physical or social needs of older persons, but these examples are not intended to be exhaustive. They include

- social and recreational programs;

- educational programs (designed to serve the interests of an older population);

- property maintenance and referral services;

- a physically accessible environment;

- information and counseling about services for older people;

- emergency and preventive health care services;

- transportation within the community and to social services, shopping, etc.; and

- congregate dining facilities and other services designed to encourage residents to use the services available to them.

The facilities and services provided in conjunction with senior housing must be significant. The legislative history of the 1988 amendment to the Act states that the installation of a ramp at the front entrance to a building or the provision of minor amenities such as placing a couch in a laundry room and calling the room a recreation center are not significant.

The proposed regulations to the Act state that the facilities and services must meet the current and future health, safety, or leisure needs of an aging population. One of the basic premises behind the proposed regulations is that as the population ages, the facilities and services must be made accessible to them. The proposed regulations require that a housing provider show a willingness to accommodate the special needs of an aging population.

The proposed regulations use the accessibility requirements under the Americans with Disabilities Act (ADA) as a threshold test. If a facility or service does not satisfy the ADA, it will not count toward meeting the significant facilities and services requirement of the Act. This should not create a problem for developers of new housing since all new construction must meet the requirements of the ADA.

Once the threshold test of accessibility is met, HUD will consider whether other factors demonstrate that the facility or service is specifically designed to meet the physical or social needs of older persons. This inquiry will focus on whether the facility or service is generally beneficial to all people (such as a swimming pool) or whether it is particularly helpful to older persons (such as arthritis relief classes that are taught in the swimming pool). HUD will then evaluate the facilities and services designed to meet the needs of older persons in the aggregate to determine if they are significant.

Irrespective of whether the proposed regulations are adopted, it is clear that Congress intended the exemption from the Act for housing for older persons to apply to bona fide senior housing facilities. A developer's provision of facilities and services demonstrates that the community is meant for seniors and makes the community more attractive to its target market. Additional facilities and services a developer could provide in a senior housing community include

- handicap-accessible amenities such as swimming pool ramps rather than stairs or ladders;

- handrails in all bathroom facilities in common areas and units;

- laundry and housekeeping services;

- trash pickup from each unit;

- sidewalks, benches, and rest areas throughout the community;

- landscaping services for each unit;

- emergency call buttons for emergency health care and security; and

- "neighborhood watch-"type programs where, in addition to security awareness, neighbors check in on each other daily and contact the property manager if a neighbor misses check-in or the mail for a unit has not been collected.

The developer itself can provide the facilities and services to the community, or it can create or contract with another entity to do so. It is essential, however, that the developer demonstrate that it supports (either financially or otherwise) the facilities and services. Many developers transfer responsibility for providing facilities and services to a homeowners' or condominium association. Others have successfully created tax-exempt entities under Section 501(c)(3) of the Internal Revenue Code to provide these facilities and services. The developer may be able to donate land, buildings, or equipment to the 501(c)(3) entity and deduct the value of such donation from its income for federal income tax purposes. Some developers also have been able to qualify land dedicated to the provision of facilities and services as exempt from state property taxes. The donated land, buildings, or equipment is then used as the base for providing facilities and services to the community.

3. Policies and Procedures

In addition to meeting the 80 percent requirement and providing significant facilities and services in conjunction with housing, the developer, and eventually the community, must publish and adhere to policies and procedures that demonstrate an intent to provide housing for people age 55 or older.

The regulations to the Act provide several examples of places where policies and procedures demonstrating an intent to provide senior housing should be included. These are

- descriptions of the community;

- marketing materials and other sales representations;

- age verification procedures;

- covenants or lease provisions;

- written rules and regulations; and

- actual practices in enforcing the relevant lease provisions or rules and regulations.

All representations about the community should indicate that it is a senior housing community. In addition, the age restriction must be enforced against all prospective residents who are not 55 or older; HUD has charged many communities with violation of the Act because the age restriction was enforced against children but not against adults under 55.

In addition, the developer or community association must create policies and procedures for verifying the residents' ages in order to ensure that the 80 percent requirement is met. In a case brought against a Florida homeowners' association, one factor cited by the federal appeals court in ruling that the association violated the Act was the failure to use reliable procedures for verifying the age of residents. Rather than merely asking the residents how old they were, the association should have kept copies of driver's licenses, birth certificates, or some other independent proof of age (*Massaro*, 3 F.3d 1472).

■ III. Complying with the Act

Developers should ensure that they satisfy the Act at every stage of the development of a senior community. When the community is in the initial stages of development, the developer should consider creating restrictive covenants establishing the property as an age-restricted community, requiring residents to comply with the age restriction and age verification procedures, and giving a homeowners' association or some other entity the authority to enforce the age restrictions. If a developer creates a declaration of covenants, conditions, and restrictions for the community, it is imperative that a covenant restricting the age of the residents also be included. If the developer is not going to include other restrictive covenants, a deed restriction restricting age is still important to put the world on notice that the property is part of an age-restricted community and, in the event that an enforcement action is brought against the developer, to demonstrate to HUD or the courts that the community is intended to provide housing for older people.

When creating restrictive covenants, it is important to preserve the flexibility to change the community's policies in the event that the requirements of the Act change. The developer, homeowners' association, or other entity responsible for complying with the Act should have the flexibility to create reasonable rules and provide additional facilities and services if necessitated by changes in the Act. The Act is subject to careful scrutiny by HUD, Congress, and the courts, and it is essential for developers to preserve their flexibility to satisfy the requirements of the Act as it evolves.

The following are some sample provisions a developer might consider including in the recorded covenants for a senior housing community:

Age Restriction. Community X is intended to provide housing for persons 55 years of age or older. In this regard, each unit, if occupied, shall be occupied by at least one person 55 years of age or older; provided, however, that in the event that such an occupant dies or otherwise ceases to reside in the unit, the unit may be occupied by such person's cohabitant or successor-in-title, subject to the terms of this section. No person under 19 years of age shall reside in any unit for more than 90 days in any calendar year.

The properties shall be operated as an age-restricted community in compliance with all applicable state and federal laws. As required by federal law, at no time shall less than 80 percent of the units subject to this declaration be occupied by single families where at least one member of the family is 55 years of age or older. The board may establish age verification procedures and enforce this age restriction in accordance with the terms of the enforcement provisions of the bylaws. The association shall provide, or contract for the provision of, significant facilities and services specifically designed to meet the physical and social needs of older persons as may be required by state or federal law. The board may establish additional policies and procedures from time to time, as necessary, to maintain Community X's status as an age-restricted community under state and federal law.

Age Restriction. Community Y is intended to provide housing for persons 55 years of age or older, and each unit in Community Y, if occupied, shall be occupied by at least one person 55 years of age or older (qualifying occupant). No person under 19 years of age shall reside in any unit for more than 90 days in any calendar year.

The Properties shall be operated in an age-restricted community in compliance with all applicable state and federal laws. In the event that any qualifying occupant dies or otherwise ceases to reside in the unit, the unit may be occupied by such person's cohabitant or successor-in-title to the extent permitted by applicable federal and state laws regarding age-restricted communities and provided that at no time shall less than 80 percent of the units subject to this declaration be occupied by single families where at least one member of the family is a qualifying occupant. The board may establish policies and procedures from time to time as necessary to maintain Community Y's status as an age-restricted community under state and federal law. The association shall provide, or contract for the provision of, those facilities and services designed to meet the physical and social needs of older persons as may be required under such laws.

The developer of a senior housing community should not assume that its responsibility for complying with the terms of the Act is complete when restrictive covenants intended to comply with the Act are recorded. The developer should also ensure that all marketing materials indicate that the community is intended for older persons. In addition, the developer's contracts for the sale or lease of property should indicate that the housing must be occupied by a person 55 or older.

Finally, the developer should give the community the framework it needs to ensure continued compliance with the Act. This involves creating age verification procedures (such as a policy requiring the property manager or sales agent to photocopy a birth certificate, driver's license, AARP membership card, or other document showing proof that the resident is 55 or over), establishing facilities and services to serve the needs of older persons, and providing a mechanism for adapting these facilities and services to the needs of its aging community.

Enforcement actions under the Act can be brought by HUD or the United States attorney general. In addition, individuals who claim they have been discriminated against in the provision of housing can sue the housing provider. Once a claim that a community violates the Act is made, the community or developer has the burden of proving that all elements of the Act have been satisfied. For this reason, good record keeping by the developer, the homeowners' association, or another entity is essential. In the event that a developer or community is found to be in violation of the Act, penalties can include fines, significant monetary damages, injunctive relief, and imprisonment. (A federal jury recently awarded $390,500 in compensatory and punitive damages to families that brought suit under the Act against a 336-home community: *Baby Girl Sarah Bradley* v. *Lime Tree Village Community Club*, No. 90-703-CIV- URL-19 (M.D. Fla. 10-27-93).)

■ IV. Conclusion

The Fair Housing Act must be addressed by developers of senior housing when initial plans for the community are made. Developers should consider how they will qualify for an exemption from the Act and what mechanisms they can create to ensure that every element of the Act is satisfied. For many developers of new senior housing communities, record keeping will be the most challenging part of complying with the Act because the facilities, services, and restrictive covenants will be necessary to make the community marketable. Developers of senior housing communities can successfully create marketable age-restricted communities that comply with the Fair Housing Act by considering the requirements of the Act at the beginning of development planning, by keeping careful records, and by giving the community the facilities, enforcement power, and flexibility it needs to comply with the Act as it may change over time.

APPENDIX 6

Creating Community And Governance: A New Perspective

©1994 by Hyatt & Stubblefield, P.C.

■ I. Introduction

The menace to America today is the emphasis on what separates us rather than on what brings us together. I am wary of the emphasis on power rather than on the sense of community.—Daniel J. Boorstin

How does one maintain the sense of community while properly exercising the power of governance within that community? What principles and procedures guide persons responsible for administering the community association governance structure as they seek to discharge increasingly weighty obligations while, at the same time, protecting the delicate balance between the needs and rights of the community and the needs and rights of the individuals residing therein? Acknowledging that governance systems are designed to govern and that community associations are far more than collectives of free spirits vested with total individual rights, one must seek new approaches to allow community associations to evolve and to achieve and maintain this delicate balance.

In the context of this paper, "community association" refers not to a neighborhood or civic group but rather to a mandatory membership entity comprised of all property owners in a real estate development. However, in a larger sense, the term "community" reflects a generally accepted definition of a group of people living together and having interests in common as in a "society"; in both, it indicates a sharing of common interests. Successful community associations are ones that have a workable, internal society as well as working relationships with the larger, external society. They have a social structure that is, of course, at least in part a function of governance.

In approaching a discussion of governance systems, it is important to recognize the impact of "governance" on various facets of community association activity. First, there is the obvious concern of the balance of the rights of the "community" and the rights of the individual residing within that community. While simplicity and flexibility are highly desirable qualities, particularly from the association's perspective, the individual will look for and expect a degree of certainty that will provide both a sense of what the rules are and a reasonable assurance that the rules will not so drastically change during a period of ownership as to make that ownership no longer desirable.

Beyond those directly involved with community associations, there are broader societal concerns. Should the public become convinced that community association living is a lifestyle of conformity, control, and constraint, buyers will avoid it. This, in turn, will reduce significantly the available housing stock and will damage producers, consumers, and local governments. Sadly, the damage would have no compensating benefit. There is no technical or anecdotal evidence to support the conclusion that the more highly regulated a community, the better that community is. There is, however, an increasing body of evidence that excessive regulation results in a diminution of the quality of life.

Quality of life and lifestyle present the third area of concern on the impact of governance. The highly egocentric individual perhaps does not belong in a community association where his or her interests run clearly and strongly counter to the degrees of conformity that are required in any "community." By the same token, community is not synonymous with conformity, and the challenge for those involved in creation and operation is making one consistent with the other. Highly regulated and formalized governance structures are, perhaps, inconsistent with the flexibility necessary to make a community successful; historically, well-settled—ancient perhaps—principles of property law have made this flexibility even more difficult to achieve.

The concern, then, for the community developer and the lawyer drafter should be the development of a system that works. Within the context of this discussion, "what works" means a system that contains a governance mechanism that balances multiple interests, preserves the functions of the community association, protects the flexibility necessary to permit an association to remain dynamic during periods of change, and reasonably protects the property owners' expectations for an appropriate degree of certainty and reliance interests.

This paper seeks to explore these issues and to recommend an approach to reconcile them. The approach offered is neither the exclusive nor necessarily perfect solution; in reality, experience tells us that few solutions are. However, as with earlier articles, the author seeks to offer a workable proposal and to generate discussion and intellectual participation in order ultimately to improve the proposal itself.

The paper will follow four steps. First, it will examine current legal principles that shed light on both the concerns and possible solutions. Next, it will review the evolution of board power, adducing certain basic principles, including the limits on these powers. Third, it will acknowledge what appears to be a reasonably well-accepted view of the process for board operation and the applicable standards. Finally, the paper will suggest an alternative.

■ II. The Current Tangle of Legal Principles

The law that will work is merely the summing up in legislative form of the moral judgment that the community has already reached.—Woodrow Wilson

Two recent cases well illustrate the conflicts inherent in community association governance structures and the courts' responses to these conflicts. The two cases illustrate what might be called the "modern view" and a more "traditional" approach. Irrespective of labels, however, they do frame the discussion.

The first case[1] concerned a blanket restriction contained in the covenants, conditions, and restrictions prohibiting pets in the community. The unit owner had three kittens that clearly constituted a de facto violation of the restriction. The issue, however, became one of the validity of the restriction itself. Under applicable statutory provision,[2] a covenant restriction is enforceable if reasonable.

From a reading of the opinion, it becomes clear that the kittens were not a substantial source of disruption and annoyance outside the unit. To the contrary, the facts indicate that the association, through its manager and others, went to some pains to investigate what was transpiring inside the unit in order to support their charge that *Nahrstedt* had violated the restriction. The essential issue appeared to be whether a blanket restriction was enforceable; however, the appeals court took a different approach.

Rejecting case law from such jurisdictions as New York, Florida, and Maryland, the court pointed out that these earlier cases neither concerned blanket restrictions nor involved statutory requirements of reasonableness. The court further pointed out that none of these earlier cases "examined the particular facts . . . to see if the challenged restrictions were reasonable as applied to those facts."[3] Describing this approach of factual analysis as "the California way," the court held that the question under §1354 is a "mixed issue of law and fact that can be resolved only in the context of the particular circumstances of this case."[4] In other words, the court converted the issue of the validity of a blanket restriction to a question of the validity on a case-by-case restriction. Such an approach seems to ignore the fundamental question of the validity of a blanket restriction itself without regard to whether one kitten is acceptable whereas a rapacious tomcat might not be. The fact was that the restriction prohibited animals.

In language that is significant without regard to the issue of blanket or nonblanket restrictions, the court pointed out that covenants are "reasonable . . . when they prohibit conduct that, while otherwise lawful, in fact interferes with, or has a reasonable likelihood of interfering with, the rights of other condominium owners to the peaceful and quiet enjoyment of their property."[5] One could reasonably suggest that "the reasonable likelihood of interfering with the rights of other condominium owners" is clearly and sufficiently established by the covenants setting forth the original "plan of development" containing the pet restriction. In the case of Lakeside Village, the plan was for a "petless community."

One could argue that this court missed or ignored the basic point that there is a considerable difference in a document provision and a resolution subsequently adopted by a board of directors imposing such a restriction. In articulating what is generally accepted as an article of faith in the "traditional view," the court pointed out that the "Plaintiff's condominium home is her castle and her enjoyment of it should be by the least restrictive means possible, conducive with the harmonious living arrangement."[6] The dissenting judge pointed out that he has "never seen a condominium that even remotely resembled a castle."[7]

In rejecting the traditional approach, the dissent makes five significant points. First, it states that the question is "distinctly not" a mixed issue of fact and law. Second, it reiterates a frequently seen point that courts should leave enforcement to the associations unless constitutional principles are involved, the enforcement is arbitrary, or the board fails to follow its prescribed procedures. Third, the dissent argues for a rule of judicial economy, and fourth, it points out that there is a more modern approach that effectuates the intent of the parties at the time of the creation of the covenant. Clearly, in a covenant prohibiting pets, the intent is reasonably explicit that the community should be petless.

Finally, in language all of us should be willing to consider seriously if not immediately to accept, the dissent states that it rejects legal rules "borrowed from real property principles developed during feudal times."[8] Not only is this a shot across the battlements of the "castle," but it is also a reaffirmation of the Mississippi Supreme Court's statement that community associations were something new and different and should be judged by the emerging body of community association law rather than by real estate principles having no real applicability to the community association concept.[9]

The traditional view, perhaps "the California Way,"[10] might be summarized as follows. Free use of land is favored. Covenant interpretation should be most restrictive against those provisions that restrict an individual's free use. Intent must clearly appear from the covenant. Land use restrictions should be drafted initially and made difficult to change. This has led to the so called "bullet-proof" restriction with judicial analysis of covenants still predicated primarily upon a view that restrictive covenants are biparty and issue-specific rather than part of the dynamics of community creation.

In *Markey* v. *Wolf*,[11] Maryland's Court of Special Appeals approached the issue differently and reached a significantly different conclusion, articulating a "modern view."[12] *Markey* concerned the issue of downsizing. The builders within the community, after a number of homes were sold, sought to build smaller, less expensive houses that dropped from a 2,000-square-foot average to an 1,800-square-foot average. While unable to show direct reliance on any representation that houses would be of a certain size or a certain price, existing property owners sued to compel the developer to exercise its design review authority to ensure that no houses smaller than the existing structures would be constructed and sold.

The court first established that there was a general plan of development, thus validating the covenants, conditions, and restrictions. Second, the court asked the question of how the covenants should be interpreted. Examining and discarding the "old rule," the court announced that there was a "modern rule" and explained it as follows:

> In interpreting . . . the court should endeavor to ascertain the real purpose and intention of the parties and to discover the purpose from the surrounding

circumstances at the time of the creation of the restriction . . . .[13]

The court stated further that words should be interpreted in their ordinary sense unless the context in that they appeared plainly indicated otherwise. This seems to shift the burden traditionally applied and permits words to be given a broad, *ordinary* interpretation in the absence of some indication that they should be more restrictively interpreted.

The court examined a "historical" line of cases, and this examination provides an excellent background for further analysis. At the conclusion of that examination, the court articulated what it refers to as a "cardinal principle."

First, the court said that the express or implied intentions of the parties control. The key word in that sentence is "implied." Second, the court said that strict construction should not defeat a covenant clearly on its face or from the surrounding circumstances. Lastly, the court pointed out that one who creates a covenant may reserve the right to waive or amend that covenant if such reservation of rights is included in the instrument. The court noted that the ability to vary the general plan and the application of this power did not constitute an attempt to abrogate the plan. If it did,

> [T]he reasonableness rule might require us to reverse. We are, however, . . . concerned not with the protection of the value of the property but how much protection those values are entitled to under the restriction.[14]

Finally, the court pointed out that public policy supported lower-priced housing as preferable to no housing at all.

In rejecting the homeowners' contention that the developer had to exercise its review process to maintain the size and prices of housing, the court did more than just reinforce the modern rule. It made clear the importance of the original intention of the circumstances surrounding the creation of the covenant and of the power to alter. It echoed and reinforced the arguments raised in the *Nahrstedt* dissent and in the *Lakes at Mercer Island* case. Perhaps most important, it continued to reinforce the foundation upon which one might build an alternative approach to governance.

That foundation is one of flexibility, intent, and the capacity to adjust to meet changes in circumstances. It is not one of rigidity and of everything spelled out in "bullet-proof" language. Before looking at that alternative, however, it is appropriate to examine the existing law dealing with the power of the board.

■ III. The Evolution of Board Power

Sunlight is the best of all disinfectants.—Louis Brandeis

The Board's Power. Initially, it is worthwhile to acknowledge where board power comes from, what it is, and what is its scope. Clearly, one must embrace the concept of "power source" by articulating that the association and the board receive their powers from the existing documentation for the community association, be it the declaration or the bylaws.[15] Four cases illustrate how this power has been treated over the years.

In *Hidden Harbor Estates, Inc.* v. *Norman,*[16] often considered the "basic case," a Florida appeals court said that a community association could make rules if they were reasonable. The court also made clear that the individual's right to use her property was subordinate to the rules necessary to support the community into which the individual had purchased. The unanswered question in *Norman* was what reasonableness meant and how it was to be applied.

In a subsequent case, the appeals court dealt with the issue of board power more specifically. The case, *Hidden Harbor Estates, Inc.* v. *Basso,*[17] drew a distinction between provisions contained in the basic documentation and restrictions enacted through board resolution. In *Basso,* the court stated that provisions contained within the document did not have to be reasonable. The buyer agreed to be bound by them by purchasing in accordance with those governing documents.

Reasonableness, however, the court pointed out, became important in analyzing the postpurchase actions of a board. The rule of reasonableness acted as a "fetter" on the board's discretion and thus limited its legislative powers. This is important from several perspectives: it constitutes an important restraint on the board and acknowledges that the board does have the power to impose postpurchase restrictions, thus institutionalizing an ongoing legislative process within the community itself.

In *Laguna Royale Owners Association* v. *Darger*,[18] a California court sought to define reasonableness. In that case, the primary issue was the right of an individual to sell his unit to three others, each of whom would take a quarter ownership, thus resulting in four owners each assigned a three-month period for the use and enjoyment of the unit. Laying aside all of the issue-specific facts, the important point is that the court sought to enunciate a standard to determine what was or was not an appropriate governance action within the association.

The court said that in order to be approved, activities must bear a reasonable relationship to the protection, preservation, or proper operation of the community as defined in the "governing instruments" and that the regulations must be fair and reasonable. Rejecting legal principles "borrowed from the law of landlord and tenant developed during the feudal period of English history,"[19] the court used a balancing test to conclude, as it pertained to the facts of the particular case, that Darger's rights overwhelmed those of the association.

The fourth case not only articulates an expansive view but also is a precursor of the suggested alternative contained in the final segment of this paper. In *Beechwood Villas* v. *Poor*,[20] a Florida appeals court examined the validity of a board's action in adopting regulations limiting the rental of units. The reasonableness of the regulation itself was not in question; thus, the court's analysis was directed at determining whether the board had acted within the scope of its authority. The aggrieved homeowner had argued that the board had only such power as reasonably to be inferred from the declaration, but the court rejected this formulation as too restrictive and pointed out that the declaration was in essence "the condominium's constitution."[21] The court then articulated a far-reaching principle as follows:

Often, it [a declaration of condominium] contains broad statements of general policy with due notice that the board of directors is empowered to implement these policies and address day-to-day problems in the condominium's operation through the rulemaking process. It would be impossible to list all restrictive uses in a declaration of condominium. Parking regulations, limitations on the use of the swimming pool, tennis court, and card room—the list is endless and subject to constant modification. Therefore, we have formulated the appropriate test in this fashion: Provided that a board-enacted rule does not contravene either an express provision of the declaration or a right reasonably inferable therefrom, it will be found valid, within the scope of the board's authority. This test, in our view, is fair and functional; it safeguards the rights of unit owners and preserves unfettered the concept of delegated board management.[22]

In reviewing that language, certain phrases become extremely significant. The first is "unfettered board management." The second is "fair and functional." The third is "safeguards the rights of unit owners." The point is that the *Beechwood* court chose not only an expansive view of the board's power consistent with such cases as *Markey, Lakes at Mercer Island*, and others but also shows that "it would be impossible to list all restrictive uses in a declaration."[23] Common sense dictates that the effort to list all potential restrictions would choke the sense of community and would impose such a formalized, legalistic structure as to make living within that community highly unattractive and potentially Orwellian.

Implicit in this discussion is the nature and extent of the inherent power of a community association. Is it limited to the delegated powers? If, as *Beechwood* indicates, the answer is "no," then silence means or can mean empowerment. If "yes," the association has only expressed powers. This paper asserts that "power" to regulate once established allows, indeed requires, regulations to evolve rather than equating "power" to "listing." A governance system is based upon the power to govern rather than a recitation of rules.

In summary, these illustrative cases show that there is broad express and implied authority, that authority and regulation set forth in the governing documents are less subject to challenge, and that there is a mandate for board governance. There are, however, limits.

What Natural Limits Apply to the Board's Power? There are some "natural" limits on the board's authority and to the somewhat expansive reading contained in *Beechwood.* For example, the regulation may fail because it seeks to regulate the subject matter over which the association has no jurisdiction,[24] or the association may seek to deprive owners of their interest in the common elements that, of course, will not be permitted.[25] A regulation that is otherwise procedurally and substantively correct and reasonable may not "create invidious classifications within the ownership/membership group or unfairly diminish the rights of some owners for the benefit of others."[26]

Likewise, an association may act in good faith but find that the regulation is improper because it is outside the power source.[27] By the same token, an association through its board may seek to exercise implied powers but find that only such implied powers as are necessary to the express powers will be upheld, not those that are merely convenient or desirable.[28]

Other cases find natural limits contained within the procedures established by the documents. One such case[29] points out that when the covenants contain a detailed review and hearing procedure, the association must show that it has followed its own standards and procedures, that those procedures were fair and reasonable, and that its substantive decision was in good faith, reasonable, and not arbitrary.

What Emerging Restraints Apply? Restraints on board power emanate from many sources and may be direct as with statutes or indirect and merely persuasive as with the restatement, articles, etc. These "restraints" include statutes, the restatement of servitudes, law review and other scholarly articles, articles in the general press, legislative hearings, and statements not rising to the level of legislation but influencing public and judicial opinion nonetheless, among other sources. Restraints also come from a general misunderstanding of the process affecting some who become part of community associations as well as the occasional and perhaps increasingly seen board that is overly aggressive in the exercise of its power. It is also true, however, that this overly aggressive approach stems from documents layered with restrictions, thus inviting unnecessary, ill-advised enforcement.

These "marketplace" restraints have a substantial impact on both the community and its governance. This is particularly true as those involved in the creation and sale of community associations react to the negative publicity and the attendant impact on sales that results from news articles, popular dissatisfaction, and legislative discourse relating to "overrestrictive" communities. The effect of these influences may be hard to understand by those not involved in direct participation in either creation or operation of community associations; for the lawyer, seller, manager, board member, or other who does experience that participation, however, the restraints are real indeed.

Without perhaps being aware of it, the courts have continued to shape an evolving board power in a way that provides a response to these restraints while identifying a reasonably recognized procedure as the standard for board decision making. This standard is, of course, the business judgment rule.

The Business Judgment Rule. This rule has been widely discussed,[30] and that discussion need not be repeated. Two cases illustrate the principle. The first case is *Schoninger* v. *Yardarm Beach Homeowners Association, Inc.,*[31] a New York case in which the unit owner challenged a maintenance decision of the board. That unit owner preferred a different maintenance and repair program. The court rejected the challenge.

> What is being challenged here is a decision by the board to pursue one program of repair rather . . . than another . . . . Upon such circumstances, the application of a loosely defined reasonableness standard of review is not appropriate. Rather, the circumstances call for the application of the business-judgment rule, that acts as a restraint on judicial interference into the corporate decision-making process.[32]

The court pointed out that the business judgment rule requires that the board act within its authority and that it act with good faith and in a nondiscriminatory manner. The court said that the decision needed to further legitimate interests of the association.

This is simply another way of saying that the decision must be intra vires. So long as the board has acted in accordance with the business judgment rule, courts will not question the "wisdom or soundness" of its decision.

The second case is *Levandusky* v. *One Fifth Avenue Apartment Corp.*,[33] which concerned a dispute over steam risers within the cooperative. Although the facts are not significant for our purposes, the court's rationale certainly is. In *Levandusky*, the court made it clear that the business judgment rule was applicable to all board actions and was not limited exclusively to businesslike decisions as seen in the *Shoninger* facts.[34] In announcing the rule and its application, the court pointed out that "a governing board may severely restrict the bundle of rights a property owner normally enjoys." Therefore, a standard to control that power is appropriate: Some check on the board's "potential powers to regulate residents' conduct, life-style, and property rights is necessary to protect the individual residents from abusive exercise."[35] The court went on to issue a warning, however, by pointing out that any rule adopted and any application "must not undermine the purpose" of the community association that the court finds to be the "protection of the interest of the entire community."[36] In other words, the rule must be one that balances the competing interests contained within in the community itself.

In *Levandusky*, the court rejected the application of the rule of reasonableness as the test for board action. It pointed out that the difference between the reasonableness test and the business judgment rule is two-pronged. First, in a reasonableness standard, the burden of proof rests with the board and, second, the reasonableness test permits or indeed requires the court to evaluate the merits or wisdom of the board's decision and potentially to substitute its judgment for the board's. The court noted that boards have the expertise and the experience beyond that of the judiciary and, perhaps most important, truly understand what is or is not important within a particular community. The court pointed to emotions involved in a community association and the fact that the board rather than the court knows and understands the combined effect of the property, the owners, and the issues. Therefore, the court held, the owner should not have the opportunity to reopen a legislatively determined activity from the governing body of the association.

The application of this corporate standard to the activities of community associations and its increasing acceptance by courts reinforces the argument that so long as a governing body acts within applicable basic principles, the board has the authority to make the decisions needed. It then becomes incumbent upon one proposing a methodology for that decision making to see what the current standard is and to show that the business judgment rule in combination with current case law supports a more innovative approach.

It is also vital that one acknowledge that business judgment provides an opportunity to *make judgments*, that is to decide whether something should be done or should not be done. Inherent in this acknowledgment would be the power of the board to decide whether or not to enforce a restriction. For example, if the gravamen of the unreasonableness of a cat restriction is that no one knew the cat was even in the unit without peeking through the window, a board should have the authority to determine in its best business judgment not to institute litigation. In other words, judgment is encompassing, not limiting.

■ IV. Acknowledge a Process and a Standard

The perpetual obstacle to human advancement is custom.—
John Stuart Mill

As one discusses the governance structure for a community and uses language evermore "governmental," it is appropriate to acknowledge the potential for courts to review these actions according to constitutional standards. Although some courts have done so, the action of private communities such as condominium and homeowners' associations generally are recognized as not constituting "state action" unless there is such a close nexus between state regulation and the challenged actions of the association that those actions can be said to emanate from or to be attributed to state government.[37]

If, in the absence of extraordinary circumstances, state action and thus constitutional principles do not apply, what are the generally accepted standards? They are, first, certain elements of "fundamental fairness" in the operation of the association. These include the fact that the board has a duty to act when presented with business and governmental decisions and that the decision is to be made in accordance with the business judgment rule and, when appropriate, the rule of reasonableness. A board, of course, must act within its power source, express or implied, and must acknowledge that there are limits to its authority. The limit to the authority should not, however, be interpreted always to require that the board make a certain decision but should acknowledge that the authority relies on the board to exercise judgment.

Fairness and a successful governance structure within a community would anticipate the emotionalism involved as several courts have noted and would require all concerned to acknowledge that the governance challenge is much more complex than it first appears. Even what appears to be a simple case about three kittens can take on major ramifications.

If one assumes that the basic underlying principles are reasonableness, business judgment, and intra vires, one accepts the concept that the board is vested with discretion, power, and responsibility and that the board may be an active part of the regulatory *process* so long as it follows the rules set out in the association's governing instruments and in general principles of corporate and community association law. By the same token, one must acknowledge that the board may not make all decisions. Some decisions are reserved for the community association's membership either by majority or super-majority vote. Acknowledging these principles, however, does not diminish the justification for the board to have a more flexible approach to governance or for the initial governing documents to create and to institutionalize rule making as a dynamic process rather than a static recitation of scores of "thou shalt not's," many of which will never have relevance in a particular community. It is best, therefore, to look at a new approach.

■ V. A Suggested Alternative

Nothing will ever be attempted if all possible objections must first be overcome.—Samuel Johnson

Meadow Bridge Condominium Association v. *Bosca*[38] was a Michigan case concerning a *rule* that prohibited dogs in the community association. Under the bylaws, no animal was permitted unless approved by the board; elsewhere, the bylaws provided that the board could adopt such rules as it deemed proper. The board had adopted a rule prohibiting all dogs. The trial court ruled in favor of the dog and its owner, holding that the rule was in essence a bylaw amendment requiring a vote in accordance with the terms and conditions of the bylaws.

In a short, to-the-point opinion, the appellate court upheld the position of the board of directors and drew a distinction between a rule and an amendment. The distinction is significant as a general statement of the law but is even more significant as a predicate upon which to develop further an alternative strategy. The court said,

> A rule . . . is a tool to implement or manage existing structural law while an amendment presumptively changes existing structural law.[39]

The appeals court pointed out that the rule was not inconsistent with the bylaws and that it did not change the provisions of the bylaws. In fact, the court observed that the rule set out the board's decision to "implement or manage" the pet process by prospectively denying approval. Citing the *Hidden Harbor Estates, Inc.* v. *Norman* case discussed earlier, the court held that the board's action was proper.[40]

The important clause in this discussion is that "a rule . . . is a tool to implement or manage existing structural law." What is needed in a less restrictive, more community-friendly governance structure is a framework, a base on which a board and the association membership may operate to implement or manage existing structural law to permit the regulatory process to evolve with the needs and desires of and changes within that community. Recognizing the difference in regulation and prohibition, the alternative approach involves the creation of a more legitimate governance structure and contemplates the governing documents containing only the limited number of prohibitions or significant restrictions that the developer believes to be vital to the overall development plan for the community.

Coupled with these initial provisions would be a method to permit changes and modifications in restrictions and the adoption, modification, or abrogation of regulations to be made in the "legislative process" of the community as time passes and circumstances change. In a system that provides simplicity, flexibility, and balance, it would be unnecessary initially to promulgate restrictions and prohibitions that might be, in the final analysis, inconsistent with the plan of development and the reality of the development as the community takes form, grows, and changes. Rather, the governing body—first, the board of directors and, secondarily, the membership—would have the power according to a defined procedure to make or change these provisions. In other words, one would create a governance system truly empowered to govern.

As a part of this governance system, however, it is important to provide checks and balances, disclosure of the potential consequences, and specific protections for vested rights that might have arisen as a part of a purchaser's initial acquisition. For this reason, the alternative approach contains not only empowering sections but also sections providing a "bill of rights" for the owners as well as for the developer.[41]

Attached as an exhibit to this paper is a suggested documentary provision setting forth the alternative approach. This provision seeks to incorporate the principles discussed and to create a mechanism for implementing and managing the structural law while protecting the rights of individuals. Its provisions should be self-explanatory and reflect the discussions throughout this article.

■ VI. Conclusion

> *Chaos is the law of nature. Order is the hope of man.*—
> Henry Adams

In an earlier article,[42] the author engaged in a lengthy discussion on the body of law comprising community association law and how that law should be approached and analyzed. It is unnecessary and inappropriate to reprise that discussion in full here; rather, it seems sufficient to incorporate it by reference to the extent necessary to reinforce the general discussions of the standards and principles applicable to the governance process. The purpose of this article is not to explore the law in depth but to identify a problem and to propose a solution consistent with the law.

To the extent that the result of this article and the acceptance of the suggested premises and alternatives is that drafters must do things differently and that certainty must give way to a combination of certainty and flexibility, so be it. In fact, communities are not static, and the governance structures for communities, whether public or private, may not be static either. To those who would say that the alternative is a departure from the old way of drafting and structuring covenants, I would say it is a departure. However, the departure is consistent with the modern view of covenant law, the emerging, growing law of community associations, and the practical realities of developing, marketing, operating, and living in community associations that are truly communities.

Once again, the hope and expectation of this article is that it will provide a basis for legal drafters, scholars, and others involved in the industry to discuss needs and options. The author has been using the suggested alternative for several years in documentation, and the initial experience is positive. Community associations and community association law are both evolving, growing concepts. In the process of that evolution and growth, mistakes will be made and victories achieved. Making a mistake is no sin if we learn from it and build on it, and victories are never achieved unless we make the effort to try something new. Truly, "chaos is the law of nature and order the hope of man." It is up to those of us who are part of the process to determine how best to balance hope with reality.

■ Notes

1. *Nahrstedt v. Lakeside Village Condominium Association, Inc.*, 11 Cal. Rptr. 2d 299 (1992). The Supreme Court of California has granted review of this case, and accordingly it has been "depublished." As of the date of this writing, the case had not been docketed. Accordingly, one may only speculate as to the ultimate disposition. Nonetheless, the discussion and rationale articulated in the appeals court decision serves as a real-time exposition of judicial views reflecting the more traditional approach when examining community association governance issues.
2. See Cal. Civ. §1354, which states, "The covenants and restrictions in the declaration shall be enforceable equitable servitudes, unless unreasonable. . . ."
3. *Nahrstedt v. Lakeside Village Condominium Association, Inc.*, 11 Cal. Rptr. 2d 299 (1992) at 306.
4. Id. at 307.
5. Id.
6. **Id. at 308.**
7. Id. at 314.
8. Id.
9. *Perry v. Bridgetown Community Association*, 486 So. 2d 1230, 1232–33 (Miss. 1986).
10. One speculates as to the outcome of any case with great trepidation, and I do so here. However, at the end of the day, I believe that the dissent in *Nahrstedt* will more nearly resemble "the California Way" than the majority opinion.
11. 92 Md. App. 137, 607 A.2d 82 (1992).
12. One would benefit from reviewing an earlier decision of *Lakes at Mercer Island v. Witrak*, 810 P.2d 27 (Wash. App. 1991) that frames the issue of the modern view quite well and makes clear that the language of the covenant is not as significant as what the drafter was obviously trying to achieve. In essence, the

court said that the individual's free use of the property was not as significant as insuring that the individual freely enjoyed her property consistent with the plan of development into which she had purchased.

13. *Markey* v. *Wolf*, 92 Md. App. 137, 607 A.2d 82 (1992) at 90.
14. Id. at 97.
15. See, e.g., Wayne S. Hyatt, *Condominium and Homeowner Association Practice: Community Association Law* (1988).
16. 309 So. 2d 179 (Fla. 1975).
17. 393 So. 2d 637 (Fla. 1981).
18. 119 Cal. App. 3d 670, 174 Cal. Rptr. 136 (1981).
19. Id. at 143.
20. 448 So. 2d 1143 (Fla. Dist. Ct. App. 1984).
21. Id. at 1145.
22. Id.
23. Id.; *Iowa Realty Co.* v. *Jochims*, 503 N.W.2d 385 (1993).
24. See *Thanasoulis* v. *Winston Tower 200 Association, Inc.*, 519 A.2d 911 (N.J. Super. A.D. 1986) at 917 in which the court rejected an impairment of ownership rights in parking spaces.
25. Id.
26. Id.
27. See generally, *Seabrook Island Property Owners Association* v. *Pelzer*, 292 S.C. 343, 356 S.E.2d 411 (1987).
28. See generally, *Lovering* v. *Seabrook Island Property Owners Association*, 289 S.C. 77, 344 S.E.2d 862 (1986), aff'd 291 S.C. 201, 352 S.E.2d 707 (1987).
29. *Ironwood Owners Association IX* v. *Solomon*, 178 Cal. App. 3d 766, 224 Cal. Rptr. 18 (1986).
30. For a discussion of the business judgment rule, see Hyatt and Stubblefield, "The Identity Crisis of Community Associations: In Search of the Appropriate Analogy," 27 *Real Property Probate and Trust Journal* 589, Winter 1993, at 695.
31. 523 N.Y.S.2d 523, 134 A.D.2d 1 (1987).
32. Id. at 528.
33. 75 N.Y.2d 530, 553 N.E.2d 1317 (1990).
34. 553 N.E.2d 1317 (1990) at 1321.
35. Id.
36. Id.
37. Hyatt and Stubblefield, supra.
38. 187 Mich. App. 280 (1990).

39. Id. at 282.
40. Id. at 283.
41. See French, "The Constitution of a Private Residential Government Should Include a Bill of Rights," 27 *Wake Forest Law Review* 345 (1992) in which Professor Susan French, the reporter for the restatement of servitudes, discusses the importance of a bill of rights as a part of the governance structure. The author expresses his appreciation to Professor French for her comments and suggestions in reviewing the suggested governance structure, for her development of the proposed bill of rights, and for her willingness to accept suggestions and comments as that bill of rights draft was fine-tuned.
42. Hyatt and Stubblefield, supra.

■ Exhibit
Article XII
Use Guidelines and Restrictions

12.1. *Plan of Development; Applicability; Effect.* Declarant has created Pleasant View as a residential and recreational development and, in furtherance of its and every other Owner's interests, has established a general plan of development for Pleasant View as a master-planned community. The Properties are subject to land development, architectural, and design guidelines as set forth in Article XI (the design guidelines). The Properties are subject to guidelines and restrictions governing land use, individual conduct, and uses of or actions upon the Properties as provided in this Article XII. This Declaration and resolutions the Board or the Voting Members may adopt established affirmative and negative covenants, easements, and restrictions (the "Use Guidelines and Restrictions").

All provisions of this Declaration and of any Association rules shall also apply to all occupants, tenants, guests, and invitees of any Unit. Any lease on any Unit shall provide that the lessee and all occupants of the leased Unit shall be bound by the terms of this Declaration, the Bylaws, and the rules of the Association.

Declarant promulgates Pleasant View's general plan of development in order to protect all Owners' quality of life and collective interests, the aesthetics and environment within the Properties, and the vitality of and sense of community within Pleasant View all subject to the Board's and the Voting Members' ability to respond to changes in circumstances, conditions, needs, and desires within the master-planned community.

Declarant has prepared initial Use Guidelines and Restrictions that contain general provisions applicable to all of the Properties, as well as specific provisions that may vary within the Properties depending upon the location, characteristics, and intended use. Such initial Use Guidelines and Restrictions are set forth in Section 12.6. Based upon these Use Guidelines and Restrictions, the Board shall adopt the initial rules at its initial organizational meeting.

12.2. *Board Power.* Subject to the terms of this Article XII and to its duty of care and undivided loyalty to the Association and its Members, the Board shall implement and manage the Use

Guidelines and Restrictions through rules that adopt, modify, cancel, limit, create exceptions to, or expand the Use Guidelines and Restrictions. Earlier to any such action, the Board shall conspicuously publish notice of the proposal at least five business days earlier to the Board meeting at which such action is to be considered. Voting Members shall have a reasonable opportunity to be heard at a Board meeting earlier to action being taken.

The Board shall send a copy of any proposed new rule or amendment to each Owner at least 30 days earlier to its effective date. The rule shall become effective unless disapproved at a meeting by Voting Members representing at least two-thirds (2/3) of the total Class "A" votes and by the Class "B" Member, if any. The Board shall have no obligation to call a meeting of the Voting Members to consider disapproval except upon petition of the Voting Members as required for special meetings in Bylaws Section 2.4.

The Board shall have all powers necessary and proper, subject to its exercise of sound business judgment and reasonableness, to effect the powers contained in this Section 12.2.

The Board shall provide, without cost, a copy of the Use Guidelines and Restrictions and rules then in effect to any requesting Member or Mortgagee.

12.3. *Members' Power.* The Voting Members, at a meeting duly called for such purpose as provided in Bylaws Section 2.4, may adopt, repeal, modify, limit, and expand Use Guidelines and Restrictions and implementing rules by a vote of two-thirds (2/3) of the total Class "A" votes and the approval of the Class "B" Member, if any.

12.4. *Owners' Acknowledgment.* All Owners are subject to the Use Guidelines and Restrictions and are given notice that (a) their ability to use their privately owned property is limited thereby, and (b) the Board and/or the Voting Members may add, delete, modify, create exceptions to, or amend the Use Guidelines and Restrictions in accordance with Sections 12.2, 12.3, and 18.2.

Each Owner by acceptance of a deed acknowledges and agrees that the use and enjoyment and marketability of his or her property can be affected by this provision and that the Use Guidelines and Restrictions and rules may change from time to time.

12.5. *Rights of Owners.* Except as may be specifically set forth in Section 12.6, neither the Board nor the Voting Members may adopt any rule in violation of the following provisions:

(a) *Equal Treatment.* Similarly situated Owners and occupants shall be treated similarly.

(b) *Speech.* The rights of Owners and occupants to display political signs and symbols in or on their Units of the kinds normally displayed in or outside of residences located in single-family residential neighborhoods shall not be abridged, except that the Association may adopt reasonable time, place, and manner restrictions for the purpose of minimizing damage and disturbance to other Owners and occupants.

(c) *Religious and Holiday Displays.* The rights of Owners to display religious and holiday signs, symbols, and decorations in their Units of the kinds normally displayed in or outside of residences located in single-family residential neighborhoods shall not be abridged, except that the Association may adopt reasonable time, place, and manner restrictions for the purpose of minimizing damage and disturbance to other Owners and occupants.

(d) *Household Composition.* No rule shall interfere with the freedom of occupants of Units to determine the composition of their households, except that the Association shall have the power to require that all occupants be members of a single housekeeping unit and to limit the total number of occupants permitted in each Unit on the basis of the size and facilities of the Unit and its fair share use of the Common Area, including parking.

(e) *Activities within Unit.* No rule shall interfere with the activities carried on within the confines of Units, except that the Association may prohibit activities not normally associated with property restricted to residential use, and it may restrict or prohibit any activities that create monetary costs for the Association or other Owners, that create a danger to the health or safety of occupants of other Units, that generate excessive noise or traffic, that create unsightly conditions visible outside the Unit, that block the views from other Units, or that create an unreasonable source of annoyance.

(f) *Pets.* Unless the keeping of pets in any Village is prohibited by Supplemental Declaration at the time of the sale of the first Unit in such Village, no rule prohibiting the keeping of ordinary household pets shall be adopted thereafter over the objection of any affected Owner expressed in writing to the Association. The Association may adopt reasonable regulations designed to minimize damage and disturbance to other Owners and occupants, including regulations requiring damage deposits, waste removal, leash controls, noise controls, occupancy limits based on size and facilities of the Unit and fair share use of the Common Area. Nothing in this provision shall prevent the Association from requiring removal of any animal that presents an actual threat to the health or safety of residents or from requiring abatement of any nuisance or unreasonable source of annoyance.

(g) *Allocation of Burdens and Benefits.* Except as permitted by Section 2.2, the initial allocation of financial burdens and rights to use Common Areas among the various Units shall not be changed to the detriment of any Owner over that Owner's objection expressed in writing to the Association. Nothing in this provision shall prevent the Association from changing the Common Areas available, from adopting generally applicable rules for use of Common Areas, or from denying use privileges to those who abuse the Common Area, violate rules or this Declaration, or fail to pay assessments. This provision does not affect the right to increase the amount of assessments as provided in Article X.

(h) *Alienation.* No rule shall prohibit transfer of any Unit, or require consent of the Association or Board for transfer of any Unit, for any period greater than two months. The Association shall not impose any fee on transfer of any Unit greater than an amount reasonably based on the costs to the Association of the transfer.

(i) *Reasonable Rights to Develop.* No rule or action by the Association or Board shall unreasonably impede Declarant's right to develop in accordance with the Master Plan.

(j) *Abridging Existing Rights.* If any rule would otherwise require Owners to dispose of personal property that they owned at the time they acquired their Units, such rule shall not apply to any such Owners without their written consent.

12.6. *Initial Use Guidelines and Restrictions.*

(a) *General.* The Properties shall be used only for residential, recreational, and related purposes (that may include, without limitation, offices for any property manager retained by the Association or business offices for the Declarant or the Association consistent with this Declaration and any Supplemental

Declaration). Any Supplemental Declaration or additional covenants imposed on the property within any Village may impose stricter standards than those contained in this Article and the Association shall have standing and the power to enforce such standards.

(b) *Restricted Activities.* The following activities are prohibited within the Properties unless expressly authorized by, and then subject to such conditions as may be imposed by, the Board:

[Here should be inserted those restrictions that are considered *essential* to the development plan. Other restrictions as may be deemed desirable but less essential will be adopted at the board's first meeting.]

APPENDIX 7

Operating a Community Association

The person or entity in control of the association has a fiduciary obligation to that association and its members to act free of self-interest or self-dealing. A problem can arise because the declarant or successor is often in a position in which the issues have, once again, multiple edges such that decisions are most difficult to make without benefiting one interest at the expense of another.

The duty has best been summed up as one of "undivided loyalty" that applies when the board of directors of the association considers maintenance and repair contracts, operating budgets, creation of reserves, etc., and in which those in control may not make decisions for the association that benefit their own interest at the expense of the association or its members. This responsibility exists because of the special confidence placed in one who is in a position to control the interests of others. The members of the board of directors of an association have these responsibilities, and when those members are developer appointees, the risk of conflict of interest is great.

There are two levels of this obligation. One is best summarized as the requirement for members of a board of directors to exercise their decision making in accordance with sound business judgment. This can be met with ordinary and reasonable care and supervision over those to whom some authority has been delegated. The director, as with any good businessperson, must exercise good faith, diligence, care, and skill in making the association's business decisions.

The second requirement, sometimes referred to as the "higher" duty, requires the board member to disclose any real or potential conflicts of interest to avoid self-dealing and to ensure that decisions are made in the best interest of the association. Regrettably, sometimes the association's best interest is in direct contravention of the developer's or the successor's best interest. In those circumstances, the decision-making process is troublesome indeed.

As noted earlier, the association has two basic roles, that of a business and that of a "minigovernment." Therefore, the board of directors of an association functions as the board of a small business and as the governing body of a private government delivering public services. In each instance, there are rules and procedures governing the operation. As with any rules, there are sanctions imposed when the rules are not obeyed. There are areas of potential liability involved in the operation of the association that are fraught with a greater-than-normal likelihood of liability because, by their very nature, they present inherent conflicts. In the analysis of what has taken place and in the preparation of a plan for what is to take place, the team should pay particular attention to these matters, although the examination should certainly not be limited to them. Included as potential areas of conflict are the following:

- *Contracts and Leases.* These are agreements between the association and the declarant, the lender, or some entity related to either the declarant or the lender.

- *Assessments, Budgets, and Reserves.* This includes the entire topic of the adequacy of assessments; the necessity and adequacy of reserves; whether assessments have been collected in a timely fashion from owners unrelated to the developer; whether they have been collected from units, homes, or lots owned by the declarant; and how the funds have been handled, invested, and reported. All are examples of the types of issues that fall into this category. Here the required stewardship is great, yet the sophistication afforded to these aspects of association operation is often well below the necessary threshold.

- *"Acceptance" of Common Property.* It is common for a representative of the developer to do a punchlist walk-through of the common property with a representative of the association in order to develop a list of outstanding defects and a timeline for curing those defects before the assumption of maintenance responsibility by the association. This approach can work well and has in a number of projects. It does not work, however, when the representative of the association is a developer appointee and the "punchlist agreement" obviously is not one entered into as an arm's length transaction reflecting equality of bargaining power on both sides of the agreement.

- *Maintenance Decisions.* Decisions made by the board of directors as to whether or not a defect is a maintenance problem or a construction problem sometimes call for fine shades of judgment. When resulting from improper maintenance, the defect is the responsibility of the association and its members rather than the builder/seller/developer. The troublesome issue is who is making the decision, under what circumstances, and how. A developer controlled board of directors may make the right decision, but the appearance will be that it was made for an improper motive. These matters can be resolved properly, but they require considerable integrity, skill, documentation as to the rationale, and communication in order to educate those concerned as to why something was done.

- *Enforcing Obligations.* Too often representatives of the developer on a board of directors will forebear from taking judicial or non-judicial action to enforce the development documents or the rules. This forbearance is quite often the result of a desire to maintain tranquillity within the project and to avoid the appearance of dissension, litigation, and intra-association divisiveness. All of these are laudable objectives unless the underlying purpose of the forbearance is to enhance sales; thus the decision is made for a reason beneficial to the developer rather than to the association to that the board members owe their duty. The companion to this problem is the board's unwillingness to enforce obligations against the developer itself. There have been interesting cases showing the liability of individual board members who have failed to take actions for such reasons.

- *Architectural Issues.* The same basic principles apply in the overall issue of enforcing the architectural and design review process. Here, however, the potential divergence of interest is quite starkly drawn. The declarant sees the need to have unbridled freedom to permit builders to construct housing reflecting a marketplace willing to buy that housing. At the same time, the existing owners have a genuine aesthetic and economic interest in seeing the requirements and guidelines in place at the time they purchased and constructed their homes to be followed so as not to denigrate their housing, thus depreciating the value of both house and investment. The twin horns of the dilemma - certainty on the one hand and flexibility on the other - best summarize the problem. It presents some interesting challenges for those who are attempting to adjust a project's plan to reflect a dramatic alteration in the market while, at the same time, maintaining a collegial community free of dispute and litigation.

- *Claims against the Developer.* How can a developer controlled board deal with potential claims against the developmental entity that is their employer without a genuine potential for conflicting interest and widely divergent opinion as to how these issues should be resolved? Stating the problem frames it sufficiently. It is important to note that the courts have indicated that not every problem requires a litigious response, and that those tasked with making decisions in accordance with sound business judgment are afforded the freedom to do just that. Sound business judgment does not always require that the decision be one unanimously approved of by the plaintiffs' bar but rather requires an objective analysis of the facts and a decision made in good faith, with diligence, care, and skill.

There are ways to avoid or at least minimize exposure in these areas, and the due diligence examination that looks backward and forward at the same time must give these matters considerable thought. Well-drafted documentation, disclosure, homeowner involvement at an early, phased transition of control, a highly refined sensitivity to the nature of the community association and of the potential problems all can militate against making costly errors. Institutionalizing procedures and practices for association operation can not only reduce exposure for earlier actions but work to prevent innocent mistakes that might create future exposure. As part of this procedure, board decisions should be carefully considered, documented, and communicated. Finally, being certain that the association's structure is adequate, accurate, in place, and operational will in large measure significantly reduce the risks.

APPENDIX 8

Sample Provisions

■ Article XIV
Dispute Resolution and Limitation on Litigation

14.1. *Agreement to Avoid Litigation.* The declarant, the association, its officers, directors, committee members, all persons subject to this declaration, any builder, and any person not otherwise subject to this declaration who agrees to submit to this article (collectively, bound parties) agree to encourage the amicable resolution of disputes involving the properties, without the emotional and financial costs of litigation. Accordingly, each bound party covenants and agrees that those claims, grievances, or disputes described in Section 14.2 (Claims) shall be resolved using the procedures set forth in Section 14.3 in lieu of filing suit in any court.

14.2. *Claims.* Unless specifically exempted below, all claims, grievances, or disputes arising out of or relating to the interpretation, application, or enforcement of the governing documents, or the rights, obligations, and duties of any bound party under the governing documents or relating to the design or construction of improvements on the properties shall be subject to the provisions of Section 14.3.

Notwithstanding the above, unless all parties thereto otherwise agree, the following shall not be claims and shall not be subject to the provisions of Section 14.3:

(a) any suit by the association against any bound party to enforce the provisions of Article VIII (Assessments);

(b) any suit by the association to obtain a temporary restraining order (or equivalent emergency equitable relief) and such other ancillary relief as the court may deem necessary in order to maintain the status quo and preserve the association's ability to enforce the provisions of Article IX (Architectural Standards) and Article X (Use Restrictions and Rules);

(c) any suit between owners, that does not include the declarant or the association as a party, if such suit asserts a claim that would constitute a cause of action independent of the governing documents;

(d) any suit in which any indispensable party is not a bound party; and

(e) any suit that otherwise would be barred by any applicable statute of limitations.

With the consent of all parties thereto, any of the above may be submitted to the alternative dispute resolution procedures set forth in Section 14.3.

14.3. *Mandatory Procedures*

(a) *Notice.* Any bound party having a claim (claimant) against any other bound party (respondent) (collectively, the parties) shall notify each respondent in writing (the notice), stating plainly and concisely

1. the nature of the claim, including the persons involved and the respondent's role in the claim;

2. the legal basis of the claim (i.e., the specific authority out of which the claim arises);

3. the claimant's proposed remedy; and

4. that the claimant will meet with the respondent to discuss in good faith ways to resolve the claim.

(b) *Negotiation and Mediation*

1. The parties shall make every reasonable effort to meet in person and confer for the purpose of resolving the claim by good faith negotiation. If requested in writing, accompanied by a copy of the notice, the board may appoint a representative to assist the parties in resolving the dispute by negotiation.

2. If the parties do not resolve the claim within 30 days of the date of the notice (or within such other period as may be agreed upon by the parties) (termination of negotiations), the claimant shall have 30 additional days to submit the claim to mediation under the auspices of _____ or, if the parties otherwise agree, to an independent agency providing dispute resolution services in the _____ area.

3. If the claimant does not submit the claim to mediation within 30 days after termination of negotiations or does not appear

for the mediation, the claimant shall be deemed to have waived the claim, and the respondent shall be released and discharged from any and all liability to the claimant on account of such claim, provided that nothing herein shall release or discharge the respondent from any liability to any person other than the claimant.

4. Any settlement of the claim through mediation shall be documented in writing by the mediator. If the parties do not settle the claim within 30 days after submission of the matter to the mediation process or within such time as determined by the mediator, the mediator shall issue a notice of termination of the mediation proceedings (termination of mediation). The termination of mediation notice shall set forth that the parties are at an impasse and the date that mediation was terminated.

5. Within five days of the termination of mediation, the claimant shall make a final written settlement demand (settlement demand) to the respondent and the respondent shall make a final written settlement offer (settlement offer) to the claimant. If the claimant fails to make a settlement demand, the claimant's original notice shall constitute the settlement demand. If the respondent fails to make a settlement offer, the respondent shall be deemed to have made a "zero" or "take nothing" settlement offer.

(c) *Final and Binding Arbitration*

1. If the parties do not agree in writing to a settlement of the claim within 15 days of the termination of mediation, the claimant shall have 15 additional days to submit the claim to arbitration in accordance with the rules of arbitration contained in Exhibit __ or such rules as may be required by the agency providing the arbitrator. If not timely submitted to arbitration or if the claimant fails to appear for the arbitration proceeding, the claim shall be deemed abandoned, and the respondent shall be released and discharged from any and all liability to the claimant arising out of such claim, provided that nothing herein shall release or discharge the respondent from any liability to persons other than claimant.

2. This subsection (c) is an agreement to arbitrate and is specifically enforceable under the applicable arbitration laws of the state of _____. The arbitration award (the award) shall be final and binding, and judgment may be entered upon it in any court of competent jurisdiction to the fullest extent permitted under the laws of the state of _____.

14.4. *Allocation of Costs of Resolving Claims*

(a) Subject to Section 14.4(b), each party shall bear its own costs, including any attorney fees incurred, and each party shall share equally all charges rendered by the mediator(s) and all filing fees and costs of conducting the arbitration proceeding (postmediation costs).

(b) Any award that is equal to or more favorable to the claimant than the claimant's settlement demand shall add the claimant's postmediation costs to the award, such costs to be borne equally by all respondents. Any award that is equal to or less favorable to the claimant than any respondent's settlement offer shall award to such respondent its postmediation costs.

14.5. *Enforcement of Resolution* After the resolution of any claim, if any party fails to abide by the terms of any agreement or award, then any other party may file suit or initiate administrative proceedings to enforce such agreement or award without the need to comply again with the procedures set forth in Section 14.3. In such event, the party taking action to enforce the agreement or award shall be entitled to recover from the noncomplying party (or if more than one noncomplying party, from all such parties pro rata) all costs incurred in enforcing such agreement or award, including, without limitation, attorney fees and court costs.

■ Article XVI
General Provisions

16.4. *Litigation.* Except as provided below, no judicial or administrative proceeding shall be commenced or prosecuted by the association unless approved by a vote of 75 of the voting members. A voting member representing units owned by persons other than himself or herself shall not vote in favor of bringing or prosecuting any such proceeding unless authorized to do so by a vote of owners holding 75 of the total votes attributable to units in the neighborhood represented by the voting member. This section shall not apply, however, to (a) actions brought by the association to enforce the provisions of this declaration (including, without limitation, the foreclosure of liens); (b) the imposition and collection of assessments as provided in Article VIII; (c) proceedings involving challenges to ad valorem taxation; or (d) counterclaims brought by the association in proceedings instituted against it. This section shall not be amended unless such amendment is approved by the percentage of votes and, pursuant to the same procedures, necessary to institute proceedings as provided above. This section shall apply in addition to the provisions of Article XIV, if applicable.

APPENDIX 9

Feasibility Checklist for Acquisition of Undeveloped Land

1. Site characteristics
   A. Walk site with construction manager
      1) Views
      2) Wetlands
      3) Topography
      4) Location
      5) Natural beauty: trees; amenities (water feature)
      6) Potential site plan
      7) Potential product
      8) Potential construction problems
      9) Rock on surface
      10) Soils, clay, changes in vegetation
      11) Impact of surrounding uses
      12) Hazardous waste; past uses
      13) Traffic/congestion
      14) Schools
      15) Shopping
      16) Parks
2. Zoning/land use
   A. Consult with state and local authorities
      1) Existing zoning—comprehensive (master) plan and existing zoning; compute probable yield; status of subdivision plat processing
      2) Transportation—existing and proposed access
      3) Utilities
         a) Availability fees
         b) Off-site requirements
         c) Availability to site
      4) Proffer requirements

a) Impact fees
b) Amenity packages
c) Arborist
d) Road Improvements
e) Parking—on- and off-site requirements
f) Development timing
g) Trails
h) Public access
i) Relocate utilities
5) Political environment
a) Neighborhood groups
b) Board of supervisors
c) Adjacent landowners
6) Surrounding land uses
a) Current
b) Planned
7) Wetlands
a) County
b) Corps of Engineers
c) Any evidence from preliminary field observations?
d) Will evidence affect yield? If so, is mitigation feasible?
8) Schools
a) Elementary
b) Junior high
c) High
d) Daycare
9) Park access
3. Preliminary soils study
A. Borings to determine
1) Rock depth
2) Clay
3) Water table depth
4) Buildable soils
a) What are site characteristics?
b) Are there existing soil reports?
c) Is there evidence of rock?
d) Is there evidence of a high water table?
e) Is there evidence of existing fills?
f) Will there be excessive cuts or fills?
g) Slope analysis

      h) Will site balance?
    5) Floodplain
      a) Size and location?
      b) Will it affect density/yield calculations?
      c) Is any improvement allowed within floodplain?
      d) Will it require bridge crossings?
4. Hazardous waste study
  A. Professional Level I preliminary study
    1) Walk site with professional
      a) Vegetation impact
      b) Storage tanks
      c) Existing structures/asbestos
      d) Transformers/PCBs
      e) Adjacent uses—groundwater contamination
    2) Sampling program
    3) Title history
    4) Aerial photographs
    5) Land use history; on site and adjacent off site
  B. Notification to seller of toxic waste on site
  C. Will a Level II study be required?
5. Product
  A. Available density
  B. Location/target market
  C. Price point to serve market
  D. Product reuse?
  E. Create new product?
    1) Use comparable existing product for site plan study
6. Market study
  A. Key points
    1) In house
    2) Outside consultant's report
    3) Supply
    4) Demand
    5) Market window
    6) Target market (demographics)
    7) Comparative advantage
    8) Projected absorption
  B. New product competition (denote on map of area)
    1) Housing data reports
    2) Personal visits

3) Sales/leasing rates (absorption); seasonal?
4) Sales prices
5) Options and prices, premiums
6) Amenities
7) Sales program and organization
    a) On-site
    b) Off-site
8) Finish specifications
    a) Interior
    b) Exterior
9) Go on product review tour with director of sales/ management team
10) Location and access to employment centers

C. Existing product competition
    1) Shadow market (townhouse rental)
    2) MLS sales comparables of finished product
    3) Land sales comparables

D. Total supply
    1) Building permit totals for proposed product type
        a) Metropolitan area
        b) Submarket
        c) Three-year trend

E. Demand
    1) Projected household growth
        a) Metropolitan area
        b) Sub market
    2) Projected employment growth
        a) Metropolitan area
        b) Submarket
        c) All income levels
        d) Target market income level
    3) National Decision Systems Census update
    4) State, county, and local data
        a) Planning office
        b) Economic development office
        c) Chamber of commerce

F. Market window
    1) Household growth of target income group
    2) Less projected new submarket supply of specific product
    3) Equals market window

a) Now
b) When units delivered
G. Target market (demographics)
1) Buyer Profile
a) Income level
b) Male/female
c) Married/single
d) Age
e) Children and age characteristics
f) Entry-level singles
g) Roommates
h) Yuppies
i) Young couples/families
j) Mature families
k) Single professionals
l) Empty nesters
m) Corporate
2) Lifestyle characteristics
a) Adult component
b) Family component
c) Specify lifestyle according to market targets
d) Floorplans and square footage requirements
e) Amenity requirements
f) Landscaping requirements
3) Location profile (denote on map of area)
a) Proximity to employment centers
b) Commute/access to employment
c) Path of growth; limitations on growth
1) macro; metropolitan area—roads, commercial growth
2) micro; community
d) Schools
e) Shopping centers
f) Parks and recreation
4) Define position between existing products (distinguish market segment)
7. Comparative advantage
A. Price
B. Inventory timing
C. Product type and finish

D. Location

E. Lifestyle

8. Marketing strategy to achieve comparative advantage

    A. Price

    B. Product

    C. Promotion

    D. Place (distribution)

    E. Timing

    F. Presentation

9. Site plan/land planning

    A. Product reuse

        1) Sited by engineer—sketch plan

        2) Architect sketch elevation

    B. New product

        1) Engineer sites comparable to existing product—sketch plan

        2) Use elevation sketch from competitor's brochure

    C. Maximize project revenues

        1) Density

        2) Amenity package placement

        3) Entrance feature

        4) Integration with surrounding uses

        5) Circulation—vehicle and pedestrian

        6) Parking

        7) Waste disposal

        8) Sales/leasing center

        9) Open space

        10) Grading

        11) Utility placement

        12) Landscaping

        13) Setbacks

        14) Buffers

        15) Tree save program

        16) Proffered conditions

        17) Pedestrian and building scale

        18) Hardscape

        19) Irrigation

        20) Existing and future easements and utilities

10. Government requirements

A. Existing, pending, or proposed legislation, bans, prohibitions, etc., affecting the development of the property?
B. Water/sewer category?
C. Estimated time for any required sewer/water category change?
D. Time frame to obtain government approvals required as a condition for contract ratification, settlement date, and outside settlement date?
E. List basic steps and estimated time frame to process engineering plans and obtain site construction permits

11. Utilities
    A. Availability to site and lots
    B. Move/relocate existing utilities
    C. Who provides to site
        1) Land developer
        2) Builder
        3) Utility company
    D. How to pay for installation?
        1) Escrow agreement for third-party development services to install new utilities
        2) Pro rata share for existing utilities
        3) Ultimate owner pays
        4) Utility company pays
    E. Timing of installation
        1) Guarantees/recourse
        2) Impact on development schedule
        3) Bonding/letter of credit requirements and availability
    F. Availability letters
        1) Sewer
            a) Name of authority and contact
            b) Treatment plant or pumping station serving the site, its present capacity and flow, name of the sewershed
            c) Is capacity adequate for the development?
            d) Has sewer been authorized? If not, has processing been initiated?
            e) Are there any required tap fees?
            f) Have tap fees been prepaid by seller and are they assignable?
            g) Are there special or subdistrict charges?
            h) Are there any anticipated deficit contributions?

i) Location, size, and adequacy of existing collector, trunk, or interceptor sewers?
j) If existing lines are inadequate, can relief sewers be built? At what cost?
k) If off-site lines are to be extended to the site, are they covered by the CIP? What is the anticipated timing?
l) Identify and locate any required off-site easements
m) Will entire site sewer by gravity?
n) Will the site require a new pumping station? Force main? Grinder pumps?

2) Water mains
    a) Name of authority and its contact
    b) Is public water available?
    c) Location and size of transmission and distribution mains
    d) Is there adequate flow and pressure?
    e) What are anticipated pressure ranges?
    f) Can existing lines be tapped?
    g) Will looping be required?
    h) Is the property in a water district? If so, which district?
    i) Will off-site water main extensions be required?
    j) Will off-site easements be required?
    k) Amount of tap fees
    l) Any special district charges?

3) Natural gas
    a) Availability
    b) Location
    c) Name of gas utility company and contact
    d) Anticipated date of availability

4) Electricity
    a) Availability
    b) Location
    c) Name of utility company and contact
    d) Anticipated date of availability

5) Storm drainage/stormwater management (retention facilities)
    a) Location of existing drains
    b) Required off-site easements?
    c) Are there regional SWM facilities planned?

d) Will on-site SWM be required?

e) Will fee in lieu of SWM be permitted?

f) Are there unusual sediment control requirements?

G. Easements

1) On-site

2) Off-site

3) On-site easement to serve off-site developments

a) Utilities

b) Signage

H. On- and off-site capacity requirements

1) Existing

2) Future

I. Sewer and water tap fees

1) Any scheduled increases?

2) Any unscheduled increases possible?

3) When can taps be purchased?

12. Easements/dedications

A. On- and off-site

1) Utility: sewer, water, electricity, telephone, gas

2) Grading

a) Grading onto adjacent property

b) Jurisdictional approvals (federal, state, county, park authority, adjacent landowner, service authority)

3) Access

a) Temporary/permanent

b) Extent of public road frontage?

c) Where is access from existing roads?

d) Will easements be required for extensions from existing streets?

e) Do adjacent existing streets conform to local standards? If not, what is required to improve them?

f) Are new roads through site shown on master plans of highways?

g) Will any existing streets require abandonment?

4) Aerial

5) Underground

6) Surface

7) Stormwater management

8) Roads

9) Trails

B. Existing easements through site
    1) Effect on density and building location
    2) Can they be vacated?
13. Title report
  A. Ordered
  B. Review of title exceptions by attorney
    1) Notification of seller of exceptions
  C. Evaluation exceptions
  D. Consult attorney for course of action
  E. Specific questions/issues
    1) Is all of the property contiguous?
    2) Are there obvious existing improvements?
    3) Are there any other known legal encumbrances?
    4) Is there a current survey? Is the survey certified? Was the property ever previously subdivided? Is there a recorded boundary plat?
  F. Have surveyor/civil engineer discussed title report and exceptions with attorney regarding closing issues?
14. Other land use/marketing issues
  A. Is site in the vicinity of any known flight patterns?
  B. Are there any power lines traversing the site?
  C. Will proximity to highways or railroads require noise attenuation buffers?
  D. Does master plan indicate a need for school sites? If not, has the potential need been discussed with school board staff?
  E. Are there MPDU requirements?
  F. Historic preservation areas (e.g., structures, Civil War battlefields, etc.)?
  G. Preliminary development costs?
  H. Tentative development schedules?
15. Financing
  A. List and evaluate acceptable financing structures
    1) Purchase
    2) Joint venture
      a) Equity
      b) Debt
  B. Risk reduction
    1) Owner financing
    2) Interest rate caps/hedging
    3) Equity partner

4) Guarantees
5) Recourse limits
6) Public financing programs
7) Forward commitments
8) Timing of settlement in relation to approvals and construction start
9) Plan status
10) Equity requirement
11) Phased takedown
C. Financing scenario for this product type
1) Availability
2) Cost
D. Provide CFO with preliminary budget
16. Budget
A. Conservative approach
1) Rental rates/prices at market
2) Operating expenses at market
3) Absorption at or below documented absorption in area
B. Timeline
1) Use standard format
2) Modify for known variations
3) Use reasonable time plus 20 percent
   a) Site plan approvals
   b) Infrastructure plan approvals
   c) Grading and building permits received
   d) Is bonding required for plan approval?
   e) Construction start
   f) Site work completed
   g) Preleasing/presales
   h) First deliveries
   i) Final delivery
C. Construction costs
1) Give program to VP for construction
2) Obtain cost estimates before feasibility review
   a) Based on earlier projects
   b) Based on actual takeoffs where possible
3) Review in detail with VP, use outside estimating service
4) For extensive infrastructure, use outside estimating service
D. Soft costs

       1) Complete budget building schedule

       2) Review construction period interest and leaseup/
          presales negative cash flow computations with/CFO

       3) Review in detail with development partner

   E. Complete budget

       1) Maintain fees/profit margin

         a) Include negative cash flows in costs

       2) Review in detail with development partner

   F. Financing approach

       1) Build land profit in coordination with CFO

17. Present recommendations in feasibility review meeting